# Early Childhood Education

# Blending Theory, Blending Practice

*by*

Lawrence J. Johnson, Ph.D.
*University of Cincinnati*
*Cincinnati, Ohio*

M.J. LaMontagne, Ed.D.
*Georgia Southern University*
*Statesboro, Georgia*

Peggy M. Elgas, Ph.D.
*University of Cincinnati*
*Cincinnati, Ohio*

*and*

Anne M. Bauer, Ed.D.
*University of Cincinnati*
*Cincinnati, Ohio*

with invited contributors

·P A U L·H·
BROOKES
PUBLISHING Cº

Baltimore • London • Toronto • Sydney

**Paul H. Brookes Publishing Co.**
Post Office Box 10624
Baltimore, Maryland 21285-0624

www.pbrookes.com

Typeset by A.W. Bennett, Inc., Hartland, Vermont.
Manufactured in the United States of America by
The Maple Press Company, York, Pennsylvania.

The photographs in this book were taken and provided by Donna M. Ruiz and Maria Sanchez and are published with the written permission of the individuals appearing in the photographs or their parents.

The vignettes are composites based on the authors' experiences; these vignettes do not represent the lives or experiences of specific individuals; therefore, any similarity to actual individuals or circumstances is coincidental, and no implications should be inferred.

**Library of Congress Cataloging-in-Publication Data**

Early childhood education: blending theory, blending practice / by
    Lawrence J. Johnson . . . [et al.].
        p.   cm.
    Includes bibliographical references and index.
    ISBN 1-55766-345-9
    1. Inclusive education—United States.    2. Early childhood
education—United States.    3. Handicapped children—Education (Early
childhood)—United States.    4. Handicapped children—Services for—
United States.    5. Group work in education—United States.
I. Johnson, Lawrence J., 1955–  .
LC1201.E27   1998
372.21'0973—dc21

97-37662
                                                                    CIP

British Cataloguing in Publication data are available from the British Library.

# Contents

# About the Authors

**Lawrence J. Johnson, Ph.D.,** Associate Dean of Research and Development, Professor, College of Education, Director, Arlitt Child and Family Research and Education Center, and Senior Researcher in the Evaluation Services Center, University of Cincinnati, Post Office Box 210002, Cincinnati, Ohio 45221-0002. Dr. Johnson is widely known in the field of education as an expert in early childhood and special education. He is a leader in the understanding and promotion of collaboration in education and has expertise in program evaluation. He has served as president, editor, and reviewer for many professional organizations and journals. He is Co-editor of *Teacher Education and Special Education*. Dr. Johnson is widely published in books and professional journals of education.

**M.J. LaMontagne, Ed.D.,** Assistant Professor, Department of Leadership, Technology, and Human Development, Georgia Southern University, Post Office Box 8131, Statesboro, Georgia 30460-8131. Dr. LaMontagne has devoted herself professionally to working with young children with disabilities and their families as a classroom teacher, consultant, and university faculty member. She serves on the Executive Board of the Division for Early Childhood of the Council for Exceptional Children and maintains a research agenda with interests in teachers' perceptions of young children's play, play-based assessment, and the blending of early childhood education and early childhood special education preservice programs.

**Peggy M. Elgas, Ph.D.,** Associate Professor, Arlitt Child and Family Research and Education Center, University of Cincinnati, One Edwards Center, Post Office Box 210105, Cincinnati, Ohio 45221-0105. Dr. Elgas's primary research interests focus on young children's play and social development and their peer cultures. She has devoted herself professionally to collaborating with professionals, families, and students to improve the quality of classroom environments, teachers' interactions with students and with each other, and young children's development.

**Anne M. Bauer, Ed.D.,** Professor, Division of Teacher Education, College of Education, University of Cincinnati, 608 Teachers College, Post Office Box 210002, Cincinnati, Ohio 45221-0002. Dr. Bauer's primary research interests involve young children who are at risk for or who have been identified as having disabilities. She has been involved in many professional roles with children with disabilities, including those of teacher, head teacher, consulting teacher, and supervisor of programs. Among her many publications have been articles in the *Journal of Special Education, School Psychology Quarterly, International Journal of Qualitative Studies,* and *Topics in Early Childhood Special Education.* She is Co-editor of *Teacher Education and Special Education.* Dr. Bauer continues to devote her research and other work to improving the education and lives of children and their families and to preparing others to engage in the pursuit of excellence in their programs for children and families.

# Contributors

**Michelle Buchanan, Ph.D.**
Assistant Professor
Division of Life Long Learning and
  Instruction
College of Education
University of Wyoming
219 McWhinney Hall
Laramie, Wyoming 82070

**Victoria W. Carr, M.Ed.**
Research Associate and Associate Director
Arlitt Child and Family Research and
  Education Center
University of Cincinnati
One Edwards Center
Post Office Box 210105
Cincinnati, Ohio 45221

**Connie Corkwell, M.Ed.**
Early Childhood Education Specialist
Arlitt Child and Family Research and
  Education Center
University of Cincinnati
One Edwards Center
Post Office Box 210105
Cincinnati, Ohio 45221

**Iris R. Daigre, Ph.D.**
Assistant Professor
Arlitt Child and Family Research and
  Education Center
University of Cincinnati
One Edwards Center
Post Office Box 210105
Cincinnati, Ohio 45221

**Karen Danbom, M.A.**
Assistant Professor
Department of Elementary and Early
  Childhood Education
Moorhead State University
Lommen Hall
Moorhead, Minnesota 56563

**Dawn M. Denno, M.S.**
Administrative Educational Consultant
Arlitt Child and Family Research and
  Education Center
University of Cincinnati
One Edwards Center
Post Office Box 210105
Cincinnati, Ohio 45221

**Elizabeth George, M.Phil.**
Research Assistant and Early Childhood
  Education Specialist
Arlitt Child and Family Research and
  Education Center
University of Cincinnati
One Edwards Center
Post Office Box 210105
Cincinnati, Ohio 45221

**Brenda Hieronymus, M.Ed.**
Early Childhood Education Specialist
Arlitt Child and Family Research and
  Education Center
University of Cincinnati
One Edwards Center
Post Office Box 210105
Cincinnati, Ohio 45221

**Mary Janson**
Parent and State Transition Coordinator for
  Early Childhood Transitions
Child Advocacy Center
1821 Summit Road
Suite 110
Cincinnati, Ohio 45237

**Shobha Chachie Joseph, M.A.**
Collaboration Specialist
Gallaudet Regional Center
203 C Street
Apartment A
Saint Augustine Beach, Florida 32084

**Ellen Lynch, Ed.D.**
Coordinator
Associate Degree Program in Early Childhood
    Education
University College
University of Cincinnati
3306 French Hall
Cincinnati, Ohio 45221

**Sally Moomaw, M.Ed.**
Early Childhood Education Specialist
Arlitt Child and Family Research and
    Education Center
University of Cincinnati
One Edwards Center
Post Office Box 210105
Cincinnati, Ohio 45221

**Janice E. Noga, M.S.**
Research Assistant
Division of Teacher Education
College of Education
University of Cincinnati
608 Teachers College
Post Office Box 210002
Cincinnati, Ohio 45221

**Kimberli Rioux, B.A.**
Early Childhood Education Specialist
Arlitt Child and Family Research and
    Education Center
University of Cincinnati
One Edwards Center
Post Office Box 210105
Cincinnati, Ohio 45221

**Donna M. Ruiz, M.Ed.**
Research Assistant
Early Childhood Education Specialist
Arlitt Child and Family Research and
    Education Center
University of Cincinnati
One Edwards Center
Post Office Box 210105
Cincinnati, Ohio 45221

**Gwen Wheeler Russell, Ed.D.**
Assistant Professor
Department of Educational Studies
School of Education
University of Tennessee at Martin
240 Gooch Hall
Martin, Tennessee 38237

**Deborah Anania Smith, M.Ed.**
Research Assistant
Arlitt Child and Family Research and
    Education Center
University of Cincinnati
One Edwards Center
Post Office Box 210105
Cincinnati, Ohio 45221

**Nancy Struewing, M.Ed.**
Early Childhood Education Specialist
Arlitt Child and Family Research and
    Education Center
University of Cincinnati
One Edwards Center
Post Office Box 210105
Cincinnati, Ohio 45221

**Mary Ulrich, M.Ed.**
9155 Funderland Road
West Chester, Ohio 45069

**Sally Ann Zwicker, M.A.**
Instructor
Deaf Education Program
Western Maryland College
Thompson Hall
2 College Hill
Westminster, Maryland 21157

# Foreword

> Because the contributors to this book are a diverse group, we do not always agree on what represents recommended practice. However, because we all are committed to doing whatever needs to be done to meet the needs of the children and families we serve, we have learned to work together and have learned a great deal from our diverse perspectives. We have embraced a unified view of early childhood practices that incorporates ECE and ECSE practices.

The preceding quotation from the Preface to this book presents a model of bringing together the best of both worlds of early childhood education (ECE) and early childhood special education (ECSE) to provide effective education practices in inclusive environments. ECE environments present us with groups of children and families with diverse needs, varying abilities, varying cultures and languages, and varying experiences and resources. No one professional alone and no profession by itself is able to meet all of these individual needs. Rather, collaborations and partnerships among adults with diverse skills and knowledge are required if high-quality educational experiences for all young children are to be provided.

## RESPECTING ALL KNOWLEDGE AND SKILLS: BUILDING TRUST

In 1993, the Division for Early Childhood (DEC) of the Council for Exceptional Children (CEC) issued a position statement on the inclusion of young children with disabilities in typical early childhood environments that the National Association for the Education of Young Children (NAEYC) endorsed. This position statement contains the following guidance to the field:

> Inclusion, as a value, supports the right of all children, regardless of their diverse abilities, to participate actively in natural settings within their communities. A natural setting is one in which the child would spend time had he or she not had a disability. Such settings include but are not limited to home and family, play groups, child care, nursery schools, Head Start programs, kindergartens, and neighborhood school classrooms. . . . To implement inclusive practices DEC supports: (a) the continued development, evaluation, and dissemination of full inclusion supports, services, and systems so that options for inclusion are of *high quality*; (b) the development of preservice and in-service training programs that prepare families, administrators, and service providers to develop and work within inclusive settings; (c) collaboration among all key stakeholders to implement flexible fiscal and administrative procedures in sup-

port of inclusion; (d) research that contributes to our knowledge of state of the art services; and (e) the restructuring and unification of social, education, health, and intervention supports and services to make them more responsive to the needs of all children and families. (1993a, emphasis added)

The key concept in this position statement is *high quality*. What is high-quality inclusion? Quality consists of those practices that contribute to children's development and learning (i.e., practices that are effective and appropriate). There are at least three features of high-quality inclusive practices in early childhood:

1.  Practices are developmentally appropriate.
2.  Practices are individually appropriate.
3.  Practices represent a partnership among professionals and between professionals and families.

In ECE, there is some debate about what constitutes effective instruction goals and practices. This debate has been heightened by the trend toward inclusive environments. When separate programs, systems, and services were maintained, it was possible—though not desirable—for general ECE and ECSE professionals to keep their philosophies and practices separate. With early childhood environments including more children with a variety of special learning needs, professionals from a variety of fields are often working together or at least with the same child and family. This shared responsibility sometimes results in the successful blending of skills and talent. At other times, it results in clashes based on perceived differences or apparent contradictions in approaches. We say *perceived* because on close inspection most recommended practices in ECE and ECSE are not conflictive but rather are complementary or represent points on a continuum. For instance, some general ECE professionals may contend that structured interventions or behavioral strategies used with young children are never appropriate. Some ECSE educators may contend that structured environments and teacher-directed activities are always appropriate. A review of both the DEC and NAEYC recommendations for practice, however, reveals that neither absolute accurately represents the position of either organization. In fact, whether a teacher should employ structured, teacher-directed activities or behavioral interventions depends on the needs of the individual child and the task in which the child is engaged. Indeed, a particular child may function independently and successfully in certain free-play or gross motor activities, yet that child may not have acquired independence in language or in social skills. For those particular domains, the child may need more structured, teacher-directed strategies before he or she develops new skills at a level that permits the child to experience continued developmental growth through the teacher's use of more child-initiated strategies. *Appropriateness* represents a wide range of strategies and methods tailored to meet the individual and developmental needs of children.

DEC and NAEYC, the national associations serving ECSE and ECE professionals, respectively, embarked on several collaborative efforts in 1990 to assist the fields in facilitating collaboration rather than perpetuating ideological extremes. These collaborative efforts have included 1) developing the position statement on inclusion (DEC, 1993a), 2) issuing coordinated recommendations for professional standards for ECE and ECSE personnel (DEC, NAEYC, & ATE, 1995; NAEYC, 1995), and 3) working together on recommended practices in ECE and ECSE (Bredekamp & Copple, 1997; DEC, 1993b). In these efforts, an attempt was made to clarify that all knowledge bases and approaches in the ECE field are needed to meet the needs of all young children, particularly in environments that are inclusive of children with diverse learning needs.

The two sets of recommended practices mentioned in the preceding paragraph embody the similarities of beliefs related to effective and appropriate education of young children. DEC recommended practices include the following:

- In selecting practices, criteria should take into account whether the practice is research based or values based, family centered, multiculturally relevant, cross-disciplinary, developmentally appropriate, and normalized.
- Strategies should promote participation, choice making, autonomy, and age-appropriate abilities.
- Adaptive behavior instruction should occur within the context of daily routines; activities and materials should be modified as needed to accommodate children's developmental levels and specific impairments.
- Children should be active rather than passive recipients of information.
- Strategies and outcomes should be frequently monitored, changes should be made as needed, and services should be individualized.
- Early childhood environments should be fun; they should stimulate children's initiations, choices, and engagement.

These guidelines are the field-validated recommended practices for the field of ECSE and were developed by ECSE professionals, parents, and representatives of DEC and NAEYC.

The revised NAEYC developmentally appropriate practice (DAP) guidelines (Bredekamp & Copple, 1997) include the following:

- Teachers should work to build reciprocal relationships with parents.
- Teachers should plan and prepare a learning environment that fosters children's initiative, active exploration, and sustained engagement.
- To sustain an individual child's effort or engagement in purposeful activities, teachers should select from a range of strategies that include but are not limited to modeling; demonstration of specific skills; and providing information, focused attention, physical proximity, verbal encouragement, reinforcement, and other behavioral guidance procedures, as well as additional structure and modification of equipment or schedules as needed.
- Responsiveness to individual differences in children's abilities and interests should be evident in the curriculum, adults' interactions, and the environment.

- Children with disabilities or with special learning needs should be included in the classroom socially and intellectually as well as physically, and necessary supports should be provided to ensure that their individual needs are met in that context. As much as possible, children with disabilities should receive therapeutic or other services within the general classroom to maintain their sense of continuity.
- Teachers should use observational assessment of children's progress, examination of children's work samples, and documentation of children's development and learning to plan and adapt the curriculum to meet individual children's developmental or learning needs and to evaluate the program's effectiveness.

Again, although these NAEYC recommendations pertain to typical environments for general ECE professionals, they assume that all such environments must be prepared to include children with disabilities. These guidelines also are field validated and were constructed with input from NAEYC and DEC members and numerous other related organizations. Clearly, there are more similarities than differences in these sets of practices. Indeed, they reflect more of a continuum of appropriate practices based on children's individual needs.

## USING ALL KNOWLEDGE AND SKILLS: BUILDING PARTNERSHIPS

Wolery, Strain, and Bailey (1992) pointed out that research on teaching young children with disabilities effectively reveals that some children with special needs 1) interact with toys and materials for shorter periods of time than their peers without disabilities; 2) are less goal oriented than their peers without disabilities; 3) give up on performing tasks or play activities sooner than their peers without disabilities; 4) do not generalize skills well to other environments, times, or people; and 5) engage in less frequent and less sophisticated social play than their peers without disabilities. Therefore, the education goals for some children with special needs may contain some fundamental skills that children without disabilities do not typically require. These goals might include 1) promoting child engagement, mastery, and independence; 2) building and supporting social and play skills; and 3) facilitating the generalized use of skills (Wolery et al., 1992). Although some children may need such assistance, the activities promoting these skills can usually be integrated into those of the general group or class. There are many ways, for instance, to meet children's individual needs within small groups. Some strategies and activities meet the needs of all children in the group, some are necessary for some of the children, and some strategies or special therapeutic or education services are necessary for only one child. Sometimes these strategies vary from child to child or from activity to activity with an individual child. Some ways of conceptualizing how all of the various methods, curricula, activities, environmental modifications, and adult–child interactions might be used to meet all of these variations in learning needs in an inclusive environment might look like the models shown in Figure 1.

Can one individual—whether an ECE teacher or an ECSE teacher—possess all of the skills needed to meet all of the needs of all of the children in an inclusive, het-

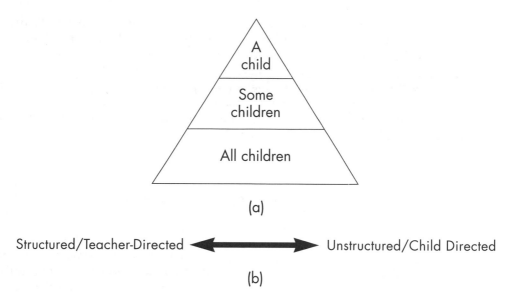

Figure 1.    Conceptual models of individual appropriateness: (a) Pyramid model. (b) Continuum model.

erogeneous environment? Not likely! Therefore, administrators, parents, and teachers need to work toward a model of collaboration and partnership that includes various personnel and parents working together. Several research and planning efforts have pointed to the importance of collaboration in meeting the complex needs of children and families. Smith and Rose (1993) reported in their national study of the major barriers to developing inclusive environments for young children that a lack of respect for differing views and resistance to collaboration were major challenges. However, they reported that some communities have successfully created inclusive opportunities and collaborative efforts. These communities reported that they had used several strategies in developing their collaborative services, including

- Building mutual respect and trust between ECE and ECSE personnel by acknowledging that each branch of the field brings diverse and necessary skills and knowledge to the early childhood environment—that is, by using the best of both worlds
- Instituting joint preservice and in-service training opportunities so that groups receive training together that builds on both sets of knowledge bases, thus validating the importance and efficacy of both
- Sharing ideas about how best to teach a particular skill to a particular child by using approaches that represent a range of degrees of structure and teacher directiveness
- Modeling collaboration at all levels so that teachers and other direct-services personnel do not feel that they are the only ones expected to undergo a paradigm shift

The early childhood field comprises many diverse branches with diverse knowledge and skills. All can learn from each other in the quest to educate all young children successfully in inclusive environments. As Bredekamp and Rosegrant stated, "It is clear that each field needs to learn from the other as we work closely together to ensure individually appropriate practice for each child" (1992, p. 93). Both fields need to accept that there is no one right way to provide appropriate, high-quality inclusive early childhood care and education. The guiding paradigm is not "either–or" but "both–and"!

*Barbara J. Smith, Ph.D.*
*Executive Director*
*Council for Exceptional Children, Division for Early Childhood*
*Denver, Colorado*

*Sue Bredekamp, Ph.D.*
*Director of Professional Development*
*National Association for the Education of Young Children*
*Washington, D.C.*

## REFERENCES

Bredekamp, S., & Copple, C. (Eds.). (1997). *Developmentally appropriate practice in early childhood programs* (Rev. ed.). Washington, DC: National Association for the Education of Young Children.

Bredekamp, S., & Rosegrant, T. (Eds.). (1992). *Reaching potentials: Appropriate curriculum and assessment for young children.* Washington, DC: National Association for the Education of Young Children.

Division for Early Childhood (DEC) of the Council for Exceptional Children (CEC). (1993a). *DEC position on inclusion.* Reston, VA: Author.

Division for Early Childhood (DEC) of the Council for Exceptional Children (CEC). (1993b). *DEC recommended practices: Indicators of quality in programs for infants and young children with special needs and their families.* Reston, VA: Author.

Division for Early Childhood (DEC), National Association for the Education of Young Children (NAEYC), & Association of Teacher Educators (ATE). (1995). *Personnel standards for early education and early intervention: Guidelines for licensure in early childhood special education.* Reston, VA: Council for Exceptional Children, Division for Early Childhood.

National Association for the Education of Young Children (NAEYC). (1995). *Guidelines for preparation of early childhood professionals.* Washington, DC: Author.

Smith, B., & Rose, D. (1993). *Administrator's policy handbook for preschool mainstreaming.* Cambridge, MA: Brookline Books.

Wolery, M., Strain, P., & Bailey, D.B., Jr. (1992). Reaching potentials of children with special needs. In S. Bredekamp & T. Rosegrant (Eds.), *Reaching potentials: Appropriate curricula and assessment for young children* (pp. 92–111). Washington, DC: National Association for the Education of Young Children.

# Preface

This book is the result of a collaborative effort of a group of people who care a great deal about young children and children's families. Some of the contributors to this book are parents, and others are professionals. Some of the contributors who are professionals are front-line service providers, and others are teacher educators. The training of some of the contributors was in early childhood education (ECE); for others, it was in early childhood special education (ECSE). Because the contributors to this book are a diverse group, we do not always agree on what represents recommended practice. However, because we all are committed to doing whatever needs to be done to meet the needs of the children and families we serve, we have learned to work together and have learned a great deal from our diverse perspectives. We have embraced a unified view of early childhood practices that incorporates ECE and ECSE practices.

The vast majority of the contributors work or have worked at the Arlitt Child and Family Research and Education Center at the University of Cincinnati. At the Arlitt Center, we have a model preschool program that serves more than 180 children and their families. The program strives to unify recommended practices from a strong constructivist ECE philosophy, ECSE, and Head Start. Funding for services comes from primary sources, the College of Education at the University of Cincinnati, the Hamilton County Community Action Agency Head Start Program, the Hamilton County Board of Mental Retardation and Developmental Disabilities, and tuition from spaces reserved for children with diverse issues and abilities.

The center was begun by Ada Hart Arlitt in the 1920s and is one of the oldest continuously running child development centers in the United States. The center has received numerous awards and recognition for the services that it provides to children and their families. It received the Irene Bandy-Hedden Early Childhood Education Program Award in 1993 from the Ohio Department of Education, Division of Early Childhood Education, for collaborating with the statewide preschool special education service delivery project in promoting quality ECE programs for Ohio's young children and their families. In 1995, the center received an Inclusion Network Award for the manner in which children with disabilities are included in its programs. In 1995, the center was recognized as one of Ohio's best education programs and was one of 13 programs featured at the statewide Best Conference. That award was particularly important because those programs honored as Ohio's best ranged from preschool to postsecondary programs.

We decided to write this book to share with others the practices employed at the Arlitt Center to meet the needs of the children and families that it serves. Collaboration is a major theme of this book because it is the means by which we work together to share practices. It is our hope that this book will provide a framework for professionals from a variety of disciplines to work together with families to nurture the development of children within their programs. Consistent with the theme of collaboration, each chapter was written by contributors who represent the diversity of individuals connected with the Arlitt Center. These contributors range from teacher educators to direct-services providers and parents and represent a mix of individuals with primary training in ECE and ECSE.

After reading each chapter, readers will be able to answer the questions listed after the corresponding chapter headings in the sections that follow. Before reading each chapter, readers can see how many of the questions they can answer, jot down the answers, and then compare their answers with what they have learned after reading each chapter. These questions may also help readers to study for a test.

# CHAPTER 1

- What is the definition of *collaboration*?
- Why is collaboration important to the blending of ECE and ECSE practices?
- What role do families have in collaborative groups?
- What are the four roles in which people engage when they are collaborating?
- How have collaborative practices changed over time?
- What is the definition of *interagency collaboration*?
- What are the barriers to and facilitators of interagency collaboration?

# CHAPTER 2

- Why is communication important to the development of collaborative environments?
- What are the barriers that can inhibit communication and collaboration?
- What are the facilitators that can enhance communication and collaboration?
- What are the key steps in group processing?
- How can people benefit from conflict?
- What are the elements of problem solving?
- What are some of the characteristics of collaborative environments?

# CHAPTER 3

- What are the historical roots of ECE practices?
- What are some of the differences between the histories and the beliefs that undergird ECE and ECSE practices?

- What are some of the similarities between the histories and the beliefs that undergird ECE and ECSE practices?
- What are some of the reasons that we must blend ECE and ECSE practices?

## CHAPTER 4

- Who are the key partners in the education of young children?
- What are the rights of all young children?
- Do young children with disabilities have different rights from other children?
- What is a primary role of partners in the education of young children?

## CHAPTER 5

- What is the definition of *developmentally and individually appropriate practices*?
- What are some of the common themes in ECE and ECSE practices?
- What are some of the themes that are unique to ECE practice and ECSE practice?
- When selecting a specific practice, what are some of the factors that you should consider? Is any one factor any more important than other factors?

## CHAPTER 6

- What are the characteristics and benefits of play?
- In what key developmental areas is play critical?
- Why is play so important to an early childhood classroom?
- Who is the primary facilitator of play in the early childhood classroom?

## CHAPTER 7

- Who is the constructor of knowledge?
- What are the key concepts in the principle of active learning?
- What is the teacher's role in scaffolding?
- What does it mean to characterize a classroom as a communicative context?
- Who constructs the rules for participation in the classroom?

## CHAPTER 8

- What are the foundations of quality programs and curriculum?
- What are the key components of a quality early childhood curriculum?
- What are the elements to consider when designing an early childhood classroom?
- How do program goals and child goals affect classroom practices?

# CHAPTER 9

- What is the definition of *prosocial skills*?
- How do inclusive environments benefit the prosocial skills of all learners?
- How are collaborative environments important to the development of children?
- What are the characteristics of classrooms in which prosocial skills are valued?
- What are the strategies that can be used to facilitate prosocial skills in children?

# CHAPTER 10

- What are some of the benefits of small-group time on young children?
- What are the classroom management strategies that can help teachers manage small-group time?
- What are the various ways to implement small-group time?
- What is the teacher's role in structuring and facilitating small-group time?
- What are some strategies that can be used to help maximize small-group time?

# CHAPTER 11

- What is the purpose of assessment?
- Why is collaboration important to the assessment process?
- Why are families important to the assessment process?
- What is transdisciplinary assessment?
- What are some problems with the instruments available to assess young children and their families?
- How is program evaluation an important part of early childhood assessment procedures?

# CHAPTER 12

- What are some of the factors that contribute to successful transitions?
- Why is planning important to transitions?
- How does collaboration relate to transition?
- Why are transition plans referred to as *road maps*?

In closing, we believe that the future of the early childhood field lies in the blending of ECE and ECSE practices to better meet the needs of the children and families that they serve. Collaboration is a process that can assist professionals as they work together to provide a unified set of blended practices. Many come to the early childhood field from a variety of other fields and have developed practices from a diverse set of theories that undergird those other fields. This diversity creates a rich set of options that can enhance professionals' abilities to better serve the increasingly diverse set of children and families in early childhood programs. Rather than focusing on differences, it is time for early childhood professionals to focus on the congruence of viewpoints and how a rich set of practices can be blended to develop recommended practices.

# Acknowledgments

As we sat down to acknowledge those who have helped us in the construction of this book, it became apparent that there have been many people who have had an influence on each of us. If we were to list each of these people, we would essentially have a telephone directory and would invariably leave someone unlisted. We thank our families, our professors, and our colleagues, who have guided our thinking throughout our careers and helped to shape the book that you see before you.

In thinking about this book, however, there are four individuals who went above and beyond the call of duty in helping us to pull things together. We extend a special "thanks" to these individuals. First, thank you, Donna, for all of the work and effort that you put into this book. Donna M. Ruiz put a great deal of time into this text; in fact, she did many of the tasks that make writing a book such as this one difficult. She tracked down references at the library, helped take photographs, and generally responded to queries from the publisher. Second, we thank Emma Carter Collins. Emma did a tremendous job in typing the manuscript and spent countless hours translating what appeared to be hieroglyphics into some kind of meaningful prose. Maria Sanchez is responsible for the great photographs herein. Thank you, Maria. The photographs are wonderful because they really illustrate what happens at the Arlitt Center. Maria and Donna spent a great deal of time thinking about taking photographs that would add meaning to the text. Finally, we thank Sue Johnson. She deserves an extra special thanks as a spouse of one of the authors. However, beyond that, she helped with the final editing and typing of the manuscript. Without a doubt, Larry will be beholden to her for a very, very long time.

We also thank the staff at Paul H. Brookes Publishing Co. Heather Shrestha and Theresa Donnelly were incredibly supportive, patient, and helpful in the process of bringing this book to press. The quality of this book is in large part a result of their careful guidance.

Thanks to all of you who have supported us in our development, and thanks to those of you who have helped us with this book.

# Early Childhood Education

# The History of Collaboration

## Its Importance to Blending Early Childhood Education and Early Childhood Special Education Practices

*Lawrence J. Johnson, Donna M. Ruiz,
M.J. LaMontagne, and Elizabeth George*

## CHAPTER ORGANIZER

In this chapter, we explore the following ideas . . .

1. The importance of collaboration to the blending of early childhood education and early childhood special education practices

2. That families are central members of collaborative groups

3. Collaboration as a coordinated, multidimensional process to meet mutually agreed-on and shared goals

4. The historical evolution from earlier collaborative practices to implementation practices

5. The nature of and barriers to interagency coordination

6. How to facilitate and maintain collaborative teams

For decades, parents and families have brought their children to community programs for a variety of educational, social, and health services. To provide these services, professionals work with children and families to nurture and promote the developmental and physical well-being of the child. Since its beginning, early childhood education (ECE) has been founded on the concept of collaboration. Parents and professionals from an assortment of disciplines come together around a single common goal: creating the best possible program for this child and this family. ECE programs have a long history of collaborating with others who have the knowledge and expertise to help create the best programs for young children and their families. It is important that the early childhood field recognize this history of collaboration and extract the valuable lessons that have emerged from years of collaborative practice. As the field moves forward into blending ECE and early childhood special education (ECSE) practices, it is critical for collaboration to remain a cornerstone of our efforts and for the art of collaboration to continue to be refined. We are at our best when we engage in this multidimensional process called collaboration to facilitate communication, problem solving, and mutual ownership of outcomes for children and families.

This chapter provides the foundation for understanding collaboration as a concept in ECE. In this chapter, *collaboration* is defined and its history is presented with an overview of what has been learned from years of practice. Next, the framework of collaboration is provided, including definitive dimensions and descriptions of practical roles for team members. The benefits and challenges of interagency collaboration efforts are explored, and the importance of the participation of parents in the collaborative process is discussed.

**Reflection:**   As you read the first section, think of two groups in which you participated that were collaborative, as well as two groups that were not collaborative. What were some of the differences between these groups?

## DEFINITION OF COLLABORATION

Bruner (1991) defined *collaboration* as a process to use for reaching goals that cannot be attained efficiently by acting alone. Similarly, Pugach and Johnson (1995) defined *collaboration* as what occurs when all members of a team are working together and supporting each other to achieve a specific goal. However, Pugach and Johnson stressed that collaboration is more than a process and that primary importance must be given to outcomes. In other words, simply engaging in collaboration is not enough; rather, the collaboration must result in improved outcomes. In ECE, the desired end is more comprehensive and appropriate services for children and families that improve outcomes for the family and the child. Bruner (1991) included all of the following elements in the promotion of successful collaboration:

- Jointly developing and agreeing to a set of common goals and directions
- Sharing responsibility for obtaining those goals
- Working together to achieve those goals, using the expertise of each collaborator

Bruner's elements provided a basis for defining the act of collaboration but focused on the mechanical aspects of this process: develop, agree, share responsibility, and achieve. However, the act of working together implies a certain level of personal interaction, and these interactions have a significant impact on successful collaboration. Pugach and Johnson suggested that the following are elements of collaboration:

- Learning and sharing the roles and responsibilities of all members of the collaborative team
- Consensus building without hierarchical impositions
- Group goal setting and decision sharing

These elements address the human side of collaboration and relate to how people interact and react during the collaborative process.

The relationships among the members of a collaborative team cannot be limited exclusively to any particular kind of interactional process. The team's collaboration occurs along a continuum from the simplest problem solving to sorting out the confusing combinations of expert input. All of the individuals participating on the team (including parents and family members) should be prepared to approach the solution in multidimensional roles because the approach to collaboration is not always a clear-cut, step-by-step process. Rather, it is a dynamic process in which team members interact through a meshing set of roles and responsibilities. Therefore, people need either to know or to learn from other members how to adapt their roles (Pugach & Johnson, 1995).

---

*Read the following example of a conversation between two collaborative team members:*

*Timika (Parent Involvement Coordinator):* Juán, hi. I'm really glad to be able to talk to you today.

*Juán (a preschool teacher):* Hey, Timika, good to see you. What's up?

*Timika:* Well, Juán, I'm afraid I won't be able to make the parent meeting on time, so could you begin the parent meeting for me?

*Juán:* I don't know. How late will you be? I'm worried that I won't be able to do what you want me to do without knowing more of what's expected. After all, I'm not the Parent Involvement Coordinator.

*Timika:* Well Juán, I'm sure you could do it. But if you want, why don't we meet beforehand to discuss our respective roles? This would help us to be able to shift our responsibilities to each other when necessary.

*Juán:* Okay, Timika. I'll give it a try if you give me some tips.

*This example illustrates Juán and Timika working as a collaborative team in which each member can effectively take on the roles of the other members, even in situations in which those roles require some additional knowledge.*

Defined as a dynamic process, *collaboration* means being able to change and adjust according to members' current needs. It becomes a flexible process that is molded to the uniqueness of every situation on any given day.

## A HISTORICAL PERSPECTIVE ON THE EVOLUTION OF COLLABORATIVE PRACTICES

Collaboration is an integral part of recommended practices in education in the 1990s. There has been a paradigm shift in the conceptual meaning of *collaboration* since the 1960s, with the first prescriptive efforts of school consultation, to the late 1990s notion of an inclusive collaborative model (Johnson, Pugach, & Devlin, 1990; Pugach & Johnson, 1995). To understand collaboration as practiced in the late 1990s, we must sketch the history and practical evolution of collaboration as well as the meaning of the term *collaboration.*

In the early 1960s, there was little collaboration as we now think of it. In the classroom, emphasis was placed on teachers' autonomy and disciplinary expertise. Teachers were thought of as the authorities in their classrooms, and the unique expertise of others from related disciplines found in schools was clearly defined and separated. Special education classrooms were completely separate from general education classrooms. Speech-language pathologists, physical therapists, and occupational therapists worked in therapy rooms and were isolated from other classrooms. Within this atmosphere of separateness, teachers and therapists struggled with skill generalization, competing priorities, and many other challenges involving communication, sharing of resources, and duplication of services.

Toward the end of the 1960s, professionals began discussing encouraging professionals from multiple disciplines to work together and share their disciplinary expertise to better serve children and families. This dialogue became the framework for the multidisciplinary teams that became prominent in the 1970s. Members of multidisciplinary teams independently completed their assigned tasks (e.g., evaluations, interventions) but shared information in order to integrate information that resulted in a more comprehensive and valid individualized education program for the child and family across all educational environments. As the 1970s

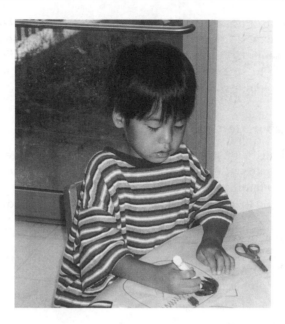

Our whole focus of collaboration should remain with the central idea of promoting recommended practices for families and children. Involving families as equal team members in decision making and working with children is important in all aspects of child development.

progressed, early collaborative efforts emerged. There were increased uses of team teaching, and school psychologists and special educators began introducing consultation as part of their service delivery for children with special needs. During the 1970s, the term *consultation* began to be used instead of *collaboration,* and the nature of the dialogue was very different from the dialogue that occurs in the course of collaboration in the 1990s. Initial consultation efforts were characterized by one-way channels of communication, with the special educator or school psychologist helping the classroom teacher solve the problem. Typically, there was a predictable flow of information: The classroom teacher talked about the problem and contributing characteristics of the environment, and the consultant made suggestions to improve or to solve the problem. These early approaches to collaboration eventually became known as the expert model of consultation.

By the end of the 1970s, consultation had become an integral part of special education services. As the 1980s began, there was a growing concern that the expert model was not fulfilling the potential of collaboration. Providing a list of expert suggestions to classroom teachers often did not meet the needs of the teachers, students, and families. Expert consultation, although useful, was not flexible and was not responsive to the inconsistencies and daily changes in a typical classroom. Johnson, Pugach, and Hammitte (1988) summarized the problems presented by an expert orientation to collaboration. They asserted that an expert orientation presents serious barriers that inhibit the potential of collaboration. Those barriers relate to strategy incongruence, giving advice, credibility conflicts, and confused problem ownership.

## Barriers to Collaboration Among Professionals

Understanding the mistakes of the past can help us avoid repeating those mistakes as we collaborate with ECE and ECSE peers to unify practices to best serve children and their families. Four barriers to effective collaboration among professionals are listed and then described in the subsections that follow (Johnson et al., 1988):

1. Strategy incongruence
2. Giving advice
3. Credibility conflicts
4. Confused problem ownership

### Strategy Incongruence

Strategy incongruence occurred when there were differences in the approaches of professionals engaging in the collaboration. For example, the approaches of special educators were often slanted toward being individualized and relied heavily on applied behavioral procedures, which were different from those of the typical general educator. Furthermore, special educators had limited experience in dealing with the problems of large-group instruction. As a result, there was an increased danger of strategies being suggested that were either unrealistic or outside the expertise of the ECE teacher, making implementation of the strategy problematic and unlikely. In the late 1990s, this problem has the potential to reemerge if we are not careful. The typical early childhood educator comes from a developmental constructivist paradigm, whereas the typical early childhood special educator comes from an applied behavioral positivist approach. These approaches embrace different strategies to support children and their families. We must work together to understand different perspectives and to incorporate those strategies that can best support children and their families.

### Giving Advice

Often expectations were placed on consultants, either internally or externally, to be in control of the situation. The consultant might have believed that he or she was ultimately responsible for the direction and outcome of the collaboration. When such a situation occurred, the consultant sometimes fell into the trap of giving advice, which, when done frequently, was a dangerous trap that was destined to lead the collaboration into failure. If the advice was successful, the result could have been the dependency of the teacher on the consultant and inhibition of the ability of the teacher to engage in independent problem solving. If the advice was unsuccessful, the result could be distrust and blame casting between professionals. Moreover, providing advice frequently resulted in strategies that the ECE teacher was unable (because it was outside of his or her area of expertise) or unwilling (because it was outside of his or her philosophical orientation) to implement. Giving advice is always a practice with potential problems. In the following discussion, the prescriptive and facilitative roles of collaboration are discussed, and suggestions for avoiding the advice-giving trap are offered.

### Credibility Conflicts

In order for collaboration to be successful, participants must have credibility with each other. Without such credibility, it is very unlikely that a successful resolution will result from the collaboration. Using an expert model increased the problems of credibility. If the recommended solution did not bring about the desired outcome, the classroom teacher no longer viewed the expert as having the necessary expertise to help him or her. When the outcome did not occur as planned in the classroom, the expert often viewed the teacher as not having the skills or the knowledge required to support the student. The literature prior to the 1990s clearly indicated dissonance among general and special educators with regard to the expectations of each group about the other group's level of expertise in addressing the needs of students with learning and behavior problems in the general classroom (Aloia & Aloia, 1983; Furey & Strauch, 1983; Johnson & Johnson, 1980; Leyser & Abrams, 1984; Ringlaben & Price, 1981; Spodek, 1982). As ECE and ECSE practices continue to be blended, educators must guard against credibility conflicts among colleagues by recognizing each other's expertise.

### Confused Problem Ownership

When collaborators took on more responsibility than the classroom teacher in identifying problems and developing strategy implementation plans, the ownership of the problem sometimes shifted to one or more of the collaborators. Once this occurred, the teacher's commitment to solve the problem was diminished. In this situation, the classroom teacher gave up control of and responsibility for the child. From the teacher's perspective, the expert was addressing the problem. As a result, the classroom teacher shifted attention to the other students in the classroom. The collaborator would therefore feel compelled to generate more ideas to help solve the problem. Unfortunately, because the suggestions were being independently developed and implemented without the teacher's input and support, failure was likely; thus, the problem often continued. To truly unify the collaborative approach to working with young children and their families, an approach that embraces mutual ownership of problems and solutions must be adopted.

## Barriers to Effective Communication Between Professionals and Families

The problems just described tended to be between professionals. Another problem inherent in the expert orientation to consultation was the tendency to exclude the family from the process. Often the child's problem was seen as a school difficulty for teachers and administrators to iron out, and thus input from family members was viewed as unnecessary. In some instances, problems were identified and addressed without the parents' being aware that their child was experiencing difficulties at school. This separation of school and home environments imposed a barrier on the family's involvement in their child's education.

By the end of the 1980s, the need for greater parity was recognized between people engaging in collaboration to maximize expertise and promote joint ownership. As the 1990s began, a new orientation in collaboration became more prominent. In this orientation, all members were seen as having the necessary expertise to solve the problem. Moreover, a sense of mutual ownership of the problem being confronted was created. Effort was directed toward developing mutual credibility and having a process in which all educators and families were seen as sources of expertise. Participants valued and practiced good listening skills to facilitate greater understanding of the problem and identification of solutions. An important role of the 1990s collaborator has emerged that supports the teacher and the parent in gaining greater understanding of the problem while being a sounding board for the pros and cons of potential solutions. Collaborators have striven to facilitate the thinking of teachers and parents about the collaborative process and to help focus their efforts on changing what can be changed rather than on what is beyond their control. In addition, approaches to collaboration in the 1990s have recognized the need for families to be included meaningfully in the collaborative process. Family members have become proactive in their roles as collaborative members of the team. This practice links the family and the program together in mutually supportive relationships (Salisbury & Dunst, 1997).

*Reflection:*   Stop for a minute and review in your mind what *collaboration* means. Do you collaborate in your profession? Do you collaborate with people in your community? How about with family members? As you read the next section, try to think of a time when you were involved in one of the dimensions of collaboration.

## COLLABORATION AS A MULTIDIMENSIONAL PROCESS

Collaborative ECE environments are places where people are committed to working together to best meet the needs of the children and families that they serve. As Pugach and Johnson (1995) asserted, the key to understanding these environments is knowing what it means to work together. That is, those working in a collaborative ECE environment must know the different ways in which adults interact in the broad context of collaboration and how various kinds of interactions relate to each other.

Johnson and Pugach (1991) studied transcripts of more than 100 teachers' collaborative dialogues to understand the manner in which teachers work together. They found four basic roles that teachers undertake as they collaborate: supportive, facilitative, informative, and prescriptive. Within this multidimensional framework, the four roles make up the continuum of interactions within any collaborative dialogue. Although the roles remain the same, the ways in which they are used and the relationships between roles change depending on the situation. The roles often overlap, and, during a single dialogue, individuals may embrace one or more of the roles. The characteristics of these roles are described in the next section.

## Supportive Role

One of the most important and fundamental dimensions of collaboration is support. Caring and being available to others, as well as their being available to you, are important in times of need and in times of joy. This dimension of support takes on many different forms. Interpersonal support represents the experiences people share. These experiences can be difficult or celebratory. Joyful events include marriages and births as well as recognition of a child's developmental progress or a special birthday. Tragic events include crises involving family members. These crises are specific to each individual and may be universal (e.g., illness, divorce, death) or unique (e.g., change in family living arrangements, car breakdown). All of these events, both happy and sad, have a profound impact on the people involved and often on their colleagues as well. Another form of support involves the recognition of growth and work well done. For example, awards and honors that create public recognition are interpersonal supports. In order to foster a collaborative environment, support from team colleagues must be present.

## Facilitative Role

The facilitative dimension of collaboration is a manner in which professionals scaffold the problem-solving process. In other words, the facilitative dimension of collaboration is a growth dimension in that the collaborator attempts to encourage colleagues to move ahead and solve a problem in spite of the colleagues' own doubts that they can do so. Within this role, the collaborator provides just enough modeling or demonstration to enable a colleague to master a new approach, come up with a new solution, and gain confidence in his or her own skills. Often, team members with greater knowledge and skills that are valuable to the team support and enhance the growth of other team members while promoting their more independent functioning. This support boosts the confidence of less experienced members of the team. The facilitative role differs substantially from advice giving or support in that the individual in this role assists colleagues in developing their own skills to a greater extent than before. It specifically focuses on modeling or demonstrating behaviors that enable a peer to master an approach, contemplate new ideas, and gain the confidence needed to implement a new practice.

## Informative Role

The information-giving dimension of collaboration is a relatively direct form of sharing expert knowledge to help with challenging situations. Information sharing promotes networking of human resources and maximizes the potential of the peo-

In early childhood environments, the desired end is increased comprehensiveness and appropriateness of services for children and families to improve desired outcomes.

ple involved with the team. From this sharing of resources, individuals and the entire team are better equipped to make decisions, which may result in communication with people who typically would not be contacted. Making contact with people not on the team promotes networking and increases the human resources available to the team. For example, a team member may feel comfortable calling an expert at an outside agency whom they would not have otherwise contacted. Then the two people begin to establish a relationship at the simplest level of an exchange of information about what each person represents. At the very least, the two learn each other's telephone numbers, addresses, and basic interests; more often they learn much more, including information about additional resources, contacts, expertise, and supports. As a result, these outside resources can become contacts that continue to be assets to the team.

## Prescriptive Role

The most direct dimension of collaboration is the prescriptive role, in which one colleague suggests a course of action to another. As discussed previously, serious problems can develop when prescription becomes the norm and one of the collaborators positions him- or herself as the expert. Although people want to avoid advice giving, providing colleagues with suggestions is often very helpful. From a multidimensional collaborative perspective, there are times when a particular practice might be just right for the situation one encounters with a colleague. As Pugach and Johnson (1995) pointed out, the trick is to know when to be prescriptive. Remember that the other roles in the collaborative process are more likely to encourage teachers to take ownership of the changes that they are trying to implement. When teachers are supported in their efforts to change, when their colleagues facilitate their use of a new practice, and when they receive useful information, the likelihood of teachers' making the change seemed to Pugach and Johnson to be greater than when someone simply tells them what to do. However, if a colleague has been trying in good faith to solve a problem and requests assistance, prescription may be in order. Prescription may also be needed when a teacher is struggling with a new practice that others have mastered. However, such help needs to be provided in a manner that empowers the teacher.

---

*Can you identify which role is being demonstrated?*

1. *Caroline (kindergarten teacher):* I have a new student in my classroom who is disruptive to the other children, and I don't know what to do at this point.

   *Reanna (preschool teacher):* What does the child do that's disruptive?

   *Caroline:* He bites the other children when they try to play with him.

   *Reanna:* I have an article that gives ideas on how to facilitate cooperative interactions between children when undesired behaviors like biting are present. I'll give you a copy of it to read.

2. *Alex (first-year preschool teacher):* Hello, Ann. I was just trying to plan for the first day of school.

   *Ann (teacher with 5 years of experience):* I remember when it was my first day teaching. I planned and planned and planned, but I still wasn't sure what to expect.

   *Alex:* Would you mind looking at what I've written?

   *Ann:* Sure, Alex. I can look at this now, and, if you like, we can also meet for lunch once each week and talk more.

3. *Jo (preschool teacher):* Hi, Lynn. I saw you asking Michael about his feelings when he left the playgroup abruptly, looking sad. What did he tell you?

   *Lynn (Michael's mother):* Oh, he said he didn't like it when the other child told him he wasn't his friend anymore. I never know what to say about this to him.

   *Jo:* Asking him his feelings is important and is a good way to approach this with him. Then, after he tells you what he is feeling, you could tell him it's okay to tell the other child how he felt when the child told him, "I'm not your friend anymore."

   *Lynn:* Thanks, Jo. I'll try that.

*Answers:*

1. Informative
2. Supportive
3. At first facilitative and then prescriptive

---

## INTERAGENCY COLLABORATION

In the previous section, the importance of individuals' collaborating to meet the needs of children and their families is stressed. Unfortunately, agencies often render services from their perspectives as experts without considering the expertise of other agencies, a situation that results in a fragmented approach to the delivery of services and thereby encourages the redundancy of some services and the absence of other services (Payzant, 1992). For example, families must tell and retell their life stories to different service providers, constantly reiterate their needs, and attempt to identify which agency wants which part of their story.

---

*Consider the following example:*

Diane and her 2-year-old son, Georgie, go to talk with a representative of the companion nurse service agency about getting in-home help for the care of Georgie. Once again, Diane must sit down with a counselor and retell her story about Georgie's disability and care needs; her home situation; her income; her family; her frustrations; and her needs, not only for Georgie but also for herself. Diane also has to fill out paperwork about all of this information. This must be the umpteenth time that she has filled out papers and has had to describe her needs and feelings. Diane thinks to herself: Couldn't the person who made the referral from the Children's Center have forwarded the information? Am I the only one who communicates with all of them? As Diane fills out the paperwork and gets ready to tell her story again, she thinks to herself, *It's so tiring and makes me feel as if no one really cares. They're just shuffling Georgie and me around until we go crazy!*

---

## Components of Interagency Collaboration

Interagency collaboration is multidimensional, interactional, and developmental in its nature and can be divided into five components:

1. *Climate:* Attitudes, priorities, and support of key decision makers as well as those of service providers may be important factors affecting the dimension of climate. They are instrumental in the degree of successful collaboration. The climate within agencies can encourage or inhibit collaboration across agencies. Typically, a climate that encourages openness and sharing is most conducive to interagency collaboration.
2. *Resources:* The three determining factors with regard to resources are money (i.e., fiscal resources available), people (i.e., number and quality of available professionals), and facilities (i.e., number and quality of intervention and specialized environments, such as diagnostic clinics, neonatal intensive care units, and surgical hospitals). Collaboration takes time and effort; resources must be committed to support collaborative efforts.
3. *Policies:* Policies, in the form of laws, regulations, standards, guidelines, licensing, certification, and interagency agreements, affect the ability of collaborative programs to function effectively. In particular, policies related to the sharing of information can be serious barriers to collaboration between agen-

cies. Policies that have the potential to inhibit interagency collaboration must be examined and changed.

4. *People:* The roles of the key people that take ownership in a cooperative endeavor may be those of a facilitator or leader, group members, and key decision makers. The facilitator or leader guides the group and is very influential in its overall success. The interagency coordination efforts of planning, developing, and influencing others to accept a given plan are the main roles of the group members. In the determination of acceptance or rejection of the overall efforts of the group, the key decision makers play a significant role and should be the primary resource as plans for interagency collaboration are being developed.

5. *Process:* The final dimension of the interagency collaboration process may be described as the series of actions and operations that critically affect interagency collaboration. Most important are the aspects of communication, proper planning, and mechanisms for conflict resolution. In order for interagency collaboration to take place, a careful plan must be put into effect that addresses channels of communication and how to resolve problems.

## Interagency Coordination Strategies

Interagency coordination strategies vary depending on the participants. Many interagency collaborative endeavors have been developed by which means multiple agencies efficiently approach a need or problem that an agency or individual could not accomplish alone. Reducing the competition to serve the child and the child's family not only promotes solidarity but also serves to strengthen the system of service delivery as a whole. Resources need to be expended, policies must be examined, and the climate must be open for interagency process to succeed. Successful interagency collaborations are developmental in nature and require preplanning and continued hard work to be successful (Johnson et al., 1997).

An understanding of the factors that facilitate and inhibit collaborative efforts is necessary. Johnson and colleagues (1997) and Steglin and Jones (1991) studied the interagency efforts of early childhood services providers across Ohio. They identified factors that facilitate or inhibit the success of interagency collaboration. Understanding these key components and barriers may allow for a successful union of individuals and agencies.

### Facilitators of Collaboration

Johnson and colleagues (1997) identified three key factors affecting interagency collaboration: commitment, communication, and strong leadership from key decision makers. *Commitment* was defined as a consensus with regard to the goals and visions of the collaborative team. If the stakeholders and significant members of the team did not have a commitment to the collaborative efforts of the team, then it would eventually fail. They provided three suggestions for building and maintaining commitment: to develop a system of compromise, to clarify issues devoid of compromise, and not to lose sight of the big picture of the important goals and positive outcomes that are made possible by the collaboration.

Johnson and colleagues (1997) also found that the component of communication was critical to collaboration. They made three suggestions with regard to the maintenance of strong communication:

1. Develop open communication that stresses awareness of information with written documentation as needed to avoid conflict.
2. Create regular communication channels such as in-person meetings, telephone conversations, correspondence, and so forth.
3. Develop informal connections such as meeting for a coffee break to promote cohesiveness.

Finally, the involvement and the commitment of key decision makers are critical to the success of an interagency collaboration. Johnson and colleagues (1997) suggested the following as elements of key personnel composition in interagency collaboration: involvement of someone who understands the agency's priorities and positions, involvement of someone empowered to make decisions on behalf of the agency, involvement of someone who can provide timely assistance, and involvement of someone who can authorize use of agency resources.

**Reflection:** Remember the previous example of the formation of a collaborative team (Juán and Timika)? The first thing team members did was to introduce themselves and talk about where they were from and why they were there, which is important to networking, making the statement of commitment, communicating, and identifying key decision makers on the collaborative team. This exercise facilitates the successful outcomes of their collaboration initially and in future relationships.

### Barriers to Interagency Collaboration

Clearly, when successful collaboration is evident, potential barriers are minimized or prevented. Steglin and Jones (1991) identified these possible barriers as lack of understanding of other agencies' policies, lack of communication between policy makers and service providers, lack of time for collaborative efforts, unclear goals and objectives, and gaps in screening and diagnostic services. Other barriers to successful collaboration include inconsistent service standards, excessive use of jargon, different definitions of *collaboration*, conflicting views on confidentiality issues, establishment of a new layer of bureaucracy, difficulty in establishing agreement among team members in defining decision-making rules, lack of sustained availability of key people, and resistance to change among members (Guthrie & Guthrie, 1991; Harbin, 1996; Johnson et al., 1988; Johnson, McLaughlin, & Christensen, 1982; Lacour, 1982).

Collaboration is not always easy but is essential and can be extremely fruitful with regard to the knowledge, policies, and practices of professionals and families.

## Interagency Coordination in Practice

The passage of the Education of the Handicapped Act Amendments of 1986 (PL 99-457) created both a climate and an opportunity for change in the manner in which interagency collaborative teams are conducted at the state and local levels. In terms of collaborative teams at the federal and state levels, Part H of the Individuals with Disabilities Education Act (IDEA) of 1990 (PL 101-476) (redesignated as Part C by the Individuals with Disabilities Education Act (IDEA) Amendments of 1997 [PL 105-17]) mandated that interagency coordinating councils (ICCs) provide coordinated services to meet the needs of families (Miller, 1992; Rosenkoetter et al., 1995). According to Rosenkoetter et al. (1995), most states have replicated the model of the local ICCs (LICCs). They utilize the ICC matrix of a collaborative system to provide a comprehensive coordinated system of services that addresses the needs of families.

There are several rationales for establishing these councils. To begin with, state interagency coordination tends to be policy or administration oriented, whereas local interagency coordination tends to be consumer and service related. Initiatives focusing on this type of local coordination have been viewed as easier to achieve than the statewide policy- and administration-oriented endeavors (Miller, 1992). One rationale for local service coordination relates to the previously mentioned concept of fragmentation. Through local service coordination efforts, there is an effort to reduce overlap of services to children and families. Service providers at the local level can then identify service needs, stop gaps from occurring in the delivery model, and simplify the process for families in gaining access to agencies. In addition, the results of local efforts include increased communication between families and all participants in the interagency collaborative team serving them (Rosenkoetter et al., 1995).

## CONCLUSIONS

The establishment of collaborative teams of professionals and families is aimed at improving the lives of children and their families. This emerging process is indicative of recommended practices for both the profession and families. Collaboration is not only mandated but also essential because of how American society is structured. The process is not always easy, but it can enhance the knowledge, policies, and practices of professionals and families. Collaboration meets the challenge of ECE by supporting the promotion of a shared goal that facilitates the growth and health of children and their families.

## REMEMBER THIS

1. ECE and ECSE professionals must work collaboratively with many professionals and parents to meet the needs of children and the children's families.

2. Collaboration is a coordinated, multidimensional process geared to meet shared goals.

3. Collaborative practices are evolving and relatively new.

4. Public policies have contributed to the establishment of collaborative service provisions.

5. Interagency coordination is an orderly development of climate, resources, policies, and people.

6. When establishing collaborative teams, developing commitment at the administrative and grassroots levels is important. Time and resources must be pledged to the effort for success to occur.

7. Families and their children are the center of the ideal vision of a collaborative culture.

## REFERENCES

Aloia, G.F., & Aloia, S.D. (1983). Teacher expectation questionnaire. *Journal of Special Education, 19*(2), 11–20.

Bruner, C. (1991). *Thinking collaboratively: Ten questions and answers to help policy makers improve children's services.* Washington, DC: Education and Human Services Consortium.

Education of the Handicapped Act Amendments of 1986, PL 99-457, 20 U.S.C. §§ 1400 *et seq.*

Furey, E.M., & Strauch, K.D. (1983). The perceptions of teachers' skills and knowledge by regular and special educators of mildly handicapped students. *Teacher Education and Special Education, 6,* 46–50.

Guthrie, G.P., & Guthrie, L.F. (1991). Streamlining interagency collaboration for youth at risk. *Educational Leadership, 49*(1), 17–22.

Harbin, G.L. (1996). The challenge of coordination. *Infants and Young Children, 8*(3), 68–76.

Individuals with Disabilities Education Act (IDEA) Amendments of 1997, PL 105-17, 20 U.S.C. §§ 1400 *et seq.*

Individuals with Disabilities Education Act (IDEA) of 1990, PL 101-476, 20 U.S.C. §§ 1400 *et seq.*

Johnson, D.W., & Johnson, R.T. (1980). Integrating handicapped students into the mainstream. *Exceptional Children, 47,* 90–99.

Johnson, L.J., & Pugach, M.C. (1991). Peer collaboration: Accommodating students with mild learning behavior problems. *Exceptional Children, 57*(5), 454–461.

Johnson, L.J., Pugach, M.C., & Devlin, S. (1990). Professional collaboration: Challenges of the next decade. *Teaching Exceptional Children, 22*(2), 9–11.

Johnson, L.J., Pugach, M.C., & Hammitte, D.J. (1988). Barriers to effective special education consultation. *Remedial and Special Education, 9*(6), 41–47.

Johnson, L.J., Tam, B., Zorn, D., LaMontagne, M.J., Oser, C., & Peters, M. (1997). *Factors that inhibit or promote successful interagency collaboration.* Cincinnati, OH: University of Cincinnati, Arlitt Child and Family Research and Education Center.

Johnson, W.H., McLaughlin, J.A., & Christensen, M. (1982). Interagency collaboration: Driving and restraining forces. *Exceptional Children, 48,* 395–399.

Lacour, J.A. (1982). Interagency agreement: A rational response to an irrational system. *Exceptional Children, 49,* 265–267.

Leyser, Y., & Abrams, P.D. (1984). Changing attitudes of classroom teachers toward mainstreaming through inservice training. *Clearinghouse, 57,* 250–255.

Miller, P.S. (1992). State interagency coordination for personnel development under Public Law 99-457: Building teams for effective planning. *Journal of Early Intervention, 16*(2), 146–154.

Payzant, T.W. (1992). New beginnings in San Diego: Developing a strategy for interagency collaboration. *Phi Delta Kappan, 74*(2), 139–146.

Pugach, M.C., & Johnson, L.J. (1995). *Collaborative practitioners, collaborative schools.* Denver: Love Publishing Co.

Ringlaben, R.P., & Price, J. (1981). Regular classroom teachers' perceptions of mainstreaming effects. *Exceptional Children, 47,* 302–304.

Rosenkoetter, S.E., Shotts, C.K., Streufert, C.A., Rosenkoetter, L.I., Campbell, M., & Torrez, J. (1995). Local interagency coordinating councils as infrastructure for early intervention: One state's implementation. *Topics in Early Childhood Special Education, 15*(3), 264–280.

Salisbury, C.L., & Dunst, C.J. (1997). Home, school, and community partnerships: Building inclusive teams. In B. Rainforth & J. York-Barr, *Collaborative teams for students with severe disabilities: Integrating therapy and educational services* (2nd ed., pp. 57–87). Baltimore: Paul H. Brookes Publishing Co.

Spodek, B. (1982). What special educators need to know about regular classrooms. *Educational Forum, 46,* 295–307.

Steglin, D.A., & Jones, S.D. (1991). Components of early childhood interagency collaboration: Results of a statewide study. *Early Education and Development, 2*(1), 54–67.

# Activities

1. Find teachers and/or administrators with a great deal of experience, and ask them to talk to you about teaming and collaboration throughout their career. Have things changed? If so, how?

2. Observe teams that are engaging in collaboration, and find examples of the four roles in which collaborators engage. How frequently are they used? Do individuals tend to engage in certain roles and not others? Why?

3. Talk with people who are participating on a collaborative team. Ask them to describe the benefits and the barriers. How did they overcome the barriers?

4. Find parents who are participating on a collaborative team. Ask them about their level of participation and their satisfaction with this level of participation.

5. Try to find parents with experience in schools over time. Ask them if their level of participation has changed. Do schools welcome parents more than they did? Are there any differences between the views of parents with a child who has a special need and those of a child without disabilities?

## chapter 2

# Key Collaborative Skills

*Lawrence J. Johnson and Janice E. Noga*

## CHAPTER ORGANIZER

In this chapter, we explore the following ideas . . .

1.  The importance of communication to the development of collaborative environments

2.  Common barriers that can inhibit communication and collaboration

3.  Active listening skills that can facilitate communication and collaboration

4.  The nature of group processes

5.  How to manage and benefit from conflict

6.  The elements of problem solving as an important component of collaboration

7.  The characteristics of collaborative environments

*Collaboration* is a process in which individuals or organizations agree to work together to achieve a set of common goals. It involves shared responsibility, consensus building, goal setting, problem solving, and decision making (Bland, 1995). Collaborative efforts require more than just personal commitment and shared vision to succeed. Collaboration is a group endeavor the success of which is dependent on effective communication and interpersonal skills (Pugach & Johnson, 1995). In turn, effective communication is an essential part of the successful use of key skills in collaboration: active listening, negotiation and mediation, networking and sharing, creative problem solving, and leadership.

Communication is the foundation of all human interactions. Without the ability to communicate, people's lives would be barren and isolated. Effective communication enables people to share experiences and establish connections with others. The ability to communicate ideas clearly and accurately is a critical component of any successful collaboration. In this chapter, we discuss communication as a key collaborative skill and examine its role in the collaborative process. We discuss the role that communication skills play as an essential component of the other key collaborative skills listed previously. Finally, we address the central role that early childhood educators can play in collaborative efforts that target children and their families.

## COMMUNICATION IN COLLABORATIVE PARTNERSHIPS

Communication is a deceivingly simple process made up of five components: sender, message, channel, environment, and receiver. A communication cycle is initiated when the sender transmits a message by way of a channel through an environment to the receiver of the message. Messages may be verbal, consisting of words, or they may be nonverbal, consisting of actions such as gestures or facial expressions or of sounds such as pitch or tone of voice. Verbal and nonverbal messages may be sent simultaneously to a receiver. The receiver acquires the message through a combination of visual and auditory means and gains meaning by interpreting the combined message. The receiver then provides direct or indirect feedback to the sender, which enables the original sender to understand whether the original message was understood. As the interaction continues, this continuous feedback loop becomes the basis of a cycle of communication between the sender and the receiver (Johnson & Pugach, 1996; U.S. Department of Agriculture, Cooperative Extension Service, 1991).

Consider the example of an individualized education program (IEP) conference between an ECE teacher and a special education consultant. The special education consultant transmits a message along a verbal channel when he or she begins to speak to the teacher about the issues that he or she has identified during his or her evaluation of a student. The teacher receives the message and sends his or her own message in return to indicate understanding of what has been said. The environment in which this communication cycle takes place may be a classroom where there is background conversation and children at play, or it may be a quiet office with few distractions. The primary verbal channel through which this message is transmitted may be augmented by supplementary messages sent through nonverbal channels such as body language; facial expression; tone of voice; and physical activity, such as indicating or underlining scores on an evaluation report.

Communication is a cyclical process that is completed only when all participants in that process understand the message. Simply sending a message is not enough. The message must also be accurately received if the cycle of communication is to reach closure. The effectiveness of communication between individuals is determined by the degree to which both the sender and the receiver achieve a mutual understanding of the messages being sent. People often believe that they are communicating whenever they send a message to another person; but if the receiver fails to understand that message, the cycle has failed and true communication does not occur. This common mistake is the one most likely to lead to problems between participants in collaborative endeavors. (For a more detailed discussion of the specific elements contributing to the cycle of communication, see Johnson & Pugach, 1996.) In the case of the IEP conference, if the teacher and the consultant fail to confirm their understanding of the messages being exchanged, they will find it difficult to design an IEP that is achievable.

**Reflection:**  Think about a meeting or conversation in which you have been involved. What was the message? Who talked to whom? How often and for how long? Which channels were used to transmit that message? Think particularly about nonverbal channels such as tones of voice, gestures, and facial expressions. Did the verbal message match the nonverbal message? What was the environment? Did it contribute to effective communication or was it a distraction?

## Elements of Effective Communication

Effective collaborative communication does not happen overnight. Reinhiller (1996) described a three-stage developmental process of communication that collaborative groups commonly go through. The first stage is marked by formal, stifled communication. During this stage, group members establish common objectives and understandings. They may be negotiating understanding of each other's motives, establishing their expertise in the eyes of the group, or feeling their way around potential turf issues. It is a period when group members are working to get to know one another.

The second stage is marked by more open and spontaneous communication. A sense of shared responsibility begins to emerge. Group members begin to establish areas of expertise, negotiate roles and responsibilities, and build interpersonal relationships that may also extend outside the collaborative activities of the group.

By the third stage, the group attains a true collaborative relationship, which is marked by open communication and interaction, mutual trust, and spontaneity. Group members have a deeper understanding and acceptance of the changing nature of power and authority that marks collaborative efforts. They learn to anticipate, delegate, and respect the specific talents and expertise of their partners. When a partnership reaches this final stage, its members are truly ready to engage in collaborative endeavors.

**Reflection:** Think about groups to which you have belonged. Can you pick out the three stages that each group went through? How easily did each group move through the three stages? Did you notice a difference based on the type of group (e.g., school based, club, social, community)? Now think about how you as a group member moved through these stages. What thoughts went through your mind? How did you view other group members? Did your views change as the group moved toward Stage 3?

If a collaborative group is to reach the third stage, members of the group must develop several key communication skills (Friend & Cook, 1996; Pugach & Johnson, 1995; Swan & Morgan, 1993). First, group members must be sensitive to others' frames of reference as well as their own. When one is able to step back from one's own values and beliefs and see and hear oneself from an outsider's perspective, one is much more aware of the multiple elements that contribute to the truly complex dynamic of communication. In stepping outside one's personal frame of reference, one is free to think broadly, explore alternative meanings, and ultimately view one's own role within the context of the collaborative mission.

A skill related to effective collaborative communication is demonstrating respect and positive regard for others, which is achieved by attending to the verbal and nonverbal messages that other partners in the group communicate, supporting and encouraging their contributions, and indicating a desire to work closely with others in the group. In this way, group members learn to trust and accept each other as they work to shape a truly collaborative effort.

Finally, the ability to understand and address conflict and resistance is an important skill for developing effective communication within the group. Typically, group members' resistance is their response to their perceptions of personal or organizational change. Because change is often a critical underlying assumption of collaborative efforts, group members' resistance to change should be considered a natural part of the process that contributes to group growth and communication. Conflict is also a natural occurrence of the group process within a collaboration. Handled in a manner grounded in trust and respect, conflict and resistance can be used to contribute to the positive growth of a collaborative effort (U.S. Department of Agriculture, Cooperative Extension Service, 1991). Unfortunately, educators and human services professionals have become masterful at avoiding conflict. Do not let this happen. Conflict and resistance are natural components of long-term group processes and occur at some point during the course of any collaborative effort. By dealing with conflict and resistance in an open, constructive manner, one is able to help the team members develop a truly collaborative partnership.

---

*Look at an exchange between an early childhood teacher and the center director:*

An early childhood teacher and the center director are discussing Caitlin, a new student at the school. The teacher has noticed that Caitlin is having difficulty with expressive language. She reports that "Caitlin just doesn't seem to be able to find the words she needs to participate in conversations with the other students in the class. I'm concerned about her progress in relation to the others. I'd like to arrange a speech screening for her." The director is coming off of a very difficult day, including an emotional session with another child's parents in which they vehemently resisted the idea of their son's being deemed in need of speech therapy. The director looks out the window and thinks, "Oh no, not another one. Caitlin's parents will never accept the idea that their daughter may need speech therapy." Looking down at her desk, the director responds to the teacher: "Are you sure you aren't overreacting? After all, you've had Caitlin in your class for only a week; perhaps she's just shy. I think you should wait a little longer." The teacher leaves the meeting frustrated and unhappy. Caitlin has never shown any signs of shyness in class. The teacher is certain that Caitlin's communication problems are due to her language delays.

*Think about the example of Caitlin's teacher and the center director. Consider the following questions:*

1. Were these two speaking from the same frame of reference? What was the teacher's concern? What was the director's?
2. What could the teacher and the director do that would change the result of their conversation?
3. How would you have managed this interaction if you were the teacher? If you were the director?

## Barriers to Effective Communication

When collaborative partners engage in an interaction style that decreases their ability to listen and communicate, they construct barriers to effective communication that may ultimately derail the collaborative effort in which they are engaged. The following eight types or aspects of communication are common barriers to maintaining collaborative dialogues:

1. Giving advice
2. Offering false reassurances
3. Misdirected questions
4. Changing the subject
5. Using clichés
6. Minimizing feelings
7. Jumping to conclusions
8. Interrupting

### Giving Advice

There is a fine line between offering suggestions and giving advice. If the director in the preceding example had given the teacher several alternative courses of action to follow before initiating a screening, the teacher would have been in control of the decision to choose any particular action. Offering suggestions is a natural activity of collaborative partnerships that reflects the give-and-take of professional expertise as warranted by a given situation or issue. Giving advice as the director did in the preceding example can carry with it the implied assumption that the advice being offered is the correct and only option. When pressed too strongly, such advice serves to disempower the individual receiving the advice, disrupting the professional balance of expertise that must exist within a collaborative partnership and creating a foundation of unequal relationships that may ultimately damage the collaboration.

### Offering False Reassurances

False reassurances usually arise during a well-meaning attempt to ease concerns of a colleague by glossing over or dismissing the true nature of a problem. In the preceding example, the director offered shyness as a possible explanation in order to reassure the teacher that there really was not a problem with Caitlin. Providing false reassurances puts partners in a difficult spot when problems are not resolved and minimizes the group's motivation to work toward a successful resolution. Ultimately, false reassurances serve only to tear down the professional's credibility in the eyes of the collaborative group and undermines professional trust.

### Misdirected Questions

Misdirected questions shift the focus to different aspects of the communication and interfere with the development of a meaningful dialogue. In the preceding example, the director shifted the focus of conversation to a consideration of whether the teacher was overreacting to Caitlin's difficulty with language, thus avoiding any discussion pertaining to Caitlin herself. The best way to avoid this pattern of negative interaction is to focus on the use of reflective listening. When one engages in reflective listening, important trends within the conversation become apparent and constructive questions flow naturally, allowing the dialogue to proceed in a coherent manner. If the director had recognized and acknowledged the teacher's concern about Caitlin rather than dismissing it, a far more substantive conversation about the teacher's perceptions of Caitlin's abilities might have occurred.

### Changing the Subject

Changing the subject during a collaborative team meeting serves to abruptly inhibit the communication between partners. It clearly indicates inattention and disinterest in the topic at hand. It is a barrier to communication best avoided by engaging in active listening techniques that help prevent inattention and keep the dialogue on track.

### Using Clichés

In collaborative discussions, responding to a colleague with a cliché is certain to inhibit communication. Clichés often are used without thought and as a result raise questions in the listener's mind about the validity of the problem. There is virtually no situation in collaborative endeavors in which the use of a cliché is appropriate.

The collaborative roles of the teachers during group times are to facilitate and to work together. These roles involve communicating and supporting each other's roles and the needs of individual children.

### Minimizing Feelings

Offering false reassurances, changing the subject, and using clichés are all examples of ways in which partners minimize the feelings of another team member. The director in the preceding example minimized the teacher's feelings when she shifted the subject to shyness as a possible source of Caitlin's difficulties. To be an effective collaborator, it is crucial that one not make judgments regarding the worth or value of a problem that is brought to the table for discussion. Rather, all partners are responsible for addressing issues and working to gain a greater understanding of the problem in order to identify a solution.

### Jumping to Conclusions

Jumping to conclusions is a reflection either of unwillingness to spend adequate time considering all factors related to a problem or of inability to view multiple perspectives. It can distract attention from the true issue at hand. As a result of jumping to conclusions, the collaborative team is unlikely to achieve successful resolution of the problem, which leads to frustration and an unwillingness to continue the use of collaboration in problem-solving situations.

### Interrupting

Interruptions disrupt the flow of the conversation and seriously inhibit the ability of participants to gain adequate understanding during the course of a collaborative interaction. Interruptions also may occur when time becomes an issue and then are used to get to the heart of the problem before time runs out on that interaction. In either case, interruptions drastically shift the focus of the interaction and serve to seriously inhibit further conversation.

**Reflection:** Pause for a moment and think about the last time you participated in a group project. Did any of the barriers to communication described in this section occur? What happened to the flow of communication when a barrier was introduced?

## COMMUNICATION SKILLS IN COLLABORATION

Good communication skills can be found at the heart of all effective collaborative partnerships. Communication is essential if partners are to establish goals and objectives, agree on roles, make decisions, resolve conflicts, or develop a shared vision of service (Melaville & Blank, 1991). Effective collaborative communications are marked by the use of common language that avoids jargon, clarifies terms and key phrases, and establishes mutually acceptable definitions. In this way, a foundation is established that can fully support the development of processes of mutual interaction, negotiation, problem solving, and decision making that are essential elements of successful collaborations.

Communication skills for effective collaboration do not come naturally to many people. As students, teachers were expected to work individually and thus were not encouraged to develop the interpersonal communication skills that support and enhance collaboration. If early childhood educators are to become successful collaborators, they need to develop interpersonal skills that are grounded in an understanding of human relationships and interpersonal communication.

Kruger (1997) found that teachers engaged in collaborative problem solving were more likely to feel confident about the value of their contributions when they perceived that their skills and abilities were appreciated by co-workers. Collaborative efforts that provided a strong element of social support from colleagues resulted in more confident and imaginative problem solving on the part of teachers. The study illustrated the importance of building strong interpersonal support mechanisms into the foundation of school-based collaborations.

Successful collaborative efforts result when members learn to blend interpersonal and communication skills to create an environment in which they devote time and effort to learning about each other's roles and responsibilities. They develop an understanding of the role that each member plays in the service system. They learn how their partners operate within their own organizations and work to gain an understanding of the needs and pressures that exist outside the bounds of the collaboration. They establish formal and informal communication structures that actively seek areas of agreement and remain open to compromise. Focus is turned early to creating an effective working climate, establishing rapport with key stakeholders, and building an atmosphere of respect among group members for each other's procedures and conventions. Emphasis is on human relationships over agency structure in the collaborative strategies being developed to solve mutual concerns. These groups focus on what is to be gained rather than on issues of power and control (Bruner, 1991; Melaville & Blank, 1991). As a result, they are far more likely to be successful at crafting a unified vision for service to children and their families.

## Active Listening to Ensure Communication

Good collaborative partners attend to both verbal and nonverbal messages. They employ active listening skills to ensure that communication is accurate, open, and natural. Active listening skills are particularly important to the establishment and maintenance of successful collaborative relationships. Use of these skills helps collaborative partners clarify and understand the messages that are being exchanged. There are eight basic skill areas that compose active listening:

1. Offering oneself
2. Broad opening statements
3. Reflection
4. Verbalization of the implied
5. Seeking clarification
6. Silence
7. Placing events in time and sequence
8. Summarization

### Offering Oneself

Offering oneself involves the ability to indicate to a colleague that one is there to listen and to help that individual work through a concern. It is an important message that indicates a readiness to be engaged and supportive.

### Broad Opening Statements

Broad opening statements create a sense of openness that encourages exploration of an issue and leaves room for multiple interpretations. It is an important technique in ensuring that collaborative dialogue does not block out the opinions and concerns of all participants.

### Reflection

Reflection enhances the receiver's understanding of the message being sent while providing the sender with the opportunity to reflect on the message's interpretation by the receiver and to modify the message as needed. This is a critical dynamic in collaborative communication because it not only clarifies the message for the receiver but also provides an opportunity for the sender to reflect on the message as it is restated, thus allowing the sender to gain a greater understanding of critical factors related to the issue being discussed.

## Verbalization of the Implied

Reflection and verbalization of the implied are similar skills. However, whereas reflection involves restatement of the overt message, verbalization of the implied seeks to get at underlying messages. This technique requires rapport and trust among collaborative partners if it is to work effectively in bringing deeper issues to the surface for examination.

## Seeking Clarification

When members engage in a collaborative dialogue, there are times when partners seek clarification. Seeking clarification is a key technique for eliminating the confusion that can result from misunderstanding, inattention, or distraction.

## Silence

Silence is an excellent way to indicate to a colleague that more information is needed. Like verbalization of the implied, however, silence is a technique that works best when there is strong rapport and a feeling of trust among participants. Used inappropriately, silence may inhibit communication and break down rapport; used skillfully, however, silence provides collaborative partners with a moment to think and reflect on salient aspects of the conversation. Silence can be a powerful tool in facilitating a dialogue that is rich in information and underlying detail.

## Placing Events in Time and Sequence

Placing an event in time and sequence is most often used when the collaborative dialogue involves substantial or complex information. This skill involves restatement and reordering of information to achieve coherence. It helps to place events in their proper order and identify those events that are unrelated to the issue under examination, thus helping the group to maintain focus and consistency within the collaborative dialogue.

## Summarization

Every collaborative interaction should end with a summary of what took place during that interaction and the actions that individuals are to take as a result of the interaction. The summary is important for two reasons: 1) It allows all individuals in the dialogue a chance to revisit key points, revise the content of the interaction and make clarifications regarding key events, and arrive at a consensus regarding outcomes; and 2) it makes public what actions are expected from each participant and thus creates a means of establishing accountability for each partner in the collaboration.

**Reflection:** Think about a conversation that you recently witnessed. Did those involved seem to be listening to one another? How did you know? Now go back over the eight elements listed in this section. Which of these skills were exhibited during the conversation you witnessed? In what way?

## Active Listening and Feedback

Active listening is a process that goes beyond the physical act of hearing. It is an intellectual and emotional process that integrates a full range of inputs in a search for the meaning of and an understanding of a sender's message. It involves listening "between the lines" to hear what is not said as well as what is said. Active listening involves interaction and participation in the cycle of communication.

Good listening skills require practice. The use of active listening skills is communicated to others through the use of feedback and reflection. A good listener concentrates on the speaker to better understand what the speaker is trying to say while also trying to determine whether the facts as they are being presented are accurate, unbiased, and complete. A good listener listens for ideas and tries to see the relationships between facts as transmitted by the speaker. Most important, a good listener suspends judgment until after all of the information has been heard. Suspending judgment is a very important part of listening. If one's attention is turned to evaluating and judging each statement as it is presented, one is distracted from the complete message that is being sent, which often results in guesswork and mutual misunderstanding.

Feedback is an important component of the communication process and plays a critical role in active listening. When delivered with care and consideration, feedback is an efficient and effective tool for confirming understanding of the message as heard. Three important criteria for giving feedback are to

1. Be considerate
2. Consider timing
3. Create a feedback loop

### Be Considerate

Active listening should provide clues about the needs and feelings of the person with whom one is communicating. Ignoring these clues can be destructive to continued effective communication.

### Consider Timing

Feedback is most useful when given as soon as possible. However, be certain that the other person is ready to hear feedback. In some cases, it is better to wait. Learn to be sensitive to the best times for feedback.

### Create a Feedback Loop

Encourage others to rephrase your comments. In this way, you ensure that they have understood both the surface and the underlying meanings of your comments.

## NEGOTIATION AND MEDIATION FOR COMMUNICATION

How a group negotiates and mediates conflict has a direct effect on its ability to integrate the different interests, skills, and goals of the group members in the shared values of the collaboration. Conflict is a natural part of the group process and should be addressed immediately and proactively. Well-managed conflict helps members increase their understanding of each other; share thoughts and feelings that might otherwise have remained hidden; and test differences of opinion in an open, safe environment (Schwarz, 1994). Groups that use effective communication strategies to resolve conflict provide group members with the opportunity to understand how the conflict arose, how it was addressed, and how they as a group were able to resolve it.

## Emotions

Collaboration on issues pertaining to young children is inevitably accompanied by strong emotions. These emotions often form the basis of conflict over issues pertaining to the goals, values, actions, and decisions of the collaboration. When left unresolved, conflict can lead to hostility, anxiety, resentment, and the ultimate dissolution of the collaborative partnership. Effective negotiation and mediation strategies can help to defuse the negative elements of conflict. The aim of such negotiation is to resolve conflict in a way that ensures that the concerns of all participants in the conflict are satisfied.

## Facilitators for Successful Negotiation

Negotiation and mediation require a specific set of communication skills to facilitate identification, processing, and resolution of a conflict. Successful negotiation of conflicts is generally conducted according to a four-step model:

1. *Diagnose the nature of the conflict:* Is this a conflict of values or specific issues or actions, or is it a combination of these?
2. *Initiate a confrontation:* As used here, *confrontation* does not mean that one should attack or demean those who disagree. Positive confrontation involves each party stating the effects of the conflict on him or her. For example, a collaboration team member might say, "I have a problem with the direction this project is taking. If we choose to pursue this particular course of action, I will find it difficult to participate because of my work schedule" rather than saying, "Obviously, you don't want me involved in this project, because you've picked activities that conflict with my work schedule!"
3. *Listen to the other person's point of view:* This point relates to understanding someone else's frame of reference. Once one's position has been stated, one should use active listening techniques to hear the response. One should not be tempted to explain or defend oneself or to make demands or threats. Listen, reflect, and clarify what the other person says in response. Once the response has been interpreted accurately, one's point of view should be restated. Avoid stating value judgments. Concentrate on outcomes and direct effects. Active listening encourages the other person to lower his or her defenses, which, in turn, makes that person more ready to truly hear another's point of view.

4.  *Use problem-solving processes to negotiate a consensus decision:* Clarify the problem, generate and evaluate possible solutions, negotiate the best solution, plan implementation of the solution, and plan for evaluation of the solution. Above all, be prepared to repeat the process if the first solution does not work out.

## Strategies for Avoiding Conflict

It is important that the collaborative groups view conflicts as offering the potential for growth, not as damaging events. Bolman and Deal (1991) offered a set of guidelines specifically designed for groups dealing with conflict. These five guidelines describe a step-by-step process for group interaction that recognizes the inevitability of conflict and suggests proactive strategies for negotiation and mediation:

1.  *Agree on the basics:* Take time to work toward consensus on group goals and how to achieve them. When group members are comfortable with their roles and with group norms, their sense of shared commitment becomes a very powerful bond that helps to hold the group together through times of stress and conflict.
2.  *Search for interests in common:* Begin the search for consensus by identifying commonalities. If group members understand what they have in common, they are then better prepared to discuss areas in which they differ. If members disagree on a particular issue, there may be other areas in which they agree.
3.  *Experiment:* Groups should not be afraid to discuss options before deciding on a specific course of action. Experimentation is a way to move beyond the stalemate created by conflict without defeat or loss of face for any group member. A test of differences can help illustrate where points of agreement do exist. Most important, however, experimentation can open new possibilities for the entire group, helping the collaboration to move forward in ways not previously considered.
4.  *Doubt your own infallibility:* During the heat of disagreement, group members need to step back, adopt a new frame of reference, and question the dysfunctional cycle of communication that supports conflict. One should ask oneself the following questions: Am I sure that I am right? Are all members of the group also sure? Are all members listening to one another? Group members who are able to question themselves and groups that value the diverse resources, ideas, and perspectives that members bring to the table are far more likely to see differences among group members as assets and as sources of learning rather than as sources of division. Such groups turn conflict into the productive discussion of differences.
5.  *Treat differences as a group responsibility:* Conflict between group members must be resolved by the entire group. It is easy to step back and leave resolution of differences in the hands of the group members who are actually in conflict. However, intragroup conflict always has the potential to affect the group's ability to achieve desired goals. It must be addressed by the group and resolved in a way that reinforces group cohesiveness and group functioning. It

These two teachers are facilitating collaborative play between two young children. One teacher also promotes the
entry of a third child into the play environment.

is in everyone's interest to make sure that the affected individuals work
through their differences.

## PROBLEM-SOLVING SKILLS FOR EFFECTIVE COLLABORATION

A common problem in collaboration is resolving the discrepancy that exists
between the way things are and the way people would like things to be. Problems
may be described as dilemmas, concerns, or challenges needing resolution—the
sooner the better, in many cases. Teachers encounter problems that are child centered, curriculum centered, teacher centered, and school centered. Participants in
collaborative teams encounter problems that may be centered in outside agencies
or in the community.

### Problem-Solving Competencies

Good problem-solving skills are crucial in effective collaboration. Regardless of the
purposes for which they are initiated, all forms of collaborative problem solving
retain common features. Chief among these are the shared nature of the interaction, the presence of two or more individuals with varying knowledge and expertise recognized as being useful for the problem at hand, and joint recognition and
acceptance of the need to engage in collaboration as an effective way of addressing
a specific problem or goal (Pugach & Johnson, 1995). Although any collaborative
problem-solving relationship will be different, depending on the individuals
involved and the problem being addressed, all collaborative problem-solving relationships are identifiable by the presence of these common features.

Silliman and Wilkinson (1991) identified four problem-solving competencies
essential for effective collaboration:

1. The capacity to communicate relevant information in a way that leads to group adoption of shared responsibility for solving problems and joint ownership for purposes of generating ideas and working solutions
2. The ability to communicate active interest in the contributions of others and understanding of the opinions and perspectives of others, both within and outside of the collaboration
3. Proficiency in obtaining information from others that is relevant to the development of joint action plans for the collaboration
4. The ability to provide explicit feedback that is directed toward identifying strengths, areas of effectiveness, weaknesses, and areas needing improvement

**Reflection:** As you read the final section on problem solving, think of a specific professional problem that you have encountered. Using the seven-step model described, define the problem, identify alternatives, select a solution, and develop an evaluation plan.

## Problem-Solving Model

Problem solving is a specific extension of collaborative communication. It underlies many key collaborative processes, such as shared decision making, goal setting, and strategic planning. Collaborative partners who consistently use the key collaborative skills discussed previously in this chapter find themselves fully prepared to incorporate the four fundamental problem-solving competencies described in the preceding section into a variety of group activities.

The problem-solving process is commonly broken down into a series of basic steps that can be used to structure group interactions. Pugach and Johnson (1995) described a process for collaborative problem solving based on their work with collaborations of school-based personnel. (For a more thorough discussion of this seven-step problem-solving model, see Pugach & Johnson, 1995, pp. 144–148.) The model suggests the following seven steps:

1. *Articulation of the problem:* Collect information about the situation or perceived need, and develop a brief statement that describes the general area to be examined. Take care not to narrow the focus too quickly—the broader the better at this stage. The challenge at this point is to identify the problem in such a way that full examination and exploration of the issues at hand are encouraged.
2. *Consideration of contributing factors:* It is important to build time for reflection into any problem-solving process. Try to identify factors that you feel contribute to the problem at hand. Consider the following: Do you have any control over these factors? How will these factors have an impact on the group's ability to address this problem? Who is best suited to address these factors? How do these factors relate to the issue being addressed?
3. *Development of a problem pattern statement:* This step provides you with an opportunity to review what you know about the problem up to this point. The problem pattern statement describes the problem and its underlying factors,

individual and group responses to this problem, and controllable factors relevant to the problem being addressed.

4. *Generation of possible solutions:* Once the problem and its contributing factors have been identified, brainstorm possible solutions. Brainstorming may be done as a group or as an individual activity. Refer to notes from the prior three steps, and try to develop several possible interventions. Be sure that the teacher or group member actually affected by the problem is involved.

5. *Selection of an alternative solution:* Now that you or the teacher affected by the problem have thoroughly examined all dimensions of this problem, it is time to select a reasonable intervention or a related course of action. One method for selecting an alternative is to consider the three most likely solutions and imagine the possible outcomes of each. What is likely to happen in the classroom as a result of this intervention? Is it workable for you?

6. *Development of an evaluation plan:* After an alternative is selected but before the intervention or solution is implemented, develop a means by which to evaluate whether the intervention is actually implemented (i.e., process evaluation) and, if so, whether it is successful (i.e., outcome evaluation). Do not bypass this step. Good evaluations yield important information about both the problem and the intervention employed. You may find that you need to rearticulate your problem or try another solution. This does not amount to failure; it just means that the problem is more complex or difficult than originally thought. If this is the case, the best step is to go back and refine your understanding of the problem by repeating earlier steps as necessary.

7. *Implementation and monitoring of the accepted solution:* Establish a time line for the intervention. When should you implement it? How long should it take to discover whether the solution has worked? How often should you meet with your group to discuss progress? If things do not work out as projected, you may need to repeat this process to identify a more successful strategy.

Problem solving takes time, a precious commodity in schools. One of the advantages of collaborative problem solving is the availability of a group of individuals who can bring diverse experiences, expertise, and understanding to bear on the problem. Group problem solving contributes to the creative pooling of many ideas, more realistic forecasting, and greater availability of expert resources (Johnson & Pugach, 1996).

**Reflection:**  As you read the next section, think about groups in which you have participated. What were the leaders like? What effect did the leader's abilities have on the group's interactions? Think about a leader you particularly admire. How did that leader use effective communication and interpersonal skills to guide the group?

## LEADERSHIP AND COMMUNICATION

Power and authority are key mediating variables that can influence the success or failure of collaborative efforts. These variables are personified in the group leader.

The success of any group effort is dependent on the ability of the leader to organize group activities, create a communicative environment, and synthesize outcomes. The leader has a responsibility to maintain a positive, cohesive atmosphere among a diverse group of people embodying varying levels and types of knowledge and personal biases. He or she needs to

1. Have a clear sense of the purpose of the group and be able to communicate it clearly
2. Be a trustworthy, skilled listener who motivates and empowers group members to accomplish group goals
3. Press members to understand each other's point of view and the way each perceives the issues and problems at hand
4. Keep members focused on goals to prevent individual interests from interfering with the development of shared goals
5. Encourage members to contribute to the full extent of their abilities, thus reinforcing the value of all participants in the collaboration (Melaville & Blank, 1991)

The skills of the leader affect both the quality and the timeliness of decisions made by groups (Abelson & Woodman, 1983). When conflicts arise, appropriate problem-solving techniques must be used to guide the group through its difficulties toward defined goals. The leader must

1. Be skillful in group facilitation, arbitration, and conflict resolution
2. Have the ability and willingness to deal with complex issues while generating an atmosphere of comfort and flexibility for all group members
3. Be skilled at group development and have the capability of developing true group rapport projecting a unity of concern for all group members
4. Facilitate group interactions and be strong enough to maintain group cohesion if conflict arises
5. Be able to engender humbleness of spirit in group members so that their own individual needs do not compete with those of the group

Leadership is an interaction between group members and designated leaders. It is based on principles of mutual responsibility, shared power, and authority. It is not an attribute but an activity the success of which is grounded in the use of effective communication skills to support the collaborative group's development of a shared vision and purpose. Leadership is a shared function of the group that is predicated on service and assistance to group members (Schien, 1996). It requires active listening by all parties and careful attention to concealed or disguised motives, attitudes, and events. Most important, leadership involves building a collection of individuals into a productive, collaborative group.

Collaborative leaders combine personal commitment with interpersonal communication skills to empower group members and enable collaborative efforts. They create a dynamic structure for interaction that enhances the quality of intergroup communications and strengthens problem-solving efforts (Farrer & Kaye, 1996). Specifically, collaborative leaders

- Press group members to understand each other's perspectives of issues and problems at hand
- Facilitate group efforts to generate alternative solutions, identify those that constitute common ground, and incorporate these solutions into the collaborative strategy
- Prevent individual agendas from interfering with the development of shared goals
- Encourage group members to contribute to the full extent of their abilities
- Represent the goals and interests of the group to others outside the collaboration (Melaville & Blank, 1991)

Good collaborative leaders are both directive and facilitative. They use personal commitment to the goals of the collaborative group in combination with effective interpersonal skills to initiate and mobilize collaborative efforts while empowering the other members of the group. The result is a group environment fostered by egalitarian structures of leadership in which power and authority are diffused according to specific task-based knowledge or expertise (Kagan, 1991).

## EARLY CHILDHOOD EDUCATORS
## AS COLLABORATIVE COMMUNICATORS

Early childhood educators are a natural choice as key players in shaping collaborative strategies that focus on children and families. Early childhood educators deal on a daily basis with a wide array of individuals, from specialists to students' parents, who have children's needs at heart. They must negotiate the differing goals, needs, and roles that each new adult brings to the classroom. They serve as advocates for their students' families, provide support and encouragement to their students' parents, and build structures for classroom participation and involvement on the part of these other adults that meld the many purposes for which they have come into an early childhood education (ECE) classroom (Stahlman, 1994).

Friend and Cook (1996) noted that collaboration is a defining feature of early childhood special education (ECSE) programs. Key characteristics of many ECSE programs include the articulation of goals that involve long-term, in-depth services; multiple perspectives that include the child, the child's family, and the service environment in the design and development of educational programs; broad community involvement in all aspects of operation; and a focus on proactive process in planning for the future and averting potential problems. Early childhood educators work as partners with parents and service providers in children's education programs. They recognize that each partner has a contribution to make that is different from the others but that is equally valuable in supporting children (Friend & Cook, 1996).

Early childhood educators, whether in general or special education, are called on to coordinate a wide range of services for children in the classroom. They need to tap into a knowledge and skills base that includes familiarity with family systems, service coordination, and special knowledge pertaining to ECE (Fantuzzo et al., 1996) and ECSE. They find themselves developing expertise in the integration of goals from multiple developmental perspectives within the context of activity-based interventions; the use of comprehensive, systematic approaches to child services in which assessment, intervention, and evaluation are coordinated to create holistic education programs; and advocacy for children and families with external service professionals, community leaders, and funding sources (McCollum & Maude, 1994).

The parallels between these points and the key collaborative skills presented previously in this chapter make apparent the key role that early childhood educators should assume in collaborative efforts designed to serve children and families. Outside of the immediate family, the early childhood teacher is one of the most consistent, objective adults in students' lives. The early childhood teacher is certainly the most consistent human services or education professional that students encounter. By virtue of regular, long-term contact with children, the early childhood teacher has the advantage of a perspective on children's needs for educational and support services that transcend the categorical service criteria that bind specialists. The early childhood teacher is the natural center to guide and coordinate team-based collaborations focused on serving students' needs.

McCollum and Maude (1994), in an article on the training and preparation needs of ECE and ECSE educators, looked closely at the day-to-day functioning of ECE educators to identify key role demands for teachers. They described activities such as

- Conducting screening and identifying children at risk of school failure
- Assessing developmental competence of students
- Planning and providing developmental interventions and services
- Coordinating interdisciplinary services for children
- Integrating and implementing recommendations made by interdisciplinary teams serving children in classrooms
- Assessing family needs and strengths
- Planning and implementing family support services
- Coordinating services from multiple agencies for families
- Evaluating program implementation and effectiveness of overall services for young children and their families
- Advocating in multiple arenas for young children and their families
- Consulting with professionals, families, and other caregivers about child needs
- Working effectively as a team member

Notice the parallels between this list and the key skills for collaboration mentioned previously. By virtue of the day-to-day role demands that are placed on them, early

Good problem-solving skills are crucial to effective collaboration.
These children demonstrate this concept as they negotiate roles and
communicate with each other.

childhood educators find themselves becoming adept at many of the key skills that
underlie effective collaboration. By further developing their understanding of the
nature and process of collaborations and how these skills contribute to collaborative efforts, early childhood educators can begin to position themselves as central,
coordinating figures in interagency collaborations that focus on children and their
families (Jones, White, Aeby, & Benson, 1997).

## THE COLLABORATIVE ENVIRONMENT

In her exemplary study of the organization of schools, Rosenholtz (1989) identified
several characteristics of schools in which schoolwide collaboration was the professional norm. She characterized such schools as vital and energetic organizations
that offer teachers the opportunity to work together and expand their professional
skills. Staff members at these schools had identified clear goals for student outcomes with classroom instruction and activities clearly related to a set of mutually
defined schoolwide expectations. As a means of reaching these goals, teachers provided assistance to their peers without hesitation. Teachers were no longer
expected to find their own answers to problems or to struggle in isolation to
acquire new methods. Structurally, time was made for teachers to share technical
knowledge, observe each other's classrooms, and coach each other in the acquisition of methodology consistent with schoolwide goals. Finally, teachers' ongoing
learning was expected and supported. Structurally, professional growth opportunities were developed that allowed teachers to practice new instructional skills

and receive feedback on their progress. These underlying structures were accompanied by an increase in teacher commitment and certainty that was operationalized in a general belief in the potential for positive change that was attainable within the collective powers of teachers and staff.

## CONCLUSIONS

The essence of collaboration for ECE and ECSE is that, for any specific situation that might arise, the ethos of a collaborative environment dictates that ingenuity and experimentation on the part of the collective professionals are expected and supported within the context of the program's goals. Actively practiced, collaborative problem solving helps to create an environment of professional support and interdependence that is centered on children and their families (Thousand, Villa, Paolucci-Whitcomb, & Nevin, 1996). As teachers gain more experience with collaborative professional relationships, problems associated specifically with hierarchical school structures and patterns of communication should diminish considerably. A collaborative ethos is self-renewing and professionally energizing. It builds on the fundamentals of communication, leadership, and problem solving to foster a professional community committed to active problem solving and mutual interdependence and support.

## REMEMBER THIS

1. Communication is a cyclical process that involves a sender, a message, a channel, an environment, and a receiver.

2. Collaborative groups generally pass through three developmental stages in the process of developing effective collaborative communication: formal, stifled communication; open, spontaneous communication; and true collaboration as evidenced by open communication and interaction, mutual trust, and spontaneity.

3. Barriers to communication disrupt the flow of interactions and redirect communication away from the original focus of the interaction.

4. Active listening is an intellectual and emotional process that goes beyond the physical action of hearing in a search for meaning and understanding.

5. There are eight basic skills that compose active listening: offering oneself, use of broad opening statements, reflection, verbalization of the implied, seeking clarification, silence, placing events in time and sequence, and summarization.

6. Conflict is a natural part of any group process, usually arising from issues that trigger strong emotional responses.

7. Well-managed conflict contributes to the overall growth and development of a group, increasing its potential for successful collaboration.

8. All forms of collaborative problem solving retain three common features: the shared nature of the interaction, the presence of two or more individuals with

knowledge and expertise useful for the problem at hand, and joint recognition and acceptance of the need to engage in collaboration to address the problem.

9. Leadership is an interaction between designated leaders and group members that is based on principles of mutual responsibility, shared power, and authority.

# REFERENCES

Abelson, M.A., & Woodman, R.W. (1983). Review of research on team effectiveness: Implications for teams in schools. *School Psychology Review, 12*(2), 125–136.

Bland, L. (1995). *Factors contributing to the successful collaboration between speech-language pathologists and classroom teachers.* Doctoral dissertation, University of Cincinnati, OH.

Bolman, L.G., & Deal, T.E. (1991). *Reframing organizations.* San Francisco: Jossey-Bass.

Bruner, C. (1991). *Thinking collaboratively: Ten questions and answers to help policy makers improve children's services.* Washington, DC: Education and Human Services Consortium.

Fantuzzo, J., Childs, S., Stevenson, H., Coolahan, K.C., Ginsburg, M., Gay, K., Debnam, D., & Watson, C. (1996). The Head Start teaching center: An evaluation of an experiential, collaborative training model for Head Start teachers and parent volunteers. *Early Childhood Research Quarterly, 11,* 79–99.

Farrer, C., & Kaye, B.L. (1996). New skills for new leadership roles. In F. Hesselbein, M. Goldsmith, & R. Beckhard (Eds.), *The leader of the future: New visions, strategies and practices for the next era* (pp. 175–188). San Francisco: Jossey-Bass.

Friend, M., & Cook, L. (1996). *Interactions: Collaboration skills for school professionals* (2nd ed.). Reading, MA: Addison Wesley Longman.

Johnson, L.J., & Pugach, M.C. (1996). The emerging third wave of collaboration: Beyond problem solving. In W. Stainback & S. Stainback (Eds.), *Controversial issues confronting special education: Divergent perspectives* (2nd ed., pp. 197–204). Needham Heights, MA: Allyn & Bacon.

Jones, I., White, C.S., Aeby, V., & Benson, B. (1997). Attitudes of early childhood teachers toward family and community involvement. *Early Education and Development, 8*(2), 153–168.

Kagan, S.L. (1991). *United we stand: Collaboration for child care and early education services.* New York: Teachers College Press.

Kruger, L.J. (1997). Social support and self-efficacy in problem solving among teacher assistance teams and school staff. *Journal of Educational Research, 90*(3), 164–168.

McCollum, J.A., & Maude, S.P. (1994). Issues and emerging practice in preparing educators to be early interventionists. In P.L. Safford, B. Spodek, & O.N. Saracho (Eds.), *Early childhood special education* (pp. 218–241). New York: Teachers College Press.

Melaville, A.I., & Blank, M.J. (1991). *What it takes: Structuring interagency partnerships to connect children and families with comprehensive services.* Washington, DC: Education and Human Services Consortium.

Pugach, M.C., & Johnson, L.J. (1995). *Collaborative practitioners, collaborative schools.* Denver: Love Publishing Co.

Reinhiller, N. (1996). Coteaching: New variations on a not-so-new practice. *Teacher Education and Special Education, 19*(1), 34–38.

Rosenholtz, S.J. (1989). *Teachers' workplace: The social organization of schools.* Reading, MA: Addison Wesley Longman.

Schien, E.H. (1996). Leadership and the organizational culture. In F. Hesselbein, M. Goldsmith, & R. Beckhard (Eds.), *The leader of the future: New visions, strategies and practices for the next era* (pp. 59–70). San Francisco: Jossey-Bass.

Schwarz, R.M. (1994). *The skilled facilitator: Practical wisdom for developing effective groups.* San Francisco: Jossey-Bass.

Silliman, E.R., & Wilkinson, L.C. (1991). *Communicating for learning: Classroom observation and collaboration*. Rockville, MD: Aspen Publishers.

Stahlman, J.I. (1994). Family and professional collaboration: Issues in early childhood special education. In P.L. Safford, B. Spodek, & O.N. Saracho (Eds.), *Early childhood special education* (pp. 26–44). New York: Teachers College Press.

Swan, W.W., & Morgan, J.L. (1993). *Collaborating for comprehensive services for young children and their families: The local interagency coordinating council*. Baltimore: Paul H. Brookes Publishing Co.

Thousand, J.S., Villa, R.A., Paolucci-Whitcomb, P., & Nevin, A. (1996). A rationale and vision for collaborative consultation. In W. Stainback & S. Stainback (Eds.), *Controversial issues confronting special education: Divergent perspectives* (2nd ed., pp. 205–218). Needham Heights, MA: Allyn & Bacon.

U.S. Department of Agriculture, Cooperative Extension Service. (1991). *Family community leadership: Teaching guide and workshop materials* [Teaching materials provided as part of a national training program for facilitators in family and community leadership programs]. Washington, DC: U.S. Government Printing Office.

# Activities

1. Practice active listening. Try to concentrate for 1 minute of every hour on one specific sound or on what any one person is saying. Keep practicing until you can hold complete concentration for at least 1 minute. This exercise is harder than you may realize. You will probably be able to concentrate totally for only a few seconds at the start.

2. Practice giving feedback to someone. The next time you listen to a message, think about how that message was communicated. Rather than evaluating the speaker's performance, describe to the speaker your reaction to the message. Think about the speaker and which behaviors the speaker could change that would improve how the message is sent. Think about how you can construct your feedback so that it describes your responses and suggests changes instead of evaluating the speaker's behavior.

3. How do you deal with conflict? Think about a conflict in which you were involved. What happened? How was it resolved? Using the five-step process described in this chapter, how might that particular conflict have been resolved?

4. Select a conflict that commonly occurs among your colleagues. Discuss strategies with them for addressing this conflict that require the use of the communication skills described in this chapter.

5. In a group of four to six people, select one person to be the problem identifier. Have that person describe a specific problem that

is student related or school related. Through discussion and by asking questions, try to articulate the actual problem. Next, identify internal and external factors that contribute to the problem and decide which of these factors are within your control as a group. Then articulate a problem pattern statement that summarizes what you have discussed. Has the problem definition changed at all from its initial introduction? Has the problem become larger or smaller than you expected? What are the implications for generating possible solutions?

6. List the various group activities in which you are involved. Circle those in which you play a leadership role. Underline those in which you would like to play a leadership role. Which characteristics of the group structure influenced your role choices? Which characteristics within yourself influenced your role choices? Identify a past experience in which you successfully assumed a leadership role. Then identify a past experience in which your leadership experience was a negative one. How did these experiences differ? How might you have adapted as a leader to make the outcome in both experiences successful?

# A History of
# Working with and for Children

*Anne M. Bauer, Lawrence J. Johnson,*
*Mary Ulrich, Dawn M. Denno, and Victoria W. Carr*

## CHAPTER ORGANIZER

In this chapter, we explore the following ideas . . .

1. Early childhood education practices have historically been grounded in efforts to support each child.

2. The education of early childhood educators and early childhood special educators has moved toward an emphasis on inclusive environments just as early childhood programs have become more inclusive.

3. There are similarities and differences among the histories of early childhood programs, programs for children at risk, and programs for children with disabilities.

4. By embracing a unified view of early childhood education, educators can learn from different perspectives and better meet the diverse needs of the children and families they serve.

The early childhood education (ECE) and the early childhood special education (ECSE) professions are both similar and different in their philosophies and practices. These similarities and differences can be traced through the respective histories of the professions. Although ECE and ECSE developed different ways of thinking about how young children develop and how ECE and ECSE programs should respond to individual students' needs, remember that both professions serve the same population of children. It is for these children that the professions are bringing their strengths and diverse points of view together to forge a continuum of recommended practices to serve all young children effectively.

Since its inception as a profession, the education of young children has been grounded in efforts to support the development of each child. This chapter begins by discussing the evolution of ECE practices, followed by a discussion of programming for young children at risk for disabilities or with disabilities. The history of collaboration on behalf of children and their families, key to any discussion of programming, is also presented. The chapter concludes with a discussion of the effort to unify and integrate the education of all young children and their families and to integrate the work of the professionals who work with them.

**Reflections:**  As you read the next section, try to identify three views from the past that are no longer generally supported and three views from the past that are still generally accepted.

## THE ORIGINS OF CURRENT PRACTICE IN EARLY CHILDHOOD EDUCATION

ECE has been influenced by the early attempts to form nursery and elementary school education programs. These two threads of education programming influenced one another. Similarities and differences between these two types of programs continue to exist.

During the early 1800s, national school systems were beginning to form in Europe (Braun & Edwards, 1972). Johann Pestalozzi (1746–1827) emerged as an education leader, contending in his book *How Gertrude Teaches Her Children* (1801) that education is for all children and emphasizing that children should learn through self-discovery and pace their own learning, with opportunities for sensory exploration and observation. Pestalozzi's book was an important milestone during a time when children were frequently viewed as passive recipients of information and flawed thinkers who needed strong authoritarian direction from adults. Children were frequently subjected to strict discipline and worked in harsh environments for long hours.

Robert Owen (1771–1858), one of Pestalozzi's disciples, was an industrialist who abolished child labor in his textile mills (Braun & Edwards, 1972). An ardent reformer, he believed that education, starting with young children and combined with a cooperative learning environment, could transform society. In 1816, Owen founded the first "infant school" for children ages 3–10 years in England. Although

Owen was considered an extremist in his time, he suggested that teachers should be provided with choices.

Another student of Pestalozzi's, Froebel (1783–1852), established the first kindergarten program in Blankenburg, Germany, in 1837 (Braun & Edwards, 1972). This kindergarten was a program for 4- to 6-year-old children that served as a transition station between home and school and also as a transition period between infancy and childhood. In kindergarten, children were to be nurtured and protected from outside influences just as plants might be in a garden. The teacher facilitated the activities in which children engaged with materials such as wooden blocks, shapes, yarn balls, and natural objects called *gifts*. In addition to these gifts, children engaged in handiwork activities such as weaving and modeling, called *occupations*. Along with this developmental curriculum, Froebel (1897) proposed training young women as kindergarten teachers.

In the United States, the first kindergarten was established in Watertown, Wisconsin, in 1855 for the children of German immigrants and was conducted in German. English-speaking kindergartens appeared as privately funded institutions in Boston beginning in 1860 and as publicly funded schools in St. Louis starting in 1873 (Maxim, 1997). These programs emphasized cleanliness, courtesy, manual skills, and physical activity. The teacher, or *kindergartner*, was an affectionate leader who supported the child in his or her transition from the home. Beginning in the 1920s, kindergarten teachers in public schools were pressured to prepare children to read. This tension between nurturing children's development and preparing children for academic subjects remains in kindergartens.

While the kindergartens were becoming more common, the nursery school movement emerged as another effort to meet the needs of young children. Rachel and Margaret McMillan established the first open-air nursery school in England in 1911. In the nursery school, education was based on the child's sense of wonder. The curriculum emphasized the value of active outdoor work and play, health and nutrition, perceptual-motor skills, and the development of the imagination. The McMillans believed that ECE should be multidisciplinary and focused on all areas of development (Braun & Edwards, 1972). This *whole-child approach*, as it came to be called, valued each area of development equally with all others so that no one area received more attention than another. Children were perceived as growing, experiencing, and learning through interactions with people and the environment. The role of the school, therefore, was to keep the paths of exploration open so that children could develop in their own ways. In the United States, the terms *nursery school*, *preschool*, and *child development center* are generally used to describe programs that developed from the nursery school movement.

In 1896, John Dewey (1859–1952) started the Laboratory School at the University of Chicago (Maxim, 1997). He proposed a progressive education for a progressive society, an education that would allow people to fulfill their full potential. He, along with the others mentioned in the preceding paragraphs, argued that children learn by doing. Education should teach the whole child by supporting the child's physical, social, emotional, and intellectual development. Dewey suggested that a curriculum should be based on observations of children's interests and needs and that the role of the teacher is that of a guide and observer rather than an instructor and disciplinarian.

From 1920 to 1950, American society changed rapidly and ECE changed with it. The Great Depression and World War II changed ECE dramatically. Unlike the early part of the 20th century, when extended families cared for and educated young children, families were required to make many accommodations to obtain work. Families were divided by distance and culture as young people traveled to large cities in search of jobs. Economic hardship required even the youngest family members to work. In addition, World War II took many men away from their families.

In 1933, the Works Progress Administration provided money to start nursery schools so that unemployed elementary and high school teachers would have jobs. This action brought together in the same profession teachers who believed in the whole-child approach and those who believed in the academic approach.

In 1940, the federal government provided funds to start full-day child care centers so that women could work in factories to support the war effort. The focus of these programs was to support mothers and the war effort. The child was seen as a secondary beneficiary.

**Reflection:** In the next section, information about the history of programs for families considered at risk is provided. As you read the next section, see if you can create a list of factors that contribute to being at risk for developmental delays and school failure. Also, the next section discusses assets of families. As you reflect on your own experiences, think about the assets of at-risk families.

## PROGRAMMING FOR YOUNG CHILDREN AT RISK

Several of the historical proponents of education for young children were actually working with families and children who would be considered at risk for disabilities today. Owen's efforts on behalf of the children of factory workers and the work of the McMillan sisters for children in poor communities indicate an early concern for children whose families had meager resources. Maria Montessori (1870–1952) began her work with young children with mental retardation and later applied the methods she had developed in her work with children from disadvantaged backgrounds. Key elements in her work were sequential visual discrimination and visual-motor integration tasks. In addition, the purpose of her psychomotor learning and sensory integration method of teaching was to teach students independence and self-control while enhancing a child's self-confidence (Bender & Bender, 1979).

In the United States, little specific attention was paid to most young children at risk for developmental delays or with disabilities. However, the privately funded kindergartens that emerged in large cities in the 1800s evolved into public school kindergartens. Until the 1960s, little attention was given to children at risk for disabilities or to young children with disabilities.

The early childhood curriculum needs to be sensitive, flexible, and supportive of diversity. This type of curriculum provides all children and families with support and opportunities to be successful.

Bloom (1964) and Hunt (1961) argued that intelligence is not fixed. Hunt argued that children's intelligence develops early and rapidly and that the child's early experiences can have a profound influence on later development. This research fueled support for Project Head Start, a federally funded ECE program designed to help children at risk for school failure. Sargent Shriver, Director of the President's War on Poverty in the Johnson administration, stated that Head Start was to be implemented immediately (U.S. Office of Economic Opportunity, 1968). Head Start provides comprehensive health, nutrition, parent involvement, social services, and education programs (U.S. Office of Economic Opportunity, 1968).

Adhering to its motto, "The parent is the child's first teacher," Head Start has set a precedent with regard to the level of parents' involvement in the education of young children in the classroom and on Head Start policy committees that has continued to influence legislators to require parent involvement in decisions involving children with disabilities. Head Start also has had a significant impact on special education for young children. As Caldwell described in the language of the early 1970s, "The implicit strategy of early Head Start was to devise a program that fits children as they are found and that institutes remedial procedures to correct whatever deficiencies they have, whether they are nutritional, experiential, or medical" (1973, p. 5). Preschool children with disabilities were first served in demonstration programs in 1968, and 2 years later Head Start was mandated to reserve 10% of its enrollment for children with disabilities (Maxim, 1997).

**Reflection:**   In the next section, the history of ECSE is discussed. While reading the next section, note that the role that legislation has played in the development of ECSE is very prominent. Can you draw parallels between the services provided to children with disabilities and the U.S. civil rights movement? How are these movements different? How are they the same?

## EARLY CHILDHOOD EDUCATION PROGRAMMING FOR CHILDREN WITH DISABILITIES

Programming for young children with disabilities is the cumulative result of American society's values, the emergence of ECE as a child-centered effort, and the work of parents and advocates on behalf of all U.S. children. The early compensatory movement and the emergence of Head Start had an impact on the development of programming for children with disabilities.

In the 18th century, there was great optimism for children with disabilities. The work of Seguin and his pupil Itard demonstrated that individuals with disabilities could indeed learn and were not possessed by demons and in need of incarceration (see Gilhool, 1995). However, during the 19th century, this optimism faded to a pessimism about "curing" mental retardation. As Gilhool reported, by the early 20th century, Goddard was administering the new Binet Intelligence Test (Binet, 1905) to those arriving in steerage at Ellis Island to identify those whom he referred to as "the immigrant feebleminded progeny of the foreign hordes that have settled and are settling among us" (Gilhool, 1995, p. 13). States established public institutions to separate the individuals with disabilities on the pretense that they were dangerous. The state of Washington made it a criminal offense for parents to refuse to institutionalize their children with disabilities (Gilhool, 1995).

World Wars I and II, which required military physical examinations and from which veterans returned to the United States with injuries or disabilities, had a positive impact on society's perceptions of people with disabilities. The physical screening of draftees revealed that thousands had physical disabilities but lived typical lives. Veterans who previously had been accepted in their communities returned after the two world wars with physical disabilities. Thus, Americans' consciousness of people with disabilities was increased, and this heightened awareness gradually extended first to children with disabilities and then to people with other types of disabilities as well (Hewett & Forness, 1974).

As Skeels (1966) and Skeels and Dye (1939) presented their studies of early stimulation of young children with mental retardation who lived in institutions, recognition of the potential impact of early intervention emerged. Kirk (1958) began a preschool for young children identified as "mentally retarded" and presented data indicating that, with enriched preschool experiences, these children demonstrated more typical development and in some cases could lose the label of mental retardation.

In 1968, the Handicapped Children's Early Education Assistance Act (HCEEAA) (PL 90-538) was enacted, providing federal funds for the First Change Network, a series of demonstration projects at child development centers that implemented new and better approaches to ECSE. At these centers, a focus on parent involvement and program evaluation systems emerged.

The Carolina Abecedarian Project began in 1972 and later evolved into the Carolina Curriculum (see Bender & Bender, 1979). The Carolina Curriculum (Johnson-Martin, Attermeier, & Hacker, 1990; Johnson-Martin, Jens, Attermeier, & Hacker, 1991) employs a longitudinal, multidisciplinary approach to the prevention of developmental disabilities in early childhood. It emphasizes Hunt's and Bloom's views (see Bender & Bender, 1979, for a description of their views) about the effect of experience on intelligence, rationalizing that children living in poverty may be deprived of learning experiences that might prevent developmental disabilities.

In 1975, the Education for All Handicapped Children Act (PL 94-142) was enacted. This law and its amendments (the Education of the Handicapped Act Amendments of 1986 [PL 99-457], the Individuals with Disabilities Education Act [IDEA] of 1990 [PL 101-476], the Individuals with Disabilities Education Act [IDEA] Amendments of 1991 [PL 102-119], and the Individuals with Disabilities Education Act [IDEA] Amendments of 1997 [PL 105-17]) have completely changed the education of young children with disabilities. These laws mandate a free appropriate public education for children with disabilities that is based on an individualized education program (IEP), provided for both preschool- and school-age children, and an individualized family service plan for infants and toddlers.

The Education for All Handicapped Children Act provided federal funding incentives to encourage states to locate and serve preschool-age children in need of early intervention services. In addition, children were to be identified through the use of a multifactored, nondiscriminatory evaluation and served in the least restrictive environment (LRE). Children were to be served with their unidentified peers unless the child could not be served in the general education environment. In addition, due process procedures were established to resolve disagreements between parents and school districts.

The Education of the Handicapped Act Amendments retained the requirements of the Education for All Handicapped Children Act. In addition, states receiving federal funds for early intervention programs were mandated to provide services. In addition, parent support services were included as related services. This legislation included provisions for discretionary use of funds for support services for infants and toddlers with developmental delays. IDEA continued funding for young children with disabilities and required the implementation of plans for the transition of young children between early intervention and preschool programs and between preschool- and school-age programs.

Throughout the federal mandates for education programs for young children with disabilities are requirements that services be provided in the LRE. In the movement toward inclusion, ECE programs that include all children are becoming more common. In 1993, the Division for Early Childhood (DEC) of the Council for Exceptional Children issued a position statement on the inclusion of young children with disabilities in ECE programs. This position paper stated that all children have the right to participate in activities in the environment in which they would spend time had they not had disabilities. In addition, the paper stated that young children and their families should have full access to health, social services, and education that promote the children's and families' full participation in natural environments. The position paper concluded with a call for the restructuring and unification of social, education, health, and intervention supports to be more responsive to the needs of all children and their families.

## DIFFERENTIATION OF EARLY CHILDHOOD EDUCATION PRACTICES

ECE and ECSE can be differentiated by the manner in which reform has been interpreted by these two groups. The push for education reform has been driven by a growing recognition that there is an increasingly diverse population of students entering schools who challenge established education practices. The inclusion of children who have historically challenged the education system, particularly those children who are considered at risk of school failure or those who have an identified disability, creates a diverse school population. Fundamental systemic changes must take place before the education system can embrace this diversity and support all children and families to have opportunities to be successful (McKenzie, 1993). Thus, the curriculum must be sensitive, flexible, and supportive of diversity. To address the issue of diversity, educators must insist that adaptations be made for the accommodation of all children as a central feature of a well-grounded curriculum.

The development of ECSE as a field paralleled ECE reform efforts. In the 1950s, services for young children with disabilities were usually designed for children with sensory or physical disabilities. Children with other types of disabilities were generally kept at home. It was often suggested that children experiencing mild developmental delays would outgrow the delays. Therefore, parents were told to wait and see whether the delays persisted long enough to warrant treatment. Children and families who were not successful in typical programs were often dismissed or excluded from the programs because the programs were not designed to serve children who require extensive supports (Peterson, 1987). The 1960s marked a shift in program orientation to one that focused on the importance of early experiences on the long-term development of children. Attention was directed toward developing services that were receptive to the needs of young children and their families that had previously not been served or that had been inadequately served in traditional programs. From this shift in thinking, Head Start and eventually ECSE emerged.

Head Start and ECSE have provided services to accommodate the needs of diverse learners, with, as mentioned previously, 10% of Head Start enrollment being reserved for children with disabilities. This allocation of services has had an important influence on the development and implementation of the curriculum. As discussed previously in this chapter, the curriculum became the tool with which to help teachers facilitate those skills that enabled the child to be more successful in his or her current environment or in a prospective environment (Bailey & Wolery, 1984; Cook, Tessier, & Klein, 1992). In addition, because ECSE emerged out of special education programs' prescriptive teaching orientation, teachers have relied on applied behavioral procedures to help children learn new behaviors. Finally, in recognition of the environmental influences affecting the children and families served by these programs, effort was directed toward involving parents in the curriculum development process. This involvement evolved from a view of parents as teachers to a view of parents as decision makers and partners in the education process with ECSE teachers (Turnbull & Turnbull, 1990).

However, early childhood educators' interpretation of reform differed from that of early childhood special educators in that the ECE curriculum focused on placing only the child, instead of both the child and the child's family, at the center of the curriculum. This focus on placing the child and the child's family at the center of the curriculum became the central theme of developmentally appropriate practice (DAP) (Bredekamp & Copple, 1997). By considering the child the critical agent in the learning process who is constructing knowledge, developing skills, gaining insights, and developing values through exploration and experimentation within the environment, the teacher facilitates the child's experiences by questioning and making suggestions as the child interacts with the environment. Therefore, within the ECE framework, the curriculum is child centered and built on a child's cognitive and psychological processes (Johnson & Carr, 1996).

The emphasis on DAP was a historical and critical milestone for ECE. It provided a powerful tool with which to combat political and social forces calling for a more academic orientation to educating children in preschool, kindergarten, and the primary grades (Johnson & Carr, 1996). The National Association for the Education of Young Children (NAEYC) position statement on DAP (Bredekamp & Copple, 1997) provided a sound theoretical foundation for opposing an emphasis on academics in programs for young children. Yet, this emphasis on DAP in ECE focused attention on the child rather than on the child's family. In addition, the conflicts between DAP and applied behavioral methods prevalent in ECSE programs have created some substantial differences in the orientation of ECE and ECSE educators. There are major differences between the ECE and ECSE fields that must be addressed if the two groups are to move toward a unified vision of ECE.

**Reflection:** As you read the next section, think of specific experiences that you have had in working with young children and their families who challenge the conventional education system. What was the reaction of service providers to these children? Were these children integrated into the school system, or were they isolated?

## UNIFYING EARLY CHILDHOOD EDUCATION AND EARLY CHILDHOOD SPECIAL EDUCATION

Truly, there is much agreement between what are considered recommended practices in ECE and ECSE. This is evidenced by similarities in the ways in which ECE and ECSE professionals design and implement educational experiences for young children (Kilgo et al., 1998). As Thorpe asserted, "Best practices in early childhood and early childhood special education are not different" (1992, p. 14). In the 1990s,

Developmentally appropriate practice (DAP) in early childhood presumes that children have a disposition to explore. The role of the teachers is to design a developmentally appropriate environment in which children can construct knowledge.

there has been an increasing emphasis on developing a unified vision for ECE (Bredekamp, 1992; Bredekamp & Copple, 1997). For example, DEC and NAEYC established a liaison committee to explore issues common to ECE and ECSE. In addition, state departments of education are increasingly moving in a direction that blurs the line between ECE and ECSE. However, although ECE and ECSE are increasingly moving toward a unified vision of early childhood education, Johnson and Carr (1996) argued that there are still fundamental differences related to child-centered versus family-centered services and the impact of variations in development on the child's disposition to explore. These differences may inhibit children's success in an inclusive ECE program.

Place (1994) suggested that the Education of the Handicapped Act Amendments of 1986 were unique because, in passing this piece of legislation, Congress recognized the critical role of the family in the education of young children. Although professionals in both ECE and ECSE agree in principle regarding the importance of families, the ECSE field has emphasized family-centered practices outlined by PL 99-457. Johnson and Carr (1996) asserted that the major difference between ECE and ECSE is the degree to which services are family centered and family goal oriented, particularly in cases in which children are in infant, toddler, and preschool programs.

DAP in ECE presumes that children have a predisposition to explore their environment. Children's voluntary or intentional actions in their environments result in insights and discoveries that promote the evolution of new cognitive schemata and new developmental behaviors. The role of the teacher is to design a developmentally appropriate environment in which children can construct knowledge and then to facilitate children's exploration and interaction within the environment. Clearly, children have varying degrees of exploratory behaviors, and, if not recognized as such, their experiences are unlikely to coincide with their developmental needs. Furthermore, if these individual variations among children are not addressed, an "uneven playing field" will develop, thus further widening the gap between children who are and are not successful in school. Johnson and Carr (1996) argued that the impact of variations in children's dispositions to explore has not been given careful consideration in ECE curricula. Yet, as inclusionary practices and unified preservice and graduate ECE programs are developed, more and more attention must be given to diversity and individualization with respect to curriculum development. A paradigm shift is imperative. When families are included in decision making and curriculum adaptations and classroom accommodations receive attention, families will become increasingly satisfied with programmatic functions and children will become increasingly successful and accepted by their peers. However, such a shift is not going to be easy, and we must keep the needs of families in the forefront as we move forward. The Arlitt Child and Family Research and Education Center program has been working very hard to blend practices, has confronted many problems, and has made some progress. Although the program is not perfect, a description of the efforts undertaken in the program might be instructive for others considering a unified approach.

## ARLITT CHILD AND FAMILY RESEARCH AND EDUCATION CENTER

The preschool program at the Arlitt Child and Family Research and Education Center at the University of Cincinnati in Ohio strives to unify recommended practices from a strong, constructivist ECE philosophy, ECSE practices, and Head Start programs. Blended funding from Head Start, the Hamilton County Board of Mental Retardation and Developmental Disabilities (HCBMRDD), and tuition provides spaces reserved for children with diverse abilities and a variety of developmental and education-related issues. This endeavor results in many successes, as well as challenges that must be overcome.

### Background

The Arlitt Center preschool highly values its diverse enrollment of children and families. As an inclusive program, each classroom is composed of children with various cultural and economic backgrounds and disabilities. Staff at the Arlitt Center preschool have learned that the culture of each individual classroom is based on a delicate balance of diverse interests, languages, abilities, and behaviors. An ECE teacher with a bachelor's or master's degree who is an ECE specialist (i.e., with the title of Lead Teacher) and an assistant teacher who is a child development associate (CDA) or has an associate's degree work with families to enhance the development of 16–18 children and to develop the knowledge base and skills of preservice ECE educators. All of the 10 classrooms are supported by four transdisciplinary Head Start coordinators, who monitor staffing issues, fill out required forms, ensure that the program complies with Head Start performance standards, keep track of IEPs, and oversee the children's transitions to and from other programs. Additional staff include two administrators, a cook/bus driver, a family advocate, and two clerical staff. The Director and Associate Director supervise and problem-solve with staff, create partnerships with community agencies, sponsor CDA courses, approve university-related research agendas, develop and implement research projects, and attend to other university-related and fiscal duties. Itinerant support services for children with disabilities are provided by the HCBMRDD. A Head Start speech-language pathologist who is a university faculty member who also supervises students from the Department of Communication Disorders is on staff part time to serve children in the preschool who are funded by Head Start or by tuition. The Arlitt Center is also fortunate to house and have access to the services of the Ohio Early Intervention Project, which utilizes intervention-based assessment procedures to assist teachers and families as they address behavioral issues inherent in any program.

## Issues at the Arlitt Center

The expertise and support systems at the Arlitt Center preschool have produced an award-winning inclusionary model that provides exemplary services for children and families. In fact, families overwhelmingly embrace the work and dedication of the Arlitt staff. However, issues surrounding inclusion abound. Although any program may encounter funding issues and many serendipitous events that require problem solving, there are four recurring issues at the Arlitt Center preschool:

1. Philosophical disequilibrium
2. An increasing number of children with special needs
3. An increased need for knowledge of special education techniques
4. Limited time for collaboration and paperwork

### *Philosophical Disequilibrium*

Ada Hart Arlitt began engaging young children in developmental nursery school activities at the University of Cincinnati in the 1920s. In the beginning, the program served university staff and a few community families. The program has grown dramatically in size and in the 1990s serves primarily community families and some university staff and student families. Historically, the developmental program at the Arlitt Center adhered to a well-developed constructivist philosophy based on the theories of Piaget and Erickson. The university's early childhood faculty emphasized pure constructivism for curriculum development and interactions with children. Inclusion of children with disabilities has placed many staff and university faculty in a state of consternation with regard to meeting the needs of individual children and their families. Basically, constructivism states that humans construct their individual understanding of the world by acting on their own experiences. However, some children with disabilities need more scaffolding and direction in order to engage in activities that other children may choose and sustain on their own. Furthermore, some of Piaget's work no longer seems valid to many ECE educators. By emphasizing social interactions as well as experiential exploration, the gap between children with and without disabilities who have successful school experiences need not widen. In graduate programs at the master's degree level, teachers at the Arlitt Center have learned to accommodate children through environmental design and curricular adaptations. Yet, philosophical struggles that emerge as a result of direct teacher–child interactions and behavioral interventions continue to cause reflective teachers to disagree. For example, one child with significant aggressive sexual acting-out behaviors and emotional issues was identified by the Ohio Early Intervention Project as needing scripted interactions and behavior modifications that were too far out of the realm of the constructivist philosophy. The classroom teacher was successful in monitoring and facilitating some successful behavior modification for this child in the classroom, but it required so much of her time that she believed that the other children were not receiving a fair amount of her attention. The project interventionists perceived resistance to behavior modification from the classroom staff as detrimental, and attempts to engage the child's parents in the intervention were met with frustrations because of the parents' minimal follow-through in classroom involvement and obtaining outside counseling.

Although the child discussed in the preceding paragraph did not have developmental delays, programs are enrolling an increasing number of children with challenging behavioral issues. At the Arlitt Center preschool, children with cognitive or physical issues who do not have significant challenging behaviors appear to create less day-to-day stress among staff. This may be due to the staff's abilities to accommodate and scaffold development for children with developmental delays. Interventions for most children can often be implemented within a constructivist developmental philosophy.

### Children with Special Needs

In addition to the 14 children who attend the Arlitt Center preschool through an agreement with HCBMRDD, 10%–20% of the 76 children enrolled in Head Start also have developmental delays or emotional and behavioral issues. In addition, particularly because the Arlitt staff have a reputation for being sensitive to and working successfully with children with special needs, an increasing number of tuition enrollees at Arlitt have disabilities. Thus, monitoring all of the children's progress and IEPs as well as providing them with the individual attention that

Children are critical agents in the learning process as they construct knowledge. Therefore, the early childhood curriculum needs to be child centered and built on children's thinking and environmental experiences.

they need in the classroom compromise the staff's ability to provide equal attention to all students. Administration and staff debate inclusion versus integrated programming approaches and how to recruit and enroll children and families without discrimination. This concern has yet to be resolved.

### Special Education Techniques

A more easily resolved area of concern is professional development. An advantage of the Arlitt Center's university affiliation is the opportunity to train educators. An additional asset for the Arlitt Center preschool is the ECSE teacher who is on staff. She teaches a classroom that is composed of the same diverse mix of children as is found in all other classrooms and typically has the children with the most challenging behaviors and disabilities in her class. Through demonstration teaching, she provides teachers and preservice students with opportunities to observe a calm, low-key classroom that is respectful, proactive, and supportive of all children and families.

Teachers, particularly assistant teachers, are continually seeking information about working with children with disabilities and their families. Lack of skill and knowledge make teachers feel inadequate and frustrated in their ability to meet the requirements of an IEP. They appear to cause teachers to avoid documentation, ongoing assessment, intervention, and interactions with parents. Although the resources are available for technical assistance and training, teachers' ignorance of special education laws and resistance to behavior modification techniques are still major issues.

### Limited Time for Collaboration

All of the issues discussed in the preceding sections might be more easily addressed if time constraints were eliminated. As a practical matter, however, teachers must facilitate the classroom, fulfill paperwork duties, interact with families, and attend to curriculum planning and supervision of student teachers within a limited number of hours. At the Arlitt Center preschool, as in so many other education programs, teachers put in far more time to complete tasks, reflect, and plan than the time for which they are compensated. At times, teachers perceive that they are just meeting the bare minimum needs of the classroom. Teachers often request more time for providing and explaining information to families, students, coordinators, administrators, and each other. In addition, collaboration with support personnel does not occur as frequently as it should because of other commitments during the hours when itinerant staff (i.e., staff assigned to several programs) are present. Therefore, alternative methods of communication are continually sought in order to share information about children, programming, and ideas. Administratively, it is important to create time for developing mutual understanding among staff and communicating with families.

In summary, adhering to a philosophy that values diversity and inclusion of all children does not happen without challenges both small and great. Although the Arlitt Center preschool has a reputation for serving all children within the realm of recommended practices, Arlitt Center staff and administrators continually try to improve programming so that an exemplary, replicable model is available for the broader ECE community. Each challenge is met with the expectation that positive outcomes for children and families will result. This expectation is generally stressful, but inclusionary programs cannot survive without it.

## CONCLUSIONS

Although the fields of ECE and ECSE are in the process of moving toward a unified vision of the provision of services to young children and their families, the degree to which programming for young children adheres to both ECE and ECSE recommended practices is still questionable (Johnson & Carr, 1996). Collaboration and agreement on fundamental theoretical perspectives are difficult processes. In addition, implementing a family-centered program is time-consuming. Yet, even a quick study of the history of ECE and advocacy obliges us to acknowledge how far we have come in working with families and children who challenge the system.

## REMEMBER THIS

1.  The education of young children has always been founded on supporting individual children.

2.  The histories of early childhood programming, programming for children at risk of developmental delays and school failure, and programming for children with disabilities have similarities and differences. Some past differences are still contributing to the present differences among these school programs. The future lies in bridging differences between groups of children.

3.  Differences between ECE and ECSE may be related to the degree to which services are child centered versus family centered and to potential conflicts between DAP and applied behavioral perspectives.

4.  A collaborative approach that embraces differences, encourages shared commitment, and utilizes expertise from a variety of viewpoints holds the most promise for meeting the needs of the diverse children and their families being served in ECE programs.

## REFERENCES

Bailey, D.B., Jr., & Wolery, M. (1984). *Teaching infants and preschoolers with handicaps.* Columbus, OH: Charles E. Merrill.

Bender, M., & Bender, R.K. (1979). *Disadvantaged preschool children: A source book for teachers.* Baltimore: Paul H. Brookes Publishing Co.

Binet, A. (1905). *Binet Intelligence Test.* Palo Alto, CA: Stanford University.

Bloom, B.S. (1964). *Stability and change in human characteristics.* New York: John Wiley & Sons.

Braun, S.J., & Edwards, E.P. (1972). *History and theory of early childhood education.* Worthington, OH: Charles A. Jones.

Bredekamp, S. (Ed.). (1992). *Developmentally appropriate practice in early childhood programs serving children birth through age 8.* Washington, DC: National Association for the Education of Young Children.

Bredekamp, S., & Copple, C. (Eds.). (1997). *Developmentally appropriate practice in early childhood programs serving children birth through age 8* (Rev. ed.). Washington, DC: National Association for the Education of Young Children.

Caldwell, B.M. (1973). The importance of beginning early. In J.B. Jordan & R.F. Daily (Eds.), *Not all little wagons are red: The exceptional child's early years* (pp. 105–115). Reston, VA: Council for Exceptional Children.

Cook, R.E., Tessier, A., & Klein, M.D. (1992). *Adapting early childhood curricula for children with special needs* (3rd ed.). New York: Macmillan.

Division for Early Childhood (DEC) of the Council for Exceptional Children (CEC). (1993). *DEC position on inclusion.* Reston, VA: Author.

Education for All Handicapped Children Act of 1975, PL 94-142, 20 U.S.C. §§ 1400 *et seq.*

Education of the Handicapped Act Amendments of 1986, PL 99-457, 20 U.S.C. §§ 1400 *et seq.*

Froebel, F.W. (1897). *The education of man.* New York: Appleton & Co.

Gilhool, T.K. (1995). Testimony of Thomas K. Gilhool. *TASH Newsletter, 21*(6), 11–15.

Handicapped Children's Early Education Assistance Act (HCEEAA) of 1968, PL 90-538, 20 U.S.C. §§ 621 *et seq.*

Hewett, F.M., & Forness, S.R. (1974). *Education of exceptional learners.* Needham Heights, MA: Allyn & Bacon.

Hunt, J. McV. (1961). *Intelligence and experience.* New York: Ronald Press.

Individuals with Disabilities Education Act (IDEA) of 1990, PL 101-476, 20 U.S.C. §§ 1400 *et seq.*

Individuals with Disabilities Education Act (IDEA) Amendments of 1991, PL 102-119, 20 U.S.C. §§ 1400 *et seq.*

Individuals with Disabilities Education Act (IDEA) Amendments of 1997, PL 105-17, 20 U.S.C. §§ 1400 *et seq.*

Johnson, L.J., & Carr, V.W. (1996). Curriculum in early childhood education: Moving toward an inclusive specialization. In M.C. Pugach & C. Wagner (Eds.), *Curriculum trends, special education, and reform: Refocusing the conversation* (pp. 216–226). Needham Heights, MA: Allyn & Bacon.

Johnson-Martin, N.M., Attermeier, S.M., & Hacker, B.J. (1990). *The Carolina Curriculum for Preschoolers with Special Needs.* Baltimore: Paul H. Brookes Publishing Co.

Johnson-Martin, N.M., Jens, K.G., Attermeier, S.M., & Hacker, B.J. (1991). *The Carolina Curriculum for Infants and Toddlers with Special Needs* (2nd ed.). Baltimore: Paul H. Brookes Publishing Co.

Kilgo, J., LaMontagne, M.J., Johnson, L.J., Cooper, C., Cook, M., & Stayton, V. (1998). *A national study of recommended practices from early childhood and early childhood special education: Important implications for personnel preparation programs of the future.* Manuscript submitted for publication.

Kirk, S. (1958). *Early education of the mentally retarded.* Urbana: University of Illinois Press.

Maxim, G. (1997). *The very young* (5th ed.). Columbus, OH: Charles E. Merrill.

McKenzie, F. (1993). Equity: A call to action. In G. Cawelti (Ed.), *Challenges and achievements of American education: 1993 yearbook of the Association for Supervision and Curriculum Development* (pp. 47–53). Alexandria, VA: Association for Supervision and Curriculum Development.

Peterson, N. (1987). *Early intervention for handicapped and at-risk children.* Denver: Love Publishing Co.

Place, P. (1994). Social policy and family autonomy. In L.J. Johnson, R.J. Gallagher, M.J. LaMontagne, J.B. Jordan, J.J. Gallagher, P.L. Hutinger, & M.B. Karnes (Eds.), *Meeting early intervention challenges: Issues from birth to three* (2nd ed., pp. 265–278). Baltimore: Paul H. Brookes Publishing Co.

Skeels, H. (1966). Adult status of children with contrasting early life experiences. *Monographs of the Society for Research in Child Development, 32*(2), 18–28.

Skeels, H., & Dye, H.A. (1939). A study of the effects of differential stimulation on mentally retarded children. *Proceedings of the American Association on Mental Deficiency, 44,* 114–136.

Thorpe, E. (1992). A unified commitment to best practice: Point. In L.J. Johnson (Ed.), *Policy issues: Creating a unified vision. Proceedings of the Summer Institute for the Ohio Early Childhood Special Education Higher Education Consortium.* Cincinnati, OH: University of Cincinnati.

Turnbull, A.P., & Turnbull, H.R., III. (1990). *Families, professionals, and exceptionality: A special partnership* (2nd ed.). Columbus, OH: Charles E. Merrill.

U.S. Office of Economic Opportunity. (1968). *Head Start: A community action program.* Washington, DC: U.S. Government Printing Office.

# Activities

1. Select an early proponent of ECE. Describe the programs in which this individual was engaged and the population that was served.

2. Interview an ECE educator and an ECSE educator. Contrast their goals for their students, their efforts at family involvement, and their curriculum emphases.

3. Make a visit to a typical ECE classroom, a Head Start classroom, and an ECSE classroom. Make a list of five differences and five similarities among these classrooms. Identify one practice of each classroom that could be improved by being replaced with a practice from one of the other classrooms that you observed.

## chapter 4

# Supporting Collaborative Partnerships

*Anne M. Bauer, Shobha Chachie Joseph, and Sally Ann Zwicker*

## CHAPTER ORGANIZER

In this chapter, we explore the following ideas . . .

1.  The child, parents and family members, teachers, related-services personnel, adults (including adults with disabilities), and administrators are all partners in the education of young children.

2.  All children have the right to stability, security, affirmation, acceptance, time together with family and friends, values, community, and access to basic resources.

3.  Young children with disabilities have additional legal rights as well as rights to supports and control over the services that they receive.

4.  Teachers and related-services personnel also have the right to stability, security, affirmation, acceptance, time for working together, values, and access to resources, and they should be supported in their efforts to communicate and collaboratively serve young children and the children's families.

5.  Partners in the education of young children and the children's families are advocates and change agents.

The authors of this chapter did not arrive at its title easily. The term *partner* has evolved from the Middle English word *partaker,* meaning one who shares. In business, *partnerships* involve people working together to meet goals and objectives that individuals could not achieve by themselves. In dance, partnerships imply give-and-take, a quality of responsiveness in which two individual dancers support each other but are always allowed a solo, a moment to shine. The notion of partnership is the foundation of a collaborative environment. In partnerships, no one individual is the sole expert. Yet, in the education of young children, true partnerships are difficult to establish and maintain.

---

*Look at the following example, which may help clarify the need for complete parity between partners who are collaborating in the education of young children:*

Juanita has just turned 3 years old. Her mother has enrolled her in the same preschool that her sister, Victoria, 18 months older, has attended since she was 3 years old. Although Juanita has not yet developed spoken language, she is an effective communicator in her home and uses gestures and vocalizations to express herself. She stays dry throughout the day and communicates her need to use the rest room. Victoria understands Juanita well, and their relationship is similar to that of other siblings of the same age. Upon Juanita's enrollment in the early childhood program, the speech-language clinician indicated her belief that Victoria and Juanita should not be in the same multi-age classroom. It was her fear that, with a communication partner who responded to her efforts at her level of functioning, Juanita would not be pushed to develop speech. She used terms such as *zone of proximal development* and *the role of need* in developing communication. The teacher, who would have liked to have had the sisters together for their own personal comfort, bowed to the opinion of the speech-language clinician because she was not an expert in communication development. The girls' mother, who wanted what was best for her daughters, saw the teacher, whom she knew, give in to the speech-language clinician and followed suit, although she was uncomfortable with the decision. During the first day of preschool, Juanita had a toileting accident because no one could understand her request to go potty; cried all morning because she did not know where her sister was and, having visited the other room, believed that she was in the wrong place; cried through lunch because she wanted chocolate milk rather than plain milk but no one could understand her; and scratched and bit her teacher while refusing to leave the outside play area because she had found her sister. Juanita's mother was astonished to hear of such behavior by her cheerful, pleasant daughter.

---

In a true collaborative partnership, the early childhood education (ECE) teacher would have been able to say, "In Juanita's first school experience, we want her to feel safe. We want her to be able to communicate. It is necessary for her personal needs and communication needs for her to be with her sister." Victoria and Juanita's mother was knowledgeable enough about her daughters to have been able to say, "The girls need to be together. They expect to be together. Victoria does not cater to Juanita but could be a real help to the professionals around her." In addition, the speech-language clinician would have been able to listen and then reply, "In this case, you may be right. Let's try it your way." Juanita, through her behavior on the first day of school, clearly expressed her feelings about the separation from her sister, and her feelings should have been recognized. The remainder of this chapter discusses the partners in a collaborative environment, provides a description of Bronfenbrenner's (1979) Systems Model, and describes family needs and the legal rights of children with disabilities.

*Reflection:* As you read the next section, you will learn about a socioecological systems model of development. Think about your immediate and extended families and how they interact with the community. Can you identify the aspects of your family that are associated with the levels of the nested systems model?

## WHO ARE THE PARTNERS IN A COLLABORATION?

A key aspect of supporting partnerships is to identify partners and potential partners. The partners should include the child; the child's parents and family; early childhood educators and related-services personnel; adults, including those with disabilities; and administrators.

## The Child

In Bronfenbrenner's (1979) socioecological view of child development, the child develops within a series of nested contexts. In this perspective, all individuals are growing, dynamic individuals who progressively move into and restructure the environments in which they find themselves. Bronfenbrenner referred to the socioecological contexts as the microsystem, the mesosystem, the exosystem, and the macrosystem.

### The Microsystem

The microsystem is the pattern of activities, roles, and interpersonal relationships engaged in by a developing individual in the environment in which he or she is functioning. In the home, the microsystem includes relationships between the child and each parent, between the child and each sibling, and between pairs of family members. When services are being provided, the microsystem includes the relationships between the child and the service provider as well as among the child and other children in the same environment.

### The Mesosystem

The mesosystem is the interrelationships among two or more environments (i.e., microsystems) in which the individual actively participates. It may include the interrelationships between home and program, home and services agency, home and neighborhood, and a child development program and the child's peer group. For example, children of differing ethnicities may be challenged by the interrelationships between their home culture and the program culture and, as a consequence, may be overrepresented as a group in early childhood special education (ECSE). Parent–teacher collaboration and family–community service involvement are included within the mesosystem. The mesosystem also includes a consideration of either transitions or the movement of the learner from one microsystem to another.

### The Exosystem

The exosystem represents those environments that do not involve the individual directly. However, events occurring within the exosystem affect or are affected by what happens in environments (i.e., microsystems) in which the individual participates. Exosystem environments include, for example, a parent's workplace, a sibling's classroom, and the school system. The exosystem factors to be addressed include the availability of ECSE service programs, the nature of those services, and efforts to train personnel for those environments.

### The Macrosystem

The macrosystem is the majority culture's belief system. It includes broad social factors that impinge on the environments in which the individual is active. Society's general perspective on children with learning disabilities as well as families, service providers, special education, the social role of children, and community values, for example, all affect each child's education (Riegel, 1975). Policy issues may also be identified in this larger social context. Using the systems perspective requires that the child be a true partner. As Bronfenbrenner suggested, education programming for children who differ from their peers has for too long been "the study of the strange behavior of children in strange situations with strange adults for the briefest possible periods of time" (1979, p. 19). The use of the systems perspective requires ECE educators to seek relationships beyond causes and instructional strategies. It forces us to look at each child as an individual who engages in unique interpersonal interactions in a variety of developmental and community contexts and receives a variety of reactions from society, rather than looking at a child as, for example, a deaf child, a child with mental retardation, a child who uses a wheelchair, or a child who is blind.

**Reflection:** As you read the next section, think about families that come into conflict with the system. When what a family believes about what is right for their child comes into conflict with an ECE program, how should the collaborative team in the program react? If you have had experience with this type of situation, what was the outcome? Are there things that you would have done differently?

## Parents and Family

Each family shares the primary responsibility for supporting and nurturing its child. In that each family is unique, the needs of parents and families cannot be met by an ECE program providing a prescribed, inflexible set of services. Turnbull, Summers, and Brotherson (1983) suggested that professionals make four assumptions when working with parents and family members as partners in the education of a young child. First, each family should be seen as unique in terms of membership characteristics, culture, and style. Families must be viewed as "systems" in which the component parts and boundaries are constantly shifting and changing to varying degrees. Families collectively, as well as each family member individually, fulfill various functions to support the continued growth and development of the child. Finally, families experience developmental and nondevelopmental changes that produce different amounts of stress for each family member.

Although parents and family members are primarily responsible for the child, Bronfenbrenner (1970) suggested that the de facto responsibility for upbringing has shifted away from the family to others. This shift has occurred for many reasons. Families used to be bigger; older children took care of younger children; and chores were distributed throughout the family. In the past, children were well acquainted with a substantially greater number of adults in different walks of life and were more likely to be active participants in the adult environment when they interacted there. Today children do not roam freely and safely in their communities, interacting with neighborhood businesses or services providers. Children often do not walk to school, and, instead of a cohort of schoolmates, they often have small circles of friends with whom they communicate only by telephone or by being brought to each other's homes by car by a parent. Finally, parents today just do not spend as much time with their children as parents once did. Although society is changing, the child's earliest and closest alliances remain his or her parents and family. Like all parents, parents of children with disabilities assume a number of roles. As parents, they have the power to make a difference in the lives of their children. There are a number of ways in which parents can support their children; this support, especially in the lives of children with disabilities, is invaluable.

Becoming a parent has a significant impact on any individual. Relationships with a spouse, other family members, community members, and professionals change when one assumes the role of parent. Adjusting to the reality of parenting is a challenge. When a child is identified as having a disability, parents require even more time to adjust to a reality for which they were most likely unprepared. Marion (1981) suggested that parents need accurate information to develop positive and realistic expectations for their child. New parents turn to their own mothers and fathers, siblings, friends, and professionals to gather information regarding the role of parent. Parenting is a common experience, and advice and knowledge are freely shared among parents. When the child has a disability, there are fewer individuals with whom the parent may share experiences; yet, getting the facts and gaining an in-depth understanding of the child's disabilities places parents on an equal footing in discussing their child with the many professionals with whom they may interact. Informed parents have a greater voice in decisions involving their children. Knowledgeable parents are more perceptive about accommodations and resources such as closed captioning, wheelchairs that are both comfortable and convenient for car transportation, large-print materials, and feeding equipment.

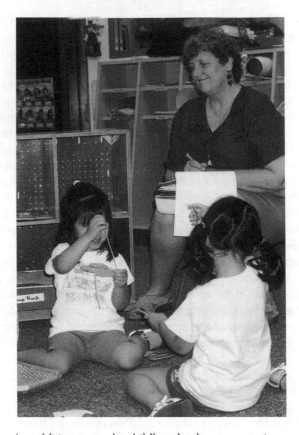

In addition to early childhood educators, various other professionals may be involved in the education of young children. The combined expertise of these professionals provides all children with successful experiences.

Parents of young children also gain information and knowledge about their children and parenting roles from interacting with individuals of various ages. These interactions provide parents with a life-span perspective of child development and the shifting roles of parents. Again, if the child has a disability, the parent is less likely to have personal contacts that support a life-span perspective. Meeting and talking with individuals with disabilities of various ages can help parents envision the future and help in planning realistic and challenging goals for their children. The accomplishments of positive role models of individuals with disabilities can be inspiring to both parents and children.

As parents become informed about their children, they feel empowered and confident. Growing sensitivity to their children's needs encourages parents and caregivers to become advocates. Active parents are essential for ensuring quality services. Although children with disabilities are legally protected regarding education-related services, parent advocacy remains essential. Whether it is a matter of arguing for consistent staff in a preschool classroom, a qualified interpreter for a deaf child, or a longer lunch period for a child with a physical disability, parents must be both knowledgeable and assertive to ensure that their children receive quality education programming. Knowing that their parents or caregivers are there for them in different contexts can make all children feel supported and strong.

Parent involvement has been consistently demonstrated to be of great benefit in the education of children with and without disabilities. Parents cannot surrender the education of their children to ECE teachers and related-services professionals. Parents know their children better than any teacher or professional does, see their children functioning in a variety of situations every day, and have practical expectations regarding their children. Supporting children at home by, for example, visiting the library; assisting in class trips and events; keeping in touch with the teachers and the school; and, most important, making children aware of parents' concern for and interest in them are the parents' responsibility.

Parents can also support their children by providing opportunities for them to interact with individuals in the community. In the same way that Bronfenbrenner (1970) described the need for children to be well acquainted with adults and to be active participants in various adult environments, children with disabilities gain great support from adults, including adults with disabilities, who truly understand them. The extent to which parents can understand and be involved with their children is related to the degree to which they can communicate and relate to their children. The ability to communicate with the child is fundamental to the parent–child relationship. Situations in which the child does not have access to his or her communication system in the home, whether it is parents who are not able to use American Sign Language (ASL), a computer or technological aid that remains at school, or a language book that parents simply do not use, impede the growth and development of the child. Although it is understandable that the daily pressures under which families function are significant, parents who cannot communicate with their child in the child's most successful mode of communication are not honoring the child's fundamental right to communicate.

**Reflection:** In the next section, a series of related-services personnel functions are listed and defined. Have you ever had contact with one or more of these individuals? What were their roles?

## Early Childhood Educators and Related-Services Personnel

The National Association for the Education of Young Children (NAEYC) (1986) provided several recommendations regarding the role of ECE educators and other adults in their interactions with young children. Adults should quickly and directly respond to children's needs and children's attempts to communicate. In addition, children should be provided with a variety of opportunities to communicate in various environments, including one-to-one interactions and groups of two to three children. Adults should provide assistance in a sensitive and appropriate manner, and children should be treated with acceptance and respect and be made comfortable regardless of their behavior. In addition, when managing behavior, ECE educators should set clear, consistent limits; redirect behavior; and support children in conflict resolution. These recommended practices for ECE educators are the same for young children with or without identified disabilities.

In addition to ECE educators, other professionals may be involved in the education of young children. The Individuals with Disabilities Education Act (IDEA) of 1990 (PL 101-476) describes special education as specially designed instruction to meet the unique needs of a student with a disability. These services are to be provided free of charge and may include related services. *Related services* are described as those services that a child requires in order to profit from his or her education. Any of the following professionals may be engaged in making plans regarding the child's education, providing direct services, working with the child's ECE educator, or evaluating the child's strengths and needs:

- *Audiologists,* who assess the range, nature, and degree of hearing loss, as well as help with amplification systems for children and developing environments that meet the child's hearing needs
- *Early interventionists,* who work with young children and their families in developing, implementing, and evaluating education programs
- *Occupational therapists,* who support children in the areas of feeding, fine motor skills, self-help skills, balance, and sensory integration
- *Physical therapists,* who support children in gross motor learning
- *Psychologists,* who may assess children; interpret assessment results; and consult with children, families, and ECE educators
- *School nurses,* who provide school health services and consultation to families and ECE educators
- *Communication specialists,* who assess children's speech, language, and communication skills; provide direct services to children; and work in consultation with parents, families, and ECE educators

Related-services personnel must be accountable for providing accurate, sensitive, unbiased evaluations of the child. They should be knowledgeable about the continuum of options and choices available to the parent and child. Related-services personnel must avoid using stereotypes and a model based on impairments and remediation, recognizing that the child develops within a given context. When working with the parents of young children, related-services personnel must be knowledgeable about disabilities throughout the life span, providing parents and caregivers with clear information regarding potential outcomes and accommodations.

## Adults, Including Those with Disabilities

Marty (cited in Brendtro, Brokenleg, & Van Bockern, 1990) suggested that, even though the family has been crucial to preserving civilization, the community rather than the nuclear family has ensured cultural survival. Children must have the opportunity to interact with various caring adults. With regard to young children with disabilities, Stainback, Stainback, East, and Sapon-Shevin (1994) suggested that young children with disabilities need to have purposeful access to other individuals with disabilities. Planned opportunities for ongoing contact among individuals who share common characteristics may support young children in developing a positive self-image and identifying themselves as individuals and as individuals with disabilities. A supportive group of individuals with disabilities may be able to serve as one of several supporting communities for the young child with disabilities. If children have contact only with their age-mates, there is no possibility for them to learn culturally established patterns of cooperation and mutual concern (Bronfenbrenner, 1970). Adults, including adults with disabilities, can be invaluable assets for programs serving young children with disabilities. They may serve as mentors, members of advisory boards, or advocates when planning education programs. Adults with disabilities can be role models and provide a life-span perspective on the disability. Adults with disabilities can provide early childhood educators with strategies to accommodate the disability.

## Administrators

Administrators of ECE programs are responsible for implementing developmentally appropriate practice (DAP) for the participants in their programs. They need to possess a strong understanding of children, families, and culture in order to provide supports that are best suited to individual and family needs. They also have the difficult challenge of explaining DAP to parents, families, and community members who seek to hurry the experience of childhood and have children engaged in rigid academic classrooms that emphasize curricula over children's learning and development.

As partners supporting young children with disabilities and their families, administrators must be knowledgeable about disabilities. In addition to recognizing the unique needs of young children, administrators should understand the life-span perspective and the wide range of outcomes possible for people with disabilities. An understanding of DAP and the ongoing tensions between DAP and the functional curriculum needs of young children with disabilities is essential. Administrators may engage in a wide range of activities as they support young children, including young children with disabilities, and their families. As advocates, they may support children, their families, and teachers and assist them as they establish networks both within and outside of the ECE program. Providing opportunities for parents and family members to interact in a safe, positive climate is essential. For example, by providing parents' rooms, brown bag lunches, morning coffees, and other opportunities for interaction, administrators can support parents as they establish networks and social supports.

---

*The following example depicts the sort of supports that can emerge as parents form networks:*

Joanna is the parent of 4-year-old Jenny, who uses a wheelchair. While working on materials in the parents' room, Joanna mentioned to Ellie, the parent of a young child who uses a walker, how uncomfortable she was when going to the mall because of the stares that she and Jenny received there. Ellie mentioned jokingly that she and Joanna should go together and "let 'em stare." Joanna, after considering the proposal for a moment, agreed. Together, they scheduled a series of afternoons out during which they and their children would go to various fast-food restaurants, ice cream parlors, and malls. Individually, they felt uncomfortable; together, they felt safer in confronting what they felt was a lack of sensitivity to them and their children in the community.

---

Perhaps the most important role of the administrator is to set the climate of the ECE program. An administrator who is knowledgeable, open, ethical, and respectful with regard to all young children, including young children with disabilities and their families, establishes the pattern of practice in the program.

**Reflection:**   In the next section, a series of children's needs are presented. As you read the section, think about how these needs were met in your own family.

## SUPPORTING THE CHILD AND THE FAMILY

Garbarino (1997) suggested that all children have the same needs. The authors of this chapter suggest that all children have the right to have these needs addressed. Using Garbarino's structure, all children have the right to

- Stability
- Security
- Affirmation and acceptance
- Time together with family and friends
- Values and community
- Access to basic resources

### Stability

Bronfenbrenner (1970) argued that stability is one of the primary needs of all children. The home is the greatest source of stability for young children. Some children have greater vulnerability to instability than others, and younger children are particularly vulnerable to family disruptions (Garbarino, 1997).

Becoming culturally competent first requires early childhood educators to clarify their own values and assumptions. Also, early childhood educators should be aware
of the values and assumptions of the families with whom
they work.

Although children and professionals often equate stability with home and
family, large numbers of young children spend much of their time outside of the
home. More than 60% of married women with children younger than age 6 are in
the labor force. More than 57% of these children were cared for outside of their own
homes (U.S. Census Bureau, 1994). In addition to the children who spend some of
their time with their families, there are many families that are so unstable that the
children are in foster care. Almost half of the confirmed cases of maltreatment are
related to child neglect rather than to child maltreatment. Nearly 500,000 children
were in foster family homes, group homes, or residential treatment centers on a
single day in 1993, and 29% of children who entered foster care before their first
birthday were still in foster care after 4 years (Children's Defense Fund, 1995).

It would be most desirable for all children to have a stable home environment.
However, for some children, the school experience is the most stable environment
that they encounter. Programs for children should emphasize stability, routine,
and ongoing contact with the same professionals. This stability allows the child to
more fully profit from the learning opportunities provided to him or her. For example, if the child's way of communication is an alternative to oral standard English,
the adults in his or her program should be consistent in supporting the child's
communication and facilitating his or her development over an extended period of
time. Rotating teachers, using fill-in staff, or scheduling activities to meet staff
needs rather than the child's needs fails to address the child's need for a stable
environment.

## Security

In one study of an inner-city neighborhood, one third of the children reported witnessing a homicide before they reached 15 years of age (Bell, 1991). Garbarino (1997) described three "secrets" that young children in violent neighborhoods learn, which have a profound, negative effect on their development. First, children may learn that the human body is quite fragile; simply encountering violence and trauma to this extent changes children. Second, children may learn that adults cannot protect them. Children learn to fend for themselves, usually through violence, when adults should be caring for them. Finally, children learn that when it comes to violence, anything is possible. Anyone may be a victim or a perpetrator. Children with disabilities are even more likely than children without disabilities to be the victims of abuse and violence. Children must feel safe in order to learn. Children must have positive relationships with adults and peers. In addition, behavior management strategies must be positive, prosocial learning strategies rather than strategies of control, deprivation, or even violence.

## Affirmation and Acceptance

A positive self-identity is central to a child's resilience (Garbarino, 1997). Children must be affirmed simply for who they are and should not be expected to be other than who they are. For children with disabilities, affirmation has a particular meaning. A parent of a child with a disability tells the story of how her and her child's lives changed when her son, who uses a wheelchair, became the running partner for one of his former teachers. The teacher, who was about to give up running because of a dismal performance in a marathon, told the class that she was quitting. The young man, who has cerebral palsy, chided her and said that he would go along and encourage her the next time that she ran. The teacher found a running stroller, and they became a running team. The mother stated that her son's bedtime prayers changed from praying to walk to thanksgiving for being able to use a wheelchair, without which he would never be able to run marathons. The mother indicated that her son had changed from asking to be removed from his wheelchair and placed in a typical chair at all times to putting stickers on his wheelchair and approaching others whom he saw in wheelchairs to chat. His attitude had changed from that of embarrassment to that of saying to the world, "I use a wheelchair, and I'm proud of who I am."

## Time Together with Family and Friends

Television has had an incredible impact on children's social interactions. Bronfenbrenner (1974) suggested that the importance of television in child development may not be the impact of television viewing on children's behavior but rather the behavior that television viewing prevents, including talks, games, family activities, and discussions—activities through which much of children's learning formerly occurred. While watching television, family social life is parallel rather than interactive, with the television set replacing the family's interactions (Maccoby, 1951).

For young children with disabilities, active engagement with family and friends may pose an additional challenge. If the child uses an alternative communication system such as ASL, language boards, or eye blinks, the parents or siblings are often cast in the role of interpreters; their pleasurable participation may be hampered by their need to work to include the young child with a disability in their conversations. If a child uses a wheelchair or has difficulty with gross motor skills, joining other members of the family may be a challenge. Constantly engaging a young child with a disability is difficult. Too often the child is physically present but ignored because of the accommodations needed to actively engage the child in the activity.

## Values and Community

Professionals who interact with young children and their families must recognize their professional values and how these values affect their interactions with children, families, and colleagues. With a commitment to DAP, early childhood educators demonstrate a value for childhood as a time of play rather than work, as a time of development rather than drill. The right of each child to a childhood, to a time of innocence and safe exploration, is an essential value. ECE educators must strive to communicate this value throughout the community to build a sense of belonging and safety for all young children.

## Access to Basic Resources

The costs of poverty, the absence of basic resources, are great. Children living in poverty are twice as likely as other children to die as a result of birth defects, four times as likely to die as a result of fire, and five times as likely to die as a result of infectious diseases and parasites. In addition, poverty leads to parents' stress and less effective parenting and, for the child, to poor nutrition, unstable living conditions, reduced access to quality education, and fewer extracurricular activities (Children's Defense Fund, 1995). At times, the ECE educator finds him- or herself providing far more than educational needs to young children. Programs such as Head Start recognize the need for basic resources and, through parent education and involvement, assist families in enhancing their health, nutrition, and life skills and in supporting their children.

## OTHER RIGHTS OF FAMILIES

The NAEYC (1986) maintained that parents have the right and the responsibility to share in decision making regarding their children's care and education. Families' views of their children's behavior and development must be obtained and respected.

Children and families of young children with disabilities, like other children and families, have legal rights and responsibilities. In addition to these rights, young children with disabilities and their families should be supported simply on the basis of their being a family. A Syracuse University Center on Human Policy (1987) position statement on families held that

- Families have the right to the supports necessary to maintain their children in their homes.
- Supports should serve entire families.
- Supports should maximize families' control over the services that they receive.

The parents and families of children with disabilities may be supported by a variety of people in different arenas. When a child is identified as having a disability, endless visits to professionals who are located in a number of places can be an overwhelming, confusing, and tiring experience for parents and caregivers. Collaborative partnerships of doctors and other professionals in the community who together can provide comprehensive information and advise parents about their children are one form of support.

Regional resource centers may also provide information about disabilities to parents and caregivers. These centers should be conveniently located and have information available on all disabilities. Information should be readily accessible and available in a variety of formats, including audiovisual aids, books, workshops, and consultations. These centers should be open at times when parents may attend special events on weekends and at other convenient times.

Community organizations managed by adults with and without disabilities also provide strong supports for parents and caregivers of children with disabilities. These organizations usually offer services for individuals with a specific disability or a specific group of disabilities. Examples of such organizations are the community service centers for the deaf in many communities. These centers support individuals who are deaf or hard of hearing and take an active role in the education and orientation of parents to the disability. Community organizations may afford parents and caregivers contact with adults with disabilities, thus providing them with role models as well as insights into accommodations. These community organizations may provide information to parents regarding the law, their rights, and their children's rights.

In terms of early intervention and preschool services, the local education agency and the school can provide a great deal of support to parents with disabilities. ECE educators can help parents understand the educational and social implications of their child's disability. Informed parents are a tremendous resource, and ECE programs should be open to and respectful of their opinions and beliefs. Their insights can contribute to the effectiveness of programs.

Parent support groups are another source of support for parents. A group of parents who can share their experiences with each other can provide great support for all members of the group. Support groups can be rich sources of information about the disability and may foster leadership skills among parents and enable them to take control of their lives and their children's lives.

The community at large must be engaged in supporting parents as well. Child care, transportation, and health care services must be affordable and available. Social services agencies should provide accurate information to parents regarding funding for technological aides, materials, and services required by children with disabilities and their families.

## Supporting Cultural Diversity

One of the roles of the family is to socialize the child to become part of the culture and the community. The cultural preferences of families must form the primary basis of program planning (Hanson, Lynch, & Wayman, 1990). The effectiveness of ECE programs, Hanson and associates suggested, largely depends on the cultural competence of ECE educators. Becoming culturally competent requires ECE educators to clarify their own values and assumptions. ECE educators should look at each family's cultural community and determine the degree to which each family operates transculturally. In addition, ECE educators should examine the family's orientation to specific child-rearing practices.

## Supporting Teachers and Related-Services Personnel

Teachers and related-services personnel also should be provided with stability, security, affirmation, acceptance, time for working together, and access to resources. In addition, teachers should be supported in their efforts to communicate with and collaboratively serve young children. With the movement toward structured, academic curricula in ECE education, teachers should be supported in their efforts to implement DAP and individually appropriate programs. Teachers should be supported in assuring both parents and administrators that children from homes and classrooms affording greater opportunities for communication and decision making not only exhibit greater initiative and independence after entering high school but also receive higher grades in high school (Epstein, 1983).

## SUPPORTING THE SYSTEM: SOCIETY'S VIEWS ON DISABILITY

On July 26, 1990, President Bush signed the Americans with Disabilities Act (ADA) of 1990 (PL 101-336) into law. Shapiro (1993), however, argued that the passage of this law was an odd victory because, as radical as the passage of the ADA might have been for individuals with disabilities, people without disabilities had little understanding that individuals with disabilities simply wanted the same rights that others had to participate in American society. People with disabilities do not want gifts or pity. Shapiro suggested that whereas African Americans had first changed Americans' attitudes toward them and then had gained equality under the law with the Civil Rights Act of 1964 (PL 88-352), the reverse occurred for peo-

Programs for children should emphasize ongoing contact and stability with professionals. This emphasis allows children to more fully profit from the daily learning opportunities provided.

ple with disabilities: They first won the passage of a law and then were confronted with the task of changing the nation's attitudes toward them. The ADA ensured the right of people with disabilities to participate in society and have the same degree of access to facilities and information as people without disabilities, such as being able to use a public toilet, being able to visually recognize a fire alarm, or entering a building via a ramp; but it did so at some financial expense. In one large midwestern city, a county commissioner argued against incurring the expense of installing braille signs in the county courthouse because he had never seen a blind person walking alone in the building. It apparently had not occurred to him that the reason why no blind people were seen walking alone in the courthouse was that blind people had to bring a companion along to read printed signs, a need that would be obviated by the installation of braille signs.

As collaborative partners in the education of young children, parents, family members, and ECE educators must work together to fight limiting attitudes toward children with disabilities, acting as educators of all individuals regarding disabilities. They need to educate the person who asks, "Who pays for the nurse to catheterize that student?" To that person the ECE educator can say that all children use the bathroom; the child with a disability just happens to use a catheter. The questioner who asks "Who pays for that interpreter?" for the child who is deaf or hard of hearing needs to be assured that everybody should know what is going on and be able to participate in the classroom.

## CONCLUSIONS

ECE educators must strive toward collaborative environments that encourage equity among partners. Families are key partners in the collaboration and must be critical players in ECE programs. Families are unique; do not assume that one set of services is appropriate for all children. By engaging in collaborative partnerships with a wide array of professionals, ECE educators gain expertise that enables them to better meet the diverse needs of the children and families that they serve.

## REMEMBER THIS

1. *Partnership* implies equality. Rather than one individual being the expert, each partner is perceived as having a valid contribution to make in supporting the young child.

2. Each family is unique and shares the primary responsibility for supporting and nurturing the child. In view of this uniqueness, ECE programs cannot be composed of a prescribed, inflexible set of services for all families.

3. Parenting is a challenge and a commitment. When the child has a disability or the family is experiencing a crisis, additional challenges are faced.

## REFERENCES

Americans with Disabilities Act (ADA) of 1990, PL 101-336, 42 U.S.C. §§ 12101 *et seq.*

Bell, C. (1991). Traumatic stress and children in danger. *Journal of Health Care for the Poor and Underserved, 2*(1), 175–188.

Brendtro, L., Brokenleg, M., & Van Bockern, S. (1990). *Reclaiming youth at risk.* Bloomington, IN: National Educational Service.

Bronfenbrenner, U. (1970). *Two worlds of childhood.* New York: Russell Sage Foundation.

Bronfenbrenner, U. (1974). Developmental research and public policy. In J. Romanshyn (Ed.), *Social science and social welfare* (pp. 159–182). New York: Council on Social Work Education.

Bronfenbrenner, U. (1979). *The ecology of human development.* Cambridge, MA: Harvard University Press.

Children's Defense Fund. (1995). *1995 yearbook on children.* Washington, DC: Author.

Civil Rights Act of 1964, PL 88-352, 20 U.S.C. §§ 241 *et seq.*

Epstein, J.L. (1983). Longitudinal effects of family–school–person interactions on student outcomes. *Research in Sociology of Education and Socialization, 4,* 101–127.

Garbarino, J. (1997). *Raising children in a socially toxic environment.* San Francisco: Jossey-Bass.

Hanson, M.J., Lynch, E.W., & Wayman, K.I. (1990). Honoring the cultural diversity of families when gathering data. *Topics in Early Childhood Special Education, 10,* 112–131.

Individuals with Disabilities Education Act (IDEA) of 1990, PL 101-476, 20 U.S.C. §§ 1400 *et seq.*

Maccoby, E.E. (1951). Television: Its impact on schoolchildren. *Public Opinion Quarterly, 15,* 421–444.

Marion, R.L. (1981). *Educators, parents, and exceptional children.* Rockville, MD: Aspen Publishers.

National Association for the Education of Young Children (NAEYC). (1986). Position statements on developmentally appropriate practice in early childhood programs. *Young Children, 41,* 3–29.

Riegel, K.F. (1975). Toward a dialectical theory of development. *Human Development, 18,* 50–64.

Shapiro, J.P. (1993). *No pity: People with disabilities forging a new civil rights movement.* New York: Times Books.

Stainback, S., Stainback, W., East, K., & Sapon-Shevin, M. (1994). A commentary on inclusion and the development of a positive self-identity by people with disabilities. *Exceptional Children, 60,* 486–490.

Syracuse University Center on Human Policy. (1987). *A statement in support of families and their children.* Syracuse, NY: Author.

Turnbull, A.P., Summers, J.A., & Brotherson, M.J. (1983). *Working with families with disabled members: A family systems approach.* Lawrence: University of Kansas Press.

U.S. Census Bureau. (1994). *Who's minding the kids? Child care arrangements: Fall 1991 Current population reports.* Washington, DC: Author.

# Activities

1. Interview two parents whose children are about the same age, with one being a parent of a child with disabilities and the other being a parent of a child without disabilities, regarding their concerns about and goals for their children. What are the similarities in their responses? What are the differences?

2. Interview the administrator of an inclusive ECE program. What issues emerged as he or she observed the application of developmentally appropriate practice to young children with disabilities?

3. Interview an ECE teacher working in an inclusive program. What are the overall goals that this individual has for his or her students? Are the goals for young children with disabilities the same as those for all other children?

4. Interview an adult with a disability about his or her experiences as a partner in his or her own education or about the participation of the individual's family in his or her education. What facilitated partnerships for this person and the person's family? What were the barriers that the individual faced?

c h a p t e r $5$

# Developmentally and Individually Appropriate Practices

*M.J. LaMontagne, Karen Danbom, and Michelle Buchanan*

## CHAPTER ORGANIZER

In this chapter, we explore the following ideas . . .

1.  Developmentally and individually appropriate practices are a combined set of strategies that reflect theory, research, and procedures from both early childhood education and early childhood special education.

2.  Early childhood education and early childhood special education share many common themes that guide services for young children and their families.

3.  Both fields have unique contributions to make in the provision of services to young children with and without disabilities and their families.

4.  When selecting an intervention strategy, early childhood education and early childhood special education professionals must determine the appropriateness of that strategy for each child and the child's family.

5.  Aspects of developmentally and individually appropriate practices include purposes and goals for early childhood education and intervention, parent—

professional partnerships, curriculum planning, instruction methods and strategies, and assessment.

6. A blending of practices from both fields provides a more holistic approach to
   early childhood education that honors the characteristics and needs that all children share as well as children's individual differences and needs.

In 1987, the National Association for the Education of Young Children (NAEYC)
articulated a set of procedures and guidelines related to developmentally appropriate practice (DAP) in early childhood education (ECE) programs (Bredekamp,
1987). In 1991, the Council for Exceptional Children (CEC) published *DEC Recommended Practices: Indicators of Quality in Programs for Infants and Young Children with
Special Needs and Their Families* (Division for Early Childhood [DEC] Task Force on
Recommended Practices, 1991) for early childhood special education (ECSE) programs serving young children with disabilities and their families. Across both professions, there has been a tendency to steer away from dogmatic proclamations
that specifically identify the "best practice" for any given ECE or ECSE program.
This perspective is based on the belief that each program serving young children
and families is unique because of the nature of the children and families, in addition to each program's having its own unique characteristics. From this view has
emerged a concept of preferred practice that provides a variety of strategies for
supporting young children and families. Preferred practice gives early childhood
educators a range of techniques to adapt and implement according to the unique
needs of their program and the families that it serves. From this perspective, developmentally and individually appropriate practices have emerged.[1] Developmentally and individually appropriate practices extend the concepts articulated by the
NAEYC (i.e., DAP) to include an emphasis on the individual characteristics and
needs of young children with disabilities.

　　Since 1991, federal education policy has focused on the importance of ECE
and the role that early learning plays in children's later school success (U.S.
Department of Education, 1991). *America 2000: An Education Strategy* presented a
challenge for ECE educators with its first goal, which simply stated that all children must enter school ready to learn. Attention is being focused on the design and
implementation of comprehensive, high-quality ECE services that meet the needs
of all young children and families. An increasing emphasis is being placed on providing services to young children with disabilities in their community environments as the preferred service delivery environment (DEC, 1993). The increased
emphasis in the 1990s on inclusive service delivery inherently suggests the blending of ECE and ECSE services in the interest of young children with and without

---

[1]In this chapter, *DAP* refers to the NAEYC guidelines of developmentally appropriate practice;
*developmentally and individually appropriate practices* refers to the combined set of strategies from NAEYC
and DEC that reflects the theory, research, and procedures from both fields.

disabilities and their families. From this blending of services comes the natural need to find congruence between the guiding practices of ECE and ECSE in order to meet the challenge of providing comprehensive, high-quality early childhood programming.

**Reflection:** As you read the next section, you will learn about some differences between ECE and ECSE with regard to the concepts of developmentally and individually appropriate practices. As you read about these viewpoints, try to identify some practical factors that contribute to these differences. How easily can the gaps created by these differences be bridged?

## DEVELOPMENTALLY AND INDIVIDUALLY APPROPRIATE PRACTICES: THE DEBATE

A generous amount of debate has occurred with regard to the applicability of developmentally and individually appropriate practices in programs serving young children with disabilities and their families. Some professionals have agreed on their use (Johnson & Johnson, 1994; Mahoney, Robinson, & Powell, 1992; Norris, 1991), and others have issued cautionary warnings on their use (Carta, Atwater, Schwartz, & McConnell, 1993; Carta, Schwartz, Atwater, & McConnell, 1991; Wolery, Strain, & Bailey, 1992).

The historical context that frames this debate centers on the origins of the respective guiding philosophies of ECE and ECSE. As is presented in Chapter 3, ECSE emerged as a downward extension of school-age special education programs to preschool-age children that relied on a behavioral perspective emphasizing impairments and a fix-it philosophy of intervention services. ECE, in contrast, has traditionally focused on cognitive development and a constructivist approach that addresses child-directed activities in the context of play.

### Intervention-Centered Early Childhood Education

In response to many years of discussion in the ECE field, Wolery and Bredekamp (1994) provided a needed examination of the debate about DAP and *DEC Recommended Practices* and described several issues that appeared to contextualize the discussion. The first issue reminded the participants that intervention practices, not the fields of ECE and ECSE, were the focus of the discussion. This distinction was important because it allowed each profession to maintain its professional status and therefore its unique contribution to young children with and without disabilities and their families. The recognition that each profession has a place in ECE allowed the debate to examine the mechanics of practices in programs for young children with disabilities. This examination led to ongoing program evaluation that addressed questions such as the following:

- Are we using preferred practices in our program?
- Are we meeting the needs of children with disabilities?
- Are we meeting the needs of children without disabilities?
- Are we meeting the needs of families of children with disabilities?
- Are we meeting the needs of families of children without disabilities?

## Acceptance of Different Viewpoints

A second issue that surfaced in the debate over DAP and *DEC Recommended Practices* deals with the acceptance of the philosophical approaches of professionals in both fields. Differences exist between the two guidelines of practice: DAP and *DEC Recommended Practices* (McLean & Odom, 1993; Wolery & Bredekamp, 1994; Wolery et al., 1992). Practitioners in each field accept their own professional practice guidelines to varying degrees, and the same is true of their acceptance of the other field's guidelines (Wolery & Bredekamp, 1994). These varying degrees of acceptance produce variations both within and among practices implemented in the two fields. Some ECE and ECSE educators might argue that some programs for young children with or without disabilities do not meet the guidelines set forth by their own professional organizations: DEC and NAEYC (Odom, 1994). In addition, ECE and ECSE practitioners are challenged to consider the concept of *preferred practices,* which includes strategies that differ from their field's historical theory of practice. In light of the advance of inclusive education practices, ECE and ECSE practitioners must explore the differences and similarities among their practices and develop the concept of preferred practice. Neither field's practices will lose its theoretical orientations or philosophical foundations; rather, each field will blend those characteristics of DAP and *DEC Recommended Practices* that meet the individual needs of young children and their families. As Carta (1994) succinctly stated, the fit between the uniqueness of the individual child and the strategies of practice determine the level of appropriateness of any set of guidelines for ECE or ECSE best practices.

From the notion of the fit between the individual child and the practices used to support that child's learning in an ECE environment emerges the third issue related to the goal of each practice. DAP and *DEC Recommended Practices* were designed to identify those strategies that provide appropriate services for young children. Discussion centers around which set of practices is appropriate for a young child with disabilities who receives services in an early childhood program for young children without disabilities. Wolery and Bredekamp (1994) defined *practice* in this context as the way in which professionals develop programs and interact with children and families to support specific outcomes in learning. If professionals arrive at a consensus on what they expect children to learn in their program, then the same professionals will gauge the suitability, individual appropriateness, efficiency, and effectiveness of practices from both fields with regard to which practices will enable them to help the child reach the identified learning outcomes. The goal of practice thus becomes the successful attainment of identified outcomes for each young child, regardless of whether the child has a disability.

*Look at the following example:*

Isabelle is a young child who is quite shy and reluctant to participate in group activities. Jerome is a boisterous young child who often dominates group activities. In order to accommodate the differences between these two typically developing children, the teacher may either structure the activity or place each child in a different group to promote balance in social exchanges. The strategies that the teacher chooses may range from direct (e.g., asking Isabelle whether she would like to lead her group in an activity) to indirect (e.g., giving Isabelle the materials for creating a piñata).

In the preceding example, the ECE educator provided learning opportunities that addressed the uniqueness of each young child. By structuring the activity to support the diversity of the children in the classroom, the teacher offered developmentally and individually appropriate practices interactions for the children in her program.

Although DAP and *DEC Recommended Practices* may have been developed to address the needs of different populations of young children (Wolery & Bredekamp, 1994), a professional's ability to choose those strategies and practices from either field that match the needs of a specific child and that child's family captures the true essence of preferred practice. In addition, the early childhood educator must know when, where, and how to make changes and adaptations in practices for diverse children, some of whom will require individual adaptations so that they can achieve success in their ECE learning environment.

## Blending of Viewpoints

The debate among ECE and ECSE professionals has led to an emerging understanding of how each profession views its role in ECE and the skills and the knowledge that each field brings to the blended practice. The next step is to define a system for blending the repertoire of knowledge and skills in order to provide appropriate programming for all young children and their families. Wolery and Bredekamp (1994) described three standards by which to gauge the appropriateness of any given practice for use with a young child with or without disabilities. These three dimensions of practice evaluation are *appropriateness, effectiveness,* and *efficiency.*

### Appropriateness

*Appropriateness* is the degree to which a practice is ethically sound and is in compliance with local, state, and federal laws and regulations. When considering the ethical appropriateness of a strategy, the standard to be used is the extent to which the practice benefits the young child, the child's family, and the child's social relationships. In addition, the practice must not violate any local, state, or federal law or regulation.

## *Effectiveness*

The *effectiveness* of a practice has a direct connection to the identified outcome for young children and/or their families. A practice is considered effective when its use results in a specifically desired outcome. A practice's effectiveness can be measured in terms of staying power, balance, and desired outcomes for individual children and the overall goals of the program. Effectiveness has a dimension of power in that some practices may produce a desired outcome, but the practices must support the desired outcome over time and across environments. Some practices promote individual, independent learning that isolates a young child from his or her peers and playmates. Early childhood educators must struggle with the issue of individual goals versus general goals of education. An individual goal is more specific and related than an identified child outcome. A general goal of education encompasses a more global result in that it may not produce a specific child outcome.

---

*Look at the following example of an individualized education program (IEP) goal:*

On Maria's IEP, her parents and teachers had decided that Maria's learning to tie her shoelaces was an important goal. For her parents, Maria's learning of the skill was a priority because Maria was either stumbling around on her loose shoelaces or constantly asking her parents to tie her shoelaces. In order to achieve this goal, the team had agreed that Maria needed as many opportunities as possible to practice tying her shoelaces. Because it was a natural part of Maria's day to remove her shoes at naptime and then put them back on before going out to play, the team decided that she would be responsible for tying her own shoelaces and that the 15-minute playtime that followed naptime would provide Maria with a high degree of motivation. Every day after her nap, Maria would work furiously to tie her shoelaces so that she could get out to the playground. Unfortunately, in her haste, she had more difficulty than previously with this task and became more frustrated than before. It usually took her 10 minutes to get her shoelaces tied and get out to the playground. After 1 week, Maria was able to get her shoelaces tied in about 8 minutes, and the teachers were hopeful that she would soon be able to tie her shoes quickly and efficiently. However, the teachers had begun to notice that Maria was not playing as much with the other children in the class as she had at the beginning of school.

---

The staff must evaluate Maria's individual needs across developmental domains so that their intervention does not increase one skill at the expense of another. The effectiveness of strategies should be examined with regard to potential future gains as well as immediate gains. Often teachers of young children with disabilities are tempted to assist that child in activities so that the child is able to achieve the desired outcome. In Maria's scenario, for example, a child may achieve an immediate goal without acquiring or practicing skills for independent learning that can be applied to other tasks. It is as important for young children with disabilities to acquire the intangible aspects of learning, such as self-initiation, perseverance, adaptation, and determination, as it is for them to achieve the objectives on their IEPs. Often these intangible aspects have an impact on 1) the approach that a young child takes toward future learning opportunities and 2) the child's eventual success as a learner.

---

*The following example illustrates intangible aspects of learning:*

Andi had been playing in the sand and water area with her friends. The theme of the day was measurement, and the children were pouring sand into and out of containers. They were busily exploring different sizes of containers and the volume of water that each was able to hold. Because Andi has cerebral palsy, she found it difficult to manipulate the containers. When she tried to pour sand from one container to another, she consistently dropped one of the containers. Observing Andi's difficulties, the teacher came to Andi's side and held one container while assisting Andi to pour the contents of the second container into the first. A week later, the children in Andi's class had the opportunity to explore the concept of measurement by using water. The teacher observed that Andi was avoiding the sand and water area and asked her why. Andi replied, "I can't do that."

---

Independence is an important aspect of learning. For Andi, independence among her peers at the sand table rather than the preciseness of her motor skills supported her learning. In the preceding scenario, the teacher attempted to support the motor skills section of Andi's IEP without realizing and respecting the adaptation section of Andi's IEP, which was being supported by Andi's attempting to perform the task on her own.

### *Efficiency*

The *efficiency* of a practice is assessed by measuring the time that it takes a young child to learn a skill. Yet speed is not the only factor that determines efficiency. The level of efficiency of a practice is measured by considering three factors:

1. Promotion of the development of the young child
2. Support of a child's acquisition of a skill in a timely manner and facilitation of the child's independence
3. The extent to which the practice reduces the chance of the appearance of secondary disabilities

First, a practice must address the interrelatedness of development in young children, recognizing that language influences cognition, which influences motor skill development, which affects socialization. Within this consideration, an early childhood educator addresses the efficiency of a practice by selecting strategies that support the higher-priority outcome. Returning to the scenario of Andi at the sand table, the teacher might have adopted a more efficient strategy of remaining in the background and allowing Andi the opportunity to adapt the learning materials and environment to her own needs and to determine her own level of success at this activity. At a later point, the teacher might have selected a strategy that would specifically address motor planning and manipulation of measurement materials during another learning opportunity.

Second, an efficient practice seeks to support a child's acquisition of a skill in a timely manner and in a way that facilitates the child's independence. Often in programs that provide services to young children with disabilities, the *dis-* in *disabilities* is enhanced by the staff's providing too much help, thus making the child dependent on others for support in activities and interactions.

---

*Look at the following example:*

Every day during lunch, Sarah sits with her friends at the table and eats the lunch that her mother has sent to school. Because she has a long bus ride to school, Sarah's mother gives her money to buy milk in the lunchroom. Sarah likes to buy her milk like the other kids in her kindergarten class do. She likes to talk to the lady who takes her money and walk with her class to the lunch table. On Sarah's IEP are several goals related to fine motor skills and language development. The IEP team members have identified several target areas: using both hands to accomplish a task, increasing muscle strength in her hands and fingers, using a pincer grasp with objects, and requesting help from peers and adults. When Sarah sits down at the lunch table, she places her milk carton in front of her and proceeds to take her lunch out of her lunch bag. Other children begin opening their milk cartons and getting prepared to eat lunch. Sarah sits patiently, and eventually a staff member comes over and opens her milk carton, saying, "Are you ready for your milk? Let me open the carton for you."

---

In the preceding example, the strategy employed was to provide Sarah with opportunities in natural environments to practice fine motor and language skills. However, in this scenario, Sarah learned that waiting appropriately will bring an adult to open her milk carton. Too much help diminishes the opportunities for young children to try, explore, manipulate, persevere, adapt strategies, and problem-solve. Without practicing these skills, children's disabilities can be accentuated and other impairments may be created. For Sarah, passive and quiet behavior may become a response that gains results (the opening of her milk carton), and her ability to use language to request help and fine motor skills may receive less attention and become weaker. As demonstrated in the preceding scenario, the third consideration of an efficient practice is the extent to which the practice reduces the chance of the development of secondary handicaps.

DAP and *DEC Recommended Practices* have created a wide range of strategies from which early childhood practitioners can choose when working with all young children. In the reality of an ECE program, young children and their families

Curricula should be designed to incorporate developmentally and individually appropriate practices and to address individual children's needs. All children should be able to gain access to and use materials in a manner consistent with their present developmental levels.

exhibit diverse cultural, linguistic, and developmental characteristics. For some young children, certain adaptations and modifications in materials, environments, interactions, and equipment are needed. These changes in the process of implementing the strategy serve only to strengthen the practice and tailor it to the individual and unique diversity of the child. Thus, the focus is on providing an exemplary intervention rather than on the source of practice (i.e., rather than on whether ECE or ECSE practices are being used).

**Reflection:** Now that you have read about the developmentally and individually appropriate practices debate, consider your philosophical orientation and determine where your position fits as you read the following discussion.

# COMMON THREADS BETWEEN DEC AND NAEYC

The DEC Task Force on Recommended Practices (1991) and NAEYC (Bredekamp, 1987) described the practices and procedures that identify the standard for quality service delivery and intervention for young children and their families. Each set of guidelines depicts a framework that an early childhood program can use as it strives to provide exemplary services to young children and their families. Before a program can meet the diverse needs of young children and their families, program staff must understand each of these frameworks, DAP, *DEC Recommended Practices*, and the manner in which all of these complement and augment each other. This understanding is based on the ECE and ECSE practices that are shared, the ones that are different, and the ones that are similar but have differing emphases or definitions.

McLean and Odom (1993) completed a comparison of the written practices articulated by NAEYC in *Developmentally Appropriate Practice in Early Childhood Programs Serving Children from Birth Through Age 8* (Bredekamp, 1987), *Reaching Potentials: Appropriate Curriculum and Assessment for Young Children, Volume I* (Bredekamp & Rosegrant, 1992), and *DEC Recommended Practices: Indicators of Quality in Programs for Infants and Young Children with Special Needs and Their Families* (DEC Task Force on Recommended Practices, 1991). Using this comparison of guidelines for practice, McLean and Odom identified seven themes that illustrate the similarities and differences between ECE and ECSE practices:

1. Inclusion
2. Family involvement
3. Assessment
4. Individualized family service plans (IFSPs) and IEPs
5. Curriculum and intervention
6. Service delivery
7. Transition

## Inclusion

Prior to discussing the theme of inclusion, a common definition of *inclusion* in the ECE context is needed. *Inclusion* is a concept that is associated with young children with disabilities and that supports the basic right of all young children to full and active engagement in their communities (DEC, 1993). In addition, the practices of inclusion are implemented under the assumption that the young child is not removed from the community or from his or her peers to begin with, and thus there is no need to integrate the child into the child's natural environment (Ferguson, 1996). Both ECE and ECSE practices refer to the individual appropriateness and age appropriateness of strategies to use with young children with disabilities.

The issue of individual appropriateness in inclusion incorporates the role of the family as the decision maker. *DEC Recommended Practices* (DEC Task Force on

Recommended Practices, 1991) identifies inclusionary programs as a place holder on the continuum of service delivery models and recognizes that families will choose which setting is optimum and most natural for them. NAEYC's DAP is viewed as appropriate for all young children, including those children with special needs (Bredekamp & Rosegrant, 1992). Furthermore, as successful inclusion practice becomes a reality, families' choices of inclusion programs as the best service delivery model for their young children with disabilities will become typical rather than being the exception. *Age appropriateness* refers to practices that consider the young child's developmental and chronological ages when planning an intervention (McLean & Odom, 1993). Both NAEYC (Bredekamp, 1987; Bredekamp & Rosegrant, 1992) and DEC (DEC Task Force on Recommended Practices, 1991) support this perspective for practice.

## Family Involvement

Family involvement is an area in which the practices that DEC and NAEYC support differ in relation to emphasis (McLean & Odom, 1993). Both sets of practices address and support family involvement. NAEYC practices provide guidelines that describe the importance of communication between families and child care providers and strategies to support this communicative link. *DEC Recommended Practices* prescribe a stronger focus on family centeredness and family and child advocacy to support the family's active role in the assessment and intervention processes.

## Assessment

Assessment in early childhood programs is another area in which both similarities and differences exist (McLean & Odom, 1993). NAEYC (Bredekamp, 1987; Bredekamp & Rosegrant, 1992) recommended that assessment be used for instructional planning, identification of children with special needs, and program evaluation. DEC (DEC Task Force on Recommended Practices, 1991) has similar guidelines with more specific consideration being given to a systematic set of procedures for information gathering. The uses of assessment have a broader range in ECSE and include screening, eligibility, program planning, monitoring, and evaluation (Neisworth, 1993). McLean and Odom (1993) made a point related to the assessment strategies of these practices when they suggested that the practices are complementary and in synchrony philosophically. Both DEC and NAEYC practices require that assessments have a purpose and result in benefits for the child and family. Both practices support the use of socioecologically valid assessment procedures and the right of families' access to all assessment information related to themselves and their child. DEC provides additional guidelines in relation to the family involvement by recommending that families determine the acceptability of assessment materials and the use of family information related to concerns and priorities as a guide to planning the assessment.

## Individualized Family Service Plans and Individualized Education Programs

IFSPs and IEPs are two documents specifically designed for young children with disabilities and their families. The components of these documents are mandated by the Individuals with Disabilities Education Act (IDEA) Amendments of 1991 (PL 102-119) and the Individuals with Disabilities Education Act (IDEA) Amendments of 1997 (PL 105-17) and are designed to systematically link assessment to an intervention plan. The purpose of an IFSP/IEP is to individualize education programs, which is reflected in both NAEYC and *DEC Recommended Practices* (McLean & Odom, 1993). The difference between practices lies in the level of specificity that the 1991 amendments to IDEA require in program planning for children identified as having special needs and the diversity of team members involved in program planning for young children with disabilities and their families. In developing early childhood education program units and activities, professionals pay attention to the diverse needs of the children whom the program serves using a curriculum that incorporates continual planning, implementation, and assessment (Rosegrant & Bredekamp, 1992). For young children with disabilities and their families, IFSPs must specifically address family priorities, concerns, and resources and include desired outcomes for the children and the children's families. An IEP provides precise goals and objectives for the child as well as a plan for achieving them and monitoring progress toward them. Each IFSP or IEP is developed by a team whose composition reflects the families' identified concerns and resources. The team members can range from professionals (e.g., occupational therapists, ECE educators, speech-language pathologists) to family members (e.g., parents, grandparents, siblings) to community members (e.g., health care professionals, child care providers, social workers). The interdisciplinary nature of IFSPs and IEPs broadens the concept of programming beyond what occurs at a center-based facility and incorporates community resources to implement appropriate programming practices for young children with disabilities and their families.

## Curriculum and Intervention

Curriculum and intervention strategies are the foundation of early childhood programs (see Chapter 8). In general, DEC and NAEYC practices demonstrate a joint perspective in recommending that curricular strategies 1) meet the needs of a wide range of children, 2) encourage and support positive relationships with members of the child's family, 3) are meaningful and functional for the child and the child's family, 4) actively support the engagement of young children with their environment, and 5) support children's physical concerns (McLean & Odom, 1993). The primary difference between the two fields of practice is the attention given to process and outcome. NAEYC practices support a focus on the cognitive and psychological processes that a child experiences while learning, and DEC practices tend to promote a greater emphasis on learning outcomes as demonstrated by a child's performance of a developmental skill (McLean & Odom, 1993). In addition, DEC practices integrate a cross-disciplinary approach that results in curricular activity that incorporates learning objectives from multiple domains.

## Service Delivery

Each set of practice guidelines addresses characteristics and components of service delivery. In relation to the components of providing services to young children and families, NAEYC describes practices that identify environments that are nurturing, safe, and accessible for young children and that meet the physical needs and support the development of young children. These practices are most commonly delivered in home-, center-, or public school–based environments. For a young child with disabilities, these components are broadened into a service delivery approach. ECSE service delivery can represent an expansion of typical ECE and community environments. Infants and toddlers may receive services in a neonatal intensive care unit or health care facility. Service delivery may occur in foster care environments, in hospital units, or at community agencies.

## Transition

Both NAEYC's and DEC's transition practices identify strategies for supporting young children and their families as they move among programs, services, and environments. Each field recognizes the importance of family involvement; preparing the child, the family, and the receiving environment for transition; and the need for communication and collaboration between the sending and the receiving environments (McLean & Odom, 1993). For young children with disabilities, a stronger emphasis is placed on formal interagency agreements and well-planned transition programs that use precise steps and procedures for all individuals and agencies involved in the transition.

***Reflection:*** As you read the next section, think about your classroom or the last several times you visited a classroom. Can you remember examples of teachers' using developmentally and individually appropriate practices? Can you think of other examples in which developmentally and individually appropriate practices should have been used but were not?

## IMPLEMENTATION OF DEVELOPMENTALLY AND INDIVIDUALLY APPROPRIATE PRACTICES

Developmentally and individually appropriate practices are based on a view of child development as dynamic, cumulative, and transformational. Each child changes in unique ways; that is, the child's developmental level and particular characteristics both contribute to how the child changes over time. This perspective emphasizes the importance to program planning, child care, and education practices of both individual differences among children and the developmental ages of children (Bredekamp, 1991; Johnson & Johnson, 1992; Katz, 1991). In discussing how to meet the needs of children with special needs and abilities within the framework of developmentally and individually appropriate practices, McCollum and Bair (1994) stated that the focus should be on adopting a developmental approach that meets the needs of diverse children.

In the effort to define the form of developmentally and individually appropriate practices for diverse groups of young learners, ECSE and ECE professionals are engaged in careful examination of practices in each field. Knowledge of ECE and ECSE practices is foundational, but not sufficient, for defining and implementing appropriate practices for individual children and their families. McCollum and Bair stated that the definition of appropriate practices for diverse groups of children does not lie in "particular practices, but rather, in the match between a particular child, a particular task, and the balance of challenge and support provided" (1994, p. 103). Implementation of developmentally and individually appropriate practices, then, requires knowledge of individual children, their families, and the nature of specific developmental tasks and contexts, as well as an appreciation of the variety of ECE and ECSE practices. In drawing on methods from the whole range of practices used by both fields, ECE and ECSE educators will find both similar and different emphases. Different emphases create a dynamic tension that may become evident in choosing and blending ECE and ECSE practices. Understanding points of congruence and tension in planning education programs appropriate for diverse groups of learners is essential for successful collaboration in inclusive education.

## Defining Purposes and Goals

ECE programs serve a variety of purposes. Although these purposes vary, goals are based on knowledge of child development and an understanding of individual children's needs and interests. Individual goals for children often take into account cultural and family characteristics.

Appropriate curriculum goals for children include the acquisition and mastery of knowledge, skills, and learning processes and the development of positive attitudes and dispositions. Important learner dispositions include focused participation, persistence, curiosity, initiative, risk taking, independence, responsibility, and self-regulation (Dodge, 1992; Katz, 1991; Rosegrant & Bredekamp, 1992; Rosegrant & Cooper, 1986). Educators should avoid limiting goals to the acquisition of specific skills at the expense of goals that focus on processes and dispositions. Children need to learn specific skills and content knowledge, and they need to build an understanding of the world by being actively, enthusiastically, and creatively engaged with it.

Children with special needs and abilities benefit from broader education goals, including those that focus on processes and dispositions and the specific intervention outcomes that families and professionals define in the IFSP/IEP process. Intervention goals serve to support the child's effective participation in the education process. Both education and intervention goals become the basis for curriculum and assessment planning. Educators provide opportunities that facilitate learning and healthy growth for all children as well as build specific opportunities for individual development related to special needs. Children's learning and growth, which are defined by the goals set forth in the IEP, are monitored frequently through ongoing assessment to determine the IEP's effectiveness. A holis-

Children need time to work alone as well as with their peers. Both kinds of opportunities are important to children's development.

tic approach to teaching recognizes that activities and behaviors in all areas of the curriculum are part of the goals for all children.

Individualized education planning commonly takes the form of designating general long-range goals that address the needs and interests of individual children. For children with special needs, the IEP or IFSP specifies behavioral and measurable goals selected by parents and professionals. The IFSP/IEP planning process may promote the selection of goals that emphasize the acquisition of specific knowledge and skills and may discourage the setting of goals that address learning processes and dispositions. Processes and dispositions are difficult to describe in behavioral terms and therefore are difficult to measure. Because intervention goals may address a narrow set of developmental issues, it is all the more important that goal setting include a balance of early education and intervention goals. Educators may not identify these processes and dispositions for goal setting purposes because traditional ECE assessment instruments do not measure these processes in young children. Although parents are an integral part of the IFSP/IEP planning process, they may not recognize that processes and dispositions are legitimate choices in intervention goal setting. This lack of knowledge may be due to parents' tendencies to address their children's behavior problems and delays in acquiring appropriate skills. IFSPs/IEPs define desirable outcomes in terms of the acquisition and mastery of new skills or the increase or decrease in any of the child's behaviors. Values related to processes and dispositions may be more likely to surface in conversations with parents about their children rather than in IEP or IFSP meetings, in which the focus is on defining behavioral and measurable objectives. For example, Elizabeth's mother shared the following information during a casual conversation with her child's educator:

> It is very important to me that Elizabeth be able to take initiative to be able to be in control of the situation . . . that she is not always manipulated and worked on, but that she initiates the play and others respond to her. It all has to do with ownership, it is important that Elizabeth feel an ownership of her interactions with others of her own learning process. (Buchanan, 1995, p. 154)

Because these parental values may not be stated in formal planning meetings, it is important that educators take time to talk to parents about their everyday thoughts about, and about their lives with, their children. When families and educators work together to define the full range of child development needs, developmentally and individually appropriate early education and intervention can be implemented in a balanced and sensitive manner.

## Considerations in Curriculum Planning

Dodge (1992) described *curriculum* as a framework for making decisions about how best to guide children's growth and development. Curriculum planners for ECE programs define goals based on consideration of the skills, dispositions, and concepts that educators want all children to acquire.

In addition to goals for groups of children, curriculum planning takes into account the individual variations among children by including goals for individual children based on their particular developmental needs, abilities, and interests. Intervention outcomes constitute a part of the children's education programs and are most appropriately addressed in the context of curriculum goals for groups of children. In this way, both ECE group goals and goals for individual children, including intervention outcomes, guide practice. Educators who focus primarily on goals for individual children and give secondary consideration to the education goals for the group may fail to adequately acknowledge and value what all young children have in common. This misguided practice is particularly important with regard to young children with special needs and abilities. A dual focus on education goals and intervention outcomes for the group in curriculum planning fosters a "children first and disabilities second" perspective in inclusive ECE practice. From that perspective, children with special needs and abilities are expected and encouraged to engage in the whole range of typical childhood activities and behaviors (e.g., playing, making friends, acting out anger) that correspond to intervention outcomes specified in their IEPs and IFSPs.

The fields of ECE and ECSE differ in curriculum content emphases (McLean & Odom, 1993). ECE curriculum emphasizes thinking and psychological processes, whereas ECSE curriculum emphasizes the performance of skills. It is especially important that educators not plan a curriculum around the individual outcomes that specify children's acquisition and mastery of certain behaviors, skills, or knowledge. Such a curriculum likely would include a predominance of adult-planned and adult-directed activities that focus on the products of learning rather than on the process of learning. An appropriate ECE curriculum provides for the construction of knowledge and understanding, processes, skills, dispositions, and attitudes (Bredekamp & Rosegrant, 1992). Such a curriculum provides rich environments that promote children's active exploration, play, and problem solving and provide ample opportunity for children to develop self-esteem; social competence; understanding of themselves and the world; dispositions such as curiosity, independence, responsibility, initiative, and creativity; and a willingness to take risks, make choices, and persevere when faced with challenges (Dodge, 1992).

Appropriate curriculum planning anticipates interests that are characteristic of young children and is responsive to or emerges from the interests that individual children demonstrate. The curriculum content reflects and is generated by the interests of children in the group (Bredekamp & Rosegrant, 1992). McLean and Odom (1993) pointed out that ECE educators often plan a curriculum based on the developmental levels and individual characteristics of children in the group and then assess the needs and interests of children in relation to curriculum goals. Curriculum goals and instruction strategies are then adapted in response to children's emerging interests. In contrast, ECSE teachers, parents, and other professionals utilize the structure of the IFSP/IEP planning process to select intervention outcomes for children and plan education content and strategies for young children with special needs and abilities. The IFSP/IEP content and strategies assist children in achieving these outcomes because the IFSP and the IEP are outcome oriented, but they may be less responsive to the changing and emerging interests of children. Developmentally and individually appropriate practices require a balance between an emergent curriculum and a curriculum based on predetermined goals. It is important that curriculum content and strategies change form in response to the emerging interests of children while continuing to support children's progress toward intervention outcomes.

**Reflection:**   As you read the following section on instruction strategies, think about ranges of diversity (e.g., cultures, disabilities, religions) and how these differences may affect service providers. Do differences among children affect how professionals interact with the child?

## INSTRUCTION STRATEGIES

Each child presents a unique developmental profile. Children vary in the pattern and timing of their development as well as in their styles of learning.

### In the Classroom

Individualizing instruction for young children within the context of the curriculum requires that the teacher have thorough knowledge of typical child development and individual variations in children's development. This understanding must include an awareness of the nature of young children and how they learn and the need to accommodate the individual variations that exist in any classroom of young learners. Valuing and appreciating the diversity that is common in all groups of young children are essential. Children differ in their approach to learning, the previous experience that they bring to learning, their understanding of concepts, their interest in ideas or in activities, and their desire or their motivation to interact with others or become engaged in a learning activity. Disabilities are one area of children's diversity that needs to be given consideration in instruction planning. Individualizing instruction requires that educators provide options for children in curriculum content, instruction, and expectations for levels of children's engagement.

There is virtual agreement among authors who discuss points of tension and convergence in ECE and ECSE that education for all young children needs to occur in a developmentally appropriate context (DEC Task Force on Recommended Practices, 1991; McCollum & Bair, 1994; McLean & Odom, 1993). One of the most important challenges for educators is the task of determining how to individualize curriculum and instruction for children without compromising the integrity of DAP. McCollum (1991) suggested that ECE educators and ECSE teachers perceive individualization in different ways. ECE educators are encouraged to focus on children's abilities and interests and to adapt the curriculum to respond to children's emerging abilities and interests. Their assumption is that what interests children is often what is on the cutting edge of their development and that that interest inspires meaningful learning in children. ECSE teachers often focus on children's needs in relation to intervention outcomes. Attempts to individualize curriculum are likely to take the form of providing children with the content, structure, and direction that they need to achieve specified outcomes. Bredekamp and Rosegrant (1992) suggested that a merger of practices requires that ECE and ECSE teachers, in individualizing curriculum, attend to both children's interests and their needs.

## In Community Environments

The inclusion of young children with special needs and abilities in community environments implies their full and active participation in those environments. In order for children to participate fully in their learning communities, instruction strategies need to support their participation in the curriculum. In speaking about blending instruction practices recommended in DAP and DEC guidelines, Atwater, Carta, Schwartz, and McConnell (1994) recommended that intervention strategies be applied in the context of classroom activities and everyday routines and include environmental adaptations and that less intrusive intervention strategies be applied before more intrusive practices are used.

## Applying Intervention Strategies

Rather than pulling the child out of the curriculum to maintain the integrity of DAP, intervention activities can be woven into the curriculum in ways that enhance the child's participation. For example, one curriculum goal may be to provide children with the opportunity to interact with their peers while climbing and playing on playground equipment. This playground activity is an important way to enhance motor development, social interaction skills, and feelings of competence. Intervention objectives and strategies that attempt to take advantage of playground activity to teach specific, targeted motor skills may interfere with children's opportunities to practice motor and social interaction skills in a natural environment and experience feelings of confidence in practicing skills independently.

---

*Look at the following example of an opportunity to work on an IEP goal:*

During outdoor play, Mario is climbing on the geodome with his peers. He is laughing and talking to several of the other children as they play together. Serena, a physical therapist, is considering intervening to work on specific motor skills designated in Mario's IEP. Serena is aware that Mario rarely interacts in social and motor play with his peers and that this opportunity is important for his development. She decides to postpone intervention for the time being.

---

In this case, addressing motor skills outcomes in the context of playground activity would have interfered with Mario's success at engaging peers in motor play. Mario might have been isolated from his peers because he would have been the only child in the group who was singled out to work with an adult on specific motor skills in the context of play. The therapist chose instead to postpone her work with Mario and chose to wait for a different opportunity to work with Mario on motor skills.

---

*Look at the IEP objective that is being addressed in the following example:*

Serena is conducting music time with a small group of children later that morning. She decides to incorporate a movement activity that addresses motor skills objectives from Mario's IEP in the course of the lesson. All children participate in some variation of the movement activity, which is designed to strengthen Mario's motor skills.

---

When all children in the classroom participate in intervention activities, each child's feeling of belonging in the group is enhanced. The practice of singling out children for specialized instruction can thus be minimized or eliminated. If educators consider the impact of the intervention on a child's current learning activity, they can better ensure that they are not interfering with the child's independent functioning, problem solving, and social engagement with peers. Children with special needs and abilities benefit from the many opportunities to learn from other children.

Educators may look for teachable moments in the course of everyday activity as opportunities for addressing an individual child's goal. Incidental instruction that is compatible with the curriculum goals for the group can enhance a particular child's participation in the curriculum. If educators look for opportunities to teach a narrow set of objectives, individual children may be distracted from focusing on broader curriculum goals and thus may be pulled out of the curriculum. During caregiving routines, educators have the opportunity to spend time with young children in a one-to-one situation. These routines provide a wealth of opportunities for supporting children's development in natural environments. If caregiving routines are not considered part of the education process, then educators are likely to miss the many teachable moments that the routines provide. Caregiving routines are particularly powerful in providing natural opportunities for learning how to behave in relationships with others, fostering a child's emotional well-being, and helping a child take pleasure in relationships with others. These developmental achievements are important for young children and should be valued equally with intervention goals.

## Environmental Adaptations

Appropriate curriculum provides creative, supportive, nurturing environments to promote exploration and learning in young children. Atwater et al. (1994) emphasized the importance of arranging the environment to accommodate the participation of all children in the classroom. These accommodations may include providing adaptive toys and materials appropriate for children with sensory and motor impairments and those functioning at different developmental levels. Environmental arrangements can also be used to promote social interaction.

When working with a community of learners with a wide range of abilities, educators must adapt environments to increase the likelihood that children will initiate an engagement and experience success. Environmental adaptation may mean arranging furniture and materials to promote access for children with sensory or motor impairments, or it may mean adjusting the group's size to provide for a higher adult-to-child ratio. Adults may need to plan for actively engaging children when children are initiating interaction with low frequency. Children who are less able to learn from actions occurring at a distance from themselves may require greater adult attention and facilitation to initiate and maintain their interactions with peers. For example, children functioning at a low cognitive level respond to objects in the environment only when those objects affect their bodies directly. When a child does not reach out for toys or objects, the toys or objects need to be brought closer to the child's body so that the child can experience an awareness of the toy (Norris, 1991). Environmental arrangement can also be used to promote appropriate behavior by the use of techniques such as dividing the classroom into well-defined areas with adequate space and materials, periodically rotating toys and equipment, including areas and materials that promote social interaction and cooperation, and designing schedules that accommodate children's attention spans and needs for variety in interactions (McEvoy, Fox, & Rosenberg, 1991).

## Choosing Instruction Strategies

The debate between ECE and ECSE professionals about appropriate instruction practices often reflects tension between those who hold behavioral or constructivist theoretical orientation. The debate often centers the relative merits of teacher-planned and teacher-directed instruction versus child-initiated learning. Bredekamp (1993) suggested a need to go beyond this simple dichotomy used to characterize practice. Bredekamp (1993) stated that interactive teaching consists of a continuum of strategies ranging from highly directive to nondirective strategies (see Figure 1). These different strategies are used to meet the individual needs of children in all of the different contexts in which learning occurs. Effective instruction consists of a range of strategies for achieving objectives because no one strategy is likely to succeed for every child or for any particular child in all situations.

In order to choose appropriate instruction strategies, teachers must be skilled observers of children so that they can adapt their approaches for individual children's abilities and interests and the task at hand. Choosing an instruction strategy often includes selecting appropriate forms of adult involvement in a child's activity. Too little or too much involvement can result in mismatching teaching behaviors with a child's need. Low levels of involvement may leave the child without adequate support for meaningful engagement. A high level of involvement such as that which occurs in direct instruction places the teacher between the child and the learning opportunity. Children with disabilities may require both higher levels of and qualitatively different types of adult involvement than typically developing children do (McCollum & Bair, 1994).

The continuum of strategies ranges from acknowledging children's activity to support their independent engagement with their peers to providing children with direct instruction so that they will perform desirable behaviors. Between these two extremes are modeling desirable behaviors for children, facilitating or assisting children temporarily as they learn the next step in the process, supporting or providing necessary assistance that allows children to participate in an activity or event, scaffolding or providing children with specific types of support that allow them to function at their highest levels of development, co-constructing with or

Figure 1.  Teaching continuum. (From Bredekamp, S., & Rosegrant, T. [1992]. *Reaching potentials: Appropriate curriculum and assessment for young children* [Vol. 1, p. 39]. Washington, DC: National Association for the Education of Young Children; reprinted by permission.)

Developmentally and individually appropriate practices include knowledge about child development in general. This realm of developmental knowledge encompasses a wide range of abilities and skills of young children. Thus, in the classroom, children can scaffold and facilitate each other's learning as they interact with each other.

joining a child as an active and equal participant in an activity, and showing the child how to do the activity (Bredekamp & Rosegrant, 1992). Co-constructing, demonstrating, and direct instruction are directive teaching strategies. These strategies should be used carefully and with consideration of what the child brings to the learning process and of the need for the child to assume responsibility for learning. Bredekamp stated that "demonstration comes naturally to adults who interact with young children, so it is important to determine whether the situation warrants demonstration or just modeling" (1993, p. 41). The discovery process that facilitates learning must not be impeded by an overly anxious teacher who is dedicated to having children do things the "right" way (Bredekamp & Rosegrant, 1992).

Educators may assume that children with disabilities are less likely to engage in their environments spontaneously. If this is so, educators may see their role as promoting active engagement, primarily through the use of directive teaching strategies. One risk inherent in the assumption that children with special needs and abilities need consistently high levels of direction to achieve optimum developmental outcomes is that adults may overwhelm and interfere with these children's learning processes by providing their experiences with excessive and unnecessary structure. In doing so, educators fail to recognize the vital importance of what the child brings to the learning process and the child's own responsibility in that process. At times, some children may require more directive instruction for engagement and learning than other children. This determination needs to be made on a case-by-case basis and must be monitored frequently so that the use of strategies that impose unnecessary or constraining forms of structure do not prove detrimental to the child's development. Because directive strategies put the teacher between the child and the child's learning, they may get in the way of the child's discovery and construction of knowledge and should be used cautiously. Johnson and Johnson (1994) maintained that the least restrictive environment for children with special needs and abilities includes the use of the least intrusive instruction strategies. They suggested that educators should first use strategies that are effective with children who are typically developing before choosing to use the more intrusive strategies. Teachers need to be able to use the full range of strategies on the teaching continuum and have the ability to use those strategies flexibly in the best interests of the children in their classrooms.

Choosing strategies is not always as straightforward as moving along the continuum from least to most intrusive strategies. When application of effective strategies for many children break down, educators need to provide developmentally appropriate adaptations. Developmentally appropriate adaptations often require adjusting adult behavior in interactive teaching. Adjustments may include more intensive recruitment of children to a task, slowing the pace of the interaction, modulating levels of stimulation, and helping children find meaning in the feedback that they are receiving. These adaptations support children's engagement by adjusting features of the environment or qualities of teacher–child interaction. Although the adaptations may constitute more active involvement in children's learning, they are not the same as directive strategies. It is important that children with special needs and abilities participate as fully as possible in free-play activities. Educators can use a variety of strategies to encourage active involvement in play if a particular child is not playing with his or her peers.

---

*Look at the following example:*

Leah is a child with cerebral palsy. She has severe physical impairments that limit movement in all four of her extremities. She has a great sense of humor and loves to interact with others. Her father shared that one of her favorite activities at home is listening to songs about everyday activities. During free play time, Leah is positioned so that she can watch other children in the room play. Leah is just beginning to reach and grasp objects. The teacher places some toys near Leah to encourage her initiation of play. After a while, Leah's teacher notices that Leah is not playing with the toys. She approaches Leah and begins to build a block tower just within Leah's reach. She shows Leah how to reach out and knock the tower down and pretends to be surprised as the blocks fall. Leah is delighted. They repeat this routine several times, until Leah loses interest. The teacher incorporates a favorite song of Leah's into the block activity to recruit Leah's attention and encourage her active participation. The song attracts not only Leah's attention but also the attention of several other children in the room, who come and join the activity. Soon the other children get into the game, singing the song and building towers for Leah to knock down.

---

In the preceding example, the teacher used positioning, environmental arrangement, and introduction of novelty to recruit Leah's attention to the play activity; then she introduced a favorite familiar routine to help Leah sustain her engagement. Incidentally, the song routine also served to attract other children to the play. Key to the teacher's use of effective and efficient strategies was her knowledge of Leah's preferences and home activities.

## CONCLUSIONS

The cornerstone of developmentally and individually appropriate practices is the educator's ability to build and maintain significant relationships with children, families, and professionals. Educators play a crucial role in supporting the development of young children in family, child care, and early education environments. For educators to be effective in that role, they must be successful in establishing working relationships with adults in children's lives, and children must view them as important or significant adults in their lives. Being a significant adult in a child's life includes knowing the child and the child's family; valuing and appreciating who the child is and what he or she can do; understanding the child's likes and dislikes; and knowing the child's favorite routines, toys, and encounters. In order to accomplish this goal, educators need to converse with the child's parents, listen to the family's stories, and appreciate the values and the culture that are a part of the child and the child's family life.

## REMEMBER THIS

1. Preferred practice is the ability to implement individualized instruction that meets the needs of all young children.

2. Practitioners must have knowledge of children in order to have knowledge of practice.

3. Meeting the needs of young children requires the balance of general education goals with specific individual outcomes.

4. Effective and efficient strategies are those that support children's development without intruding on the natural activities in which young children engage.

## REFERENCES

Atwater, J.B., Carta, J.J., Schwartz, I.S., & McConnell, S.R. (1994). Blending developmentally appropriate practice and early childhood special education. In B. Mallory & R. New

(Eds.), *Diversity and developmentally appropriate practices* (pp. 185–201). New York: Teachers College Press.

Bredekamp, S. (Ed.). (1987). *Developmentally appropriate practice in early childhood programs serving children from birth through age 8* (Expanded ed.). Washington, DC: National Association for the Education of Young Children.

Bredekamp, S. (1991). Redeveloping early childhood education: A response to Kessler. *Early Childhood Research Quarterly, 6,* 199–209.

Bredekamp, S. (1993). The relationship between early childhood education and early childhood special education: Healthy marriage or family feud? *Topics in Early Childhood Special Education, 13*(3), 258–273.

Bredekamp, S., & Rosegrant, T. (1992). *Reaching potentials: Appropriate curriculum and assessment for young children* (Vol. 1). Washington, DC: National Association for the Education of Young Children.

Buchanan, M. (1995). *The home play of toddlers with disabilities and typically developing toddlers.* Doctoral dissertation, University of Washington, Seattle.

Carta, J.J. (1994). Developmentally appropriate practices: Shifting the emphasis to individual appropriateness. *Journal of Early Intervention, 18*(4), 342–343.

Carta, J.J., Atwater, J.B., Schwartz, I.S., & McConnell, S.R. (1993). Developmentally appropriate practices and early childhood special education: A reaction to Johnson and McChesney Johnson. *Topics in Early Childhood Special Education, 13,* 243–254.

Carta, J.J., Schwartz, I.S., Atwater, J.B., & McConnell, S.R. (1991). Developmentally appropriate practice: Appraising its usefulness for young children with disabilities. *Topics in Early Childhood Special Education, 11*(1), 1–20.

Division for Early Childhood (DEC), Council for Exceptional Children (CEC). (1993). *Position statement on inclusion.* Reston, VA: Author.

Division for Early Childhood (DEC) Task Force on Recommended Practices. (1991). *DEC recommended practices: Indicators of quality in programs for infants and young children with special needs and their families.* Reston, VA: Council for Exceptional Children.

Dodge, D. (1992). *The creative curriculum for early childhood* (3rd ed.). Washington, DC: Teaching Strategies.

Ferguson, D. (1996). Is it inclusion yet? Bursting bubbles. In M. Berres, D. Ferguson, D. Knobloch, & C. Woods (Eds.), *Restructuring schools for all children.* New York: Teachers College Press.

Individuals with Disabilities Education Act (IDEA) Amendments of 1991, PL 102-119, 20 U.S.C. §§ 1400 *et seq.*

Individuals with Disabilities Education Act (IDEA) Amendments of 1997, PL 105-17, 20 U.S.C. §§ 1400 *et seq.*

Johnson, J.E., & Johnson, K. (1992). Clarifying the developmental perspective in response to Carta, Schwartz, Atwater, and McConnell. *Topics in Early Childhood Special Education, 12*(4), 439–457.

Johnson, J.E., & Johnson, K. (1994). The applicability of developmentally appropriate practice for children with diverse abilities. *Journal of Early Intervention, 18*(4), 343–346.

Katz, L. (1991). Pedagogical issues in early childhood education. In S.L. Kagan (Ed.), *The care and education of America's young children: Obstacles and opportunities: Nineteenth yearbook of the National Society for the Study of Education.* Chicago: University of Chicago Press.

Mahoney, G., Robinson, C., & Powell, A. (1992). Focusing on parent–child interaction: The bridge to developmentally appropriate practice. *Topics in Early Childhood Special Education, 12*(1), 105–120.

McCollum, J.A. (1991). At the crossroads: Reviewing and rethinking interaction coaching. In K. Marfo (Ed.), *Early intervention in transition: Current perspectives on programs for handicapped children* (pp. 137–176). New York: Praeger.

McCollum, J.A., & Bair, H. (1994). Research in parent–child interaction. In B. Mallory & R. New (Eds.), *Diversity and developmentally appropriate practices* (pp. 84–103). New York: Teachers College Press.

McEvoy, M.A., Fox, J.J., & Rosenberg, M.S. (1991). Organizing preschool environments: Suggestions for enhancing the development/learning of preschool children with handicaps. *Topics in Early Childhood Special Education, 11*(2), 18–28.

McLean, M., & Odom, S. (1993). Practices for young children with and without disabilities: A comparison of DEC and NAEYC identified practices. *Topics in Early Childhood Special Education, 13*(3), 274–292.

Neisworth, J.T. (1993). Assessment. In DEC Task Force on Recommended Practices, *DEC Recommended Practices: Indicators of quality in programs for infants and young children with special needs and their families* (pp. 11–18). Reston, VA: Council for Exceptional Children.

Norris, J.A. (1991). Providing developmentally appropriate intervention to infants and young children with handicaps. *Topics in Early Childhood Special Education, 11*(1), 21–35.

Odom, S. (1994). Developmentally appropriate practice, policies, and use for young children with disabilities and their families. *Journal of Early Intervention, 18*(4), 346–348.

Rosegrant, T., & Bredekamp, S. (1992). Reaching individual potentials through transformational curriculum. In S. Bredekamp & T. Rosegrant (Eds.), *Reaching potentials: Appropriate curriculum and assessment for young children* (Vol. 1, pp. 66–73). Washington, DC: National Association for the Education of Young Children.

Rosegrant, T., & Cooper, R. (1986). *The talking text writer: Professional guide.* New York: Scholastic.

U.S. Department of Education. (1991). *America 2000: An education strategy.* Washington, DC: Author.

Wolery, M., & Bredekamp, S. (1994). Developmentally appropriate practices and young children with disabilities: Contextual issues in the discussion. *Journal of Early Intervention, 18*(4), 331–341.

Wolery, M., Strain, P., & Bailey, D.B., Jr. (1992). Reaching potentials of children with special needs. In S. Bredekamp & T. Rosegrant (Eds.), *Reaching potentials: Appropriate curriculum and assessment for young children* (Vol. 1, pp. 92–111). Washington, DC: National Association for the Education of Young Children.

# Activities

1.  Observe young children on a playground. Record the many developmental activities in which children are participating. Take special note of problems that children encounter, the challenging nature of the problems, and the problem-solving approaches that the children use.

2.  Observe an ECE teacher and/or an ECSE teacher working with young children. Identify instructional strategies used by each, and categorize each strategy according to the teaching continuum that Bredekamp and Rosegrant (1992) presented.

3.  Using the scenario involving Leah presented in this chapter, choose one instruction strategy that is nondirective, one that is mediating, and one that is directive. Describe how you would use each strategy to support Leah's development, and provide a rationale for the use of each strategy in a learning activity.

c  h  a  p  t  e  r  6

# Play

*Peggy M. Elgas and Ellen Lynch*

## CHAPTER ORGANIZER

In this chapter, we explore the following ideas . . .

1. Play has specific characteristics and benefits.
2. Play is likened to and facilitates cognitive and social development.
3. Play is the cornerstone of curriculum in early childhood education classrooms.
4. The teacher is a facilitator of play.

As the play literature has burgeoned, so too has the discussion that is centered on a definition of *play*. Play has been described as children's work, as a process versus a product, and as what children do naturally. Various researchers (Bruner, 1974; Rubin, Fein, & Vanderberg, 1983; Singer & Singer, 1985) have defined various aspects of play, yet most would agree on the following characteristics of play that Garvey described:

- Play is pleasurable, enjoyable, or laden with positive affect.
- Play has no extrinsic goals or attention is to means rather than ends.
- Play is spontaneous and voluntary or free from externally imposed rules.
- Play is active engagement of the child.
- Play is characterized by an "as if" attitude or a nonliteral set or pretense. (1977, p. 4)

Regardless of their perspectives or theoretical orientations, theorists generally agree that play is important in the lives of young children and that play contributes to all aspects—social, emotional, cognitive, and physical—of children's development. Erickson (1963) suggested that play provides children with opportunities to deal with emotional issues ranging from ego development to hospitalization and death. Piaget (1962) suggested that play provides opportunities for children to imitate, practice, and make sense of the world around them. Vygotsky (1976) suggested that children at play have opportunities to use materials to represent other objects within a social and cultural context.

In this chapter, play is viewed as being linked to and contributing to all areas of development. Play is both influenced by the various ages and stages of development and a catalyst for developmental progression. The discussion is limited, however, to the areas of social and cognitive development because there are always concerns relating to these areas regarding children with disabilities.

**Reflection:** As you read the next section, think of specific experiences that you have had with young children in a preschool environment. Have you ever seen a child clearly benefit from an episode of play? In what ways did the child benefit from play?

## THE CONTRIBUTION OF PLAY TO CHILDREN'S DEVELOPMENT

Various researchers (Parten, 1932; Piaget, 1962; Smilansky, 1968; Vygotsky, 1976) have studied play in the context of how it relates to development. Piaget and Parten contributed to the understanding of children's play and specifically to how play is related to cognitive and social development. Each of these researchers described play behaviors in the form of a hierarchical system, with the first level being the least complex and the last level being the most complex.

### Cognitive Functioning and Play

Piaget's theory of play is greatly influenced by his broader theory of development. A child's play and cognitive functioning are inexorably linked together. The three major types of play (practice, symbolic, games with rules) correlate with the three major stages of development: sensorimotor, preoperational, and concrete operational. *Practice play* can be described as the child's engaging in repetitive physical movements and interacting with objects (e.g., shaking keys and dropping them on the floor). *Symbolic play* is characterized by representational thought as children substitute objects or actions (e.g., a child pretends to be a firefighter, a child pretends that a red rhythm stick is a fire hose). At around age 6 or 7, children engage in games with rules. These games with rules require children to adopt another person's perspective; take turns; and follow prescribed, externally imposed rules (e.g., tic-tac-toe).

**Reflection:** The next section discusses Parten's categories of play. As you read the section, try to think of one or two examples from your own experiences that fit into each category.

## Social Play

Parten's (1932) work focused on play and its link to children's social development. After studying children's interactions with each other, Parten suggested that children's social play could be categorized according to a hierarchical system and that this system was directly linked to children's development. Younger children, Parten wrote, engaged in more onlooker behavior and parallel play, whereas older preschool-age children engaged in more social play such as associative and cooperative play. Parten's categories of play have been defined as follows:

1. *Unoccupied:* In this category of play, children watch other children playing but do not enter the play themselves. They may stand near or move around the play area.
2. *Onlooker:* Children watch other children playing and may talk to the other children playing or ask them questions.
3. *Solitary:* In this play category, children play alone with objects and do not interact with other children.
4. *Parallel:* In this category of play, children play with objects like those used by children playing nearby but do not try to influence the other children's play.
5. *Associative:* Children in this group are engaged in similar activities, but specific roles and goals are not identified.
6. *Cooperative:* In this category, children play together according to coordinated roles and themes and work toward some identified goal.

Certainly, there is both anecdotal and research evidence to support this hierarchical system; however, in the 1990s, early childhood educators have found that older preschool-age children engage in all of these categories of play for various reasons and that engaging in all of the play categories contributes to healthy development.

Fein (1986) provided further insight into the nature of the substages of pretend-play and sociodramatic play. Fein determined that children move from less complicated to more complex use of objects and development of thematic plans. Young preschool-age children need more realistic props for pretend-play. For example, a 3-year-old who pretends to talk on the telephone needs a plastic replica of a telephone or a small block that in some way resembles the shape of a telephone. A 4- or 5-year-old is less concerned with the physical properties of an object and its similarities to the object that it represents in the pretend-play. Thus, the child may use, for example, a plastic banana toy from the house area or any small block from the block area to represent the telephone.

Fein (1986) further determined that young children (e.g., 3-year-olds) participate in the development of themes and scripts but that their themes are less complex than those of their older preschool counterparts. For example, the family theme is popular with young children of all age groups. However, young children might concentrate on a simple but familiar experience such as dinnertime. They might repeatedly imitate cooking and serving food. Older preschoolers often engage in the same pretend-play of dinnertime, but the play episode might also include a trip to the local grocery store to purchase the foods listed on the menu, the conversation at the dinner table, and an expanded guest list that includes a grandmother and grandfather or other relatives and friends.

## PLAY AND DEVELOPMENT

In this section, the linkage between play and development is discussed in more detail. Specific emphasis is placed on how play is linked to cognitive and social development.

### Cognitive Development

Play has been linked to cognitive development in myriad ways. These areas include creativity, convergent and divergent thinking (Pepler & Ross, 1981; Rubin et al., 1983; Singer & Singer, 1985), problem solving (Bretherton, 1984; Bruner, 1974; Smilansky, 1968; Sylva, Bruner, & Genova, 1976), language and literacy development (Bruner, 1974; Garvey, 1977; Pellegrini, 1980), and representation and concept development (Piaget, 1962; Vygotsky, 1976).

Singer and Singer (1985) suggested that imaginative play is essential to children's development of various capacities for creativity. These capacities include internal imagery, exploration, and producing alternative solutions and combinations. These capacities in turn help children develop a more flexible attitude and approach to new situations when new situations are encountered. Divergent thinking has also been linked to play (Dansky, 1980; Dansky & Silverman, 1975; Johnson, 1976; Pepler & Ross, 1981). Johnson found a relationship between children's make-believe play and their scores on tests of cognitive and divergent thinking. Children's make-believe play experiences were highly correlated with measures of children's cognitive abilities, including picture completion, fluency, and fantasy subscores. Pepler and Ross supported these findings by suggesting that play experiences lead to new problems and questions and therefore engage children in continual problem-solving situations. Continual problem solving in turn promotes children's opportunities for reflection and thus their ability to think more deeply about their experiences.

These young children are engaged in a form of sociodramatic play that allows them the opportunity to develop
themes and scripts about families. The children are developing roles for each other and pretending to be the babies'
caregivers.

Both Bretherton (1984) and Smilansky (1968) suggested that play is linked to
problem-solving and reasoning abilities. Bretherton suggested that sociodramatic
play contributes to reasoning ability because children are provided with many
opportunities to make decisions, verify outcomes, plan, reconstruct, estimate, and
reason about causes and effects. Smilansky (1968) suggested that many factors
inherent in sociodramatic play support the development of problem solving. These
factors are

- Concentrating on a given theme
- Controlling actions within the assumed theme and roles
- Being flexible about taking different approaches to the story line
- Learning new concepts and approaches through different role definitions and
  variations in theme development
- Engaging in representational thought
- Becoming more acquainted with different interpretations of roles and thematic
  definitions

## Language and Literacy Development

Various studies (Athey, 1984; Garvey, 1977; Genishi & Dyson, 1984; Pellegrini,
1980) have linked pretend-play with language and literacy development. Begin-

ning in infancy, children produce a variety of sounds. This sound production continues throughout the preschool years in the forms of rhymes, songs, and chants
(Athey, 1984). This type of play is related to language development, and rhyming
specifically is highly correlated with early reading achievement. These studies further suggested that fantasy play incorporates aspects of adult speech as well as the
opportunity for children to increase their vocabulary as they create themes and
scripts and communicate these ideas to each other.

Children's reading and writing achievements have also been correlated with
both the frequency and the complexity of their sociodramatic play (Pellegrini,
1980). Sociodramatic play also necessitates communication. In order for children's
play to develop and continue successfully, children must communicate their ideas
to others and then persuade the other players to accept their ideas. Each player
may have different ideas, and consequently communication of intent and interest
takes place within the context of ongoing negotiation regarding themes and role
assignments (Garvey, 1977). In addition to learning to communicate, Garvey found
that children also learn to manipulate the language system while playing. Children
learn about both the phonological and the pragmatic aspects of language. As children practice sounds and play with language, they learn about how language
sounds or about its phonological aspects. Preschool-age children also learn about
the pragmatic or communicative aspects of language as they learn the rule of turn
taking.

Play has also been specifically linked to literacy development. Genishi and
Dyson (1984) found that the "as if" attitude necessary in play (e.g., "Pretend you
are the zoo keeper, and I feed the animals") is similar to creating a story. Heath
(1985) supported this finding with research suggesting that children who enter
school as sophisticated players (i.e., those who can create, contribute to, and maintain sociodramatic play) were also frequently successful in all forms of reading and
writing.

## Representational Skills and Concept Development

Both Piaget (1962) and Vygotsky (1976) suggested that play provides necessary
experiences for the development of important cognitive functioning. Vygotsky
suggested that play is a zone of proximal development within which children
advance themselves toward increasingly complex levels of psychological functioning. Children's play supports the emergence of their ability to separate thought
from actions and objects.

Piaget (1962) suggested that play serves an important consolidating function
in assisting children in the construction of meaning from their experiences. He also
suggested that the organizational features of intelligence and development depend
on the processes of assimilation and accommodation. In play, children assimilate
various experiences and later incorporate them into their established cognitive
schemata. For example, children might pretend to be mommy and daddy in family play, imitating roles and behaviors that they have observed. They might also
have to engage in new behaviors that they would then have to incorporate into their

understanding of these family roles. Singer (1973) supported this idea by suggesting that play empowers children to practice and consolidate newly acquired skills and thus to assimilate new information.

Piaget (1962) further suggested that play helps children develop the ability to think about relationships between objects when they are not acting on the objects, to imagine objects that are not present, and to imitate events that are not currently taking place. He described children's development of these abilities as a transitory process that facilitates their movement from the earliest forms of sensorimotor thought to operational patterns that demonstrate more mature thinking. Athey (1984) suggested that play provides children with opportunities to classify objects and events, thus allowing them to progress from concrete physical and spatial knowledge to understanding abstract concepts that are based on relationships. Play also provides opportunities for children to develop the concept of categorization or the construction of logicomathematical knowledge at their own pace.

---

*The following example illustrates learning the concept of categorization through play:*

Lamont and Steve are sitting on the floor, building a zoo with cages for the animals. They are sorting all of the small, rectangular blocks for cages. Lamont says, "We need all of these kind." Steve says, "Yeah, but we need to get all the tall animals in a bigger cage."

---

Although Piaget (1962) and Vygotsky (1976) differed somewhat in their perspectives and interpretations, they both suggested that play was linked to thought and representational skills. In play situations, children imaginatively use objects to represent something else in their play (e.g., a child's pretending that a small rectangular block is a telephone). For Vygotsky, these object substitutions provided opportunities for children to separate an object from a thought. When children use a block to represent a telephone, for example, their perception of reality is significantly changed (Berk, 1994). Their use of the block to represent a telephone can separate the meaning of *telephone* from their understanding of a real telephone. Detaching the meanings of words used to describe the objects and behaviors that the words represent is a necessary step in children's making the transition to adult thought, which Vygotsky labeled as *abstract*, that is, as not being dependent on concrete objects and actions.

Piaget (1962), however, suggested that children's ability to represent is dependent on their levels of cognitive development and maturity. Therefore, one would not expect to see imaginative play in the earliest years of infancy. Rather, imaginative play or the ability to represent would surface later and would continue to develop and reach a peak in the preschool and primary school years. According to Piaget, children in the preschool and primary years have the cognitive capability of using an object to represent something else and can play at something that is not actually taking place but is an experience that they are reenacting.

## Social Development

Play has been linked to social development in various ways. Play is thought to promote social skills, help children adopt another's perspective, and learn social roles and cultural norms (Corsaro, 1985; Elgas, Klein, Kantor, & Fernie, 1988; Emihovich, 1981; Garvey, 1977; Isaacs, 1933). As early as 1933, Isaacs suggested the social benefits of play. Isaacs viewed play as the pathway from children's egocentrism to their socialization. In social play, two or more children start exchanging services or objects; they play at being cooperative. Children move from rivalry to discovering the benefits of cooperation.

### Social Roles and Rules

Garvey (1974, 1977, 1979) supported the notion that children gain independence from adults as they learn to work cooperatively with their peers. In Garvey's (1974) study, children demonstrated a clear awareness that social play is dependent on mutually accepted rules of procedure. Specifically, role behaviors and attributes must remain consistent throughout an episode of social play or else changes in these behaviors and attributes must be negotiated in certain ways. For example, it would not be acceptable for the daddy to cry like the baby in family pretend-play. General procedural rules such as turn taking and rules guiding behavior in particular situations were found to be essential to the conduct of play. Children continually defined and directed each other's behavior.

---

*The following example illustrates the establishment of role behaviors and attributes:*

Shontee and Maria were in the dramatic play area, which was set up as a doctor's office. Maria took her "baby" to see Shontee, who was playing the role of doctor. While waiting for "Dr. Shontee" to check her doll, Maria picked up a play syringe and pretended to give her baby a shot. Just at that time, Shontee came over to Maria and exclaimed, "You can't do that! The doctor has to give the shots!"

---

Vygotsky's (1976) description of play supports the idea that children create and negotiate rules. Vygotsky suggested that play teaches children to guide their behavior based not only on their immediate perception of the object or of the situation affecting them but also by the meaning created in the situation conjointly by the players. Denzin (1977) suggested that group participation in negotiation helps children learn about society. Society is a negotiated order wherein the participants communicate with symbolic gestures and language. Language is the medium for social interaction; it is the tool with which roles and perspectives are created.

### Social Understanding

Goncu (1993) supported the idea that play promotes social understanding. Goncu described play as a process whereby children bring different perspectives to the same activity and, in order for the play to continue, they coordinate their roles and efforts, leading them to a high level of intersubjectivity.

---

*The following example helps to illustrate the points made in the preceding paragraphs:*

Milo and Marla are playing with the large blocks. They have built a large pirate ship. They have pretend swords, pretend food, and a map to guide them on their journey. John and Samantha are playing in the same general area, building a doctor's office with the rest of the large blocks. The block supply is suddenly depleted. John grabs some of the pirate ship's blocks.

"No you can't take those—we'll sink!" say Milo and Marla.

"We have to have these for the hospital, or the babies will die," John responds.

"The babies can go to a different hospital. We're on the sea. We'll sink," Milo answers. They are still both holding the blocks.

"We need those blocks for the hospital," John replies.

After more of the same discussion, Milo has an idea.

"I know! Let's have a ship hospital. The babies and the pirates can both go," Milo says.

"Well, yeah, I guess we could do that," says John.

---

As shown in the preceding vignette, play can provide opportunities for children to learn about how society functions, develop interpersonal relationships, adopt another's perspective, and develop the social skills of negotiating and cooperation.

As already discussed, play provides opportunities for children to become socialized into the culture as they learn about adult roles and norms for behavior. Children's socialization was traditionally thought of as being provided exclusively by adults. However, Corsaro's (1985) seminal work introduced the concept of a peer culture and demonstrated its powerful force in children's lives. Similar to the adult culture, the peer culture includes a common set of values, attitudes, beliefs, and objects. Corsaro described the peer culture as children's joint attempt to gain control over their lives through the establishment of a collective identity. The establishment of a collective identity is accomplished through shared and repeated activities; for children, these activities are play. Furthermore, he suggested that these play activities both reflect the peer culture and react to the adult culture and adult-imposed rules.

### Development of Social Competence Among Peers

Building on Corsaro's (1985) work, Elgas et al. (1988), in a yearlong ethnographic study, also found the existence of a peer culture among young children. Their study provided support for the idea that children's peer culture is complex and totally developed and maintained by the children. In addition, Elgas and colleagues found that there were various small groups within the larger peer group. By studying a core peer group, the larger peer group's norms and values were identified. Examples of information that was important in the peer group were that certain objects (e.g., capes, red rhythm sticks) were used as both gatekeepers and markers of social status, that peer players (i.e., children who preferred to play with peers rather than with adults) were more well received among peers than others, and that children viewed social competence as a complex construct.

Children's attainment of social competence is a complex process in which many children experience difficulty. As a result, many children are not successful in gaining access to the playgroup and are repeatedly rejected. Kantor, Elgas, and Fernie (1993) found that children had to fulfill certain roles and use the appropriate language accompanying those roles, adapt their ideas to existing themes, coordinate their efforts with other group members, and possess and use certain objects appropriately, all within the social context that the children created. In the core group that Kantor and colleagues studied, comic book superheroes supplied the preferred themes and roles.

---

*The following example illustrates children's successful and unsuccessful attempts at entry into a playgroup:*

*Successful:* Kyle and Bob, both wearing capes, are hanging upside down on the climber. Lisa, also wearing a cape, pretends to fly over, carrying small blocks in her hands. "Here, I brought these for our Batman house." "Yeah," Bob and Kyle reply, "Drop them here."

*Unsuccessful:* Bob and Kyle are building a Batman house. They are wearing capes and saying, "We better get this built—keep the bad guys out of here." William, making a siren noise, drives over on a large wooden toy car. "I'll put the fire out," he says. Bob and Kyle stare at him for a minute and then scream, "Get out of here!"

---

Several researchers (Connolly & Doyle, 1984; Hartup, 1983; Howes, 1988; Monighan-Nourot, Scales, Van Hoorn, & Almy, 1987; Ross, 1985) described a link between social pretend-play with peers and social competence. Connolly and Doyle found a correlation between frequency of social pretend-play and measures of social competence. Hartup and Howes further suggested that children who are flexible and compromise in their play negotiations as well as work cooperatively with other players are more well liked than others by their peers. Ross also found that children's social competence was related to their ability to match an appropriate behavior with an appropriate situation. Monighan-Nourot and colleagues added to the literature, suggesting that children's interactive play is dependent partially on the socioecological features of the environment in which it takes place (e.g., room arrangement, types of activities available) and of children's interactive skills. Children's expressions of themes or new ideas had to be related to a shared understanding and had to be relevant to the ongoing "script" of the pretend-play. Monighan-Nourot and colleagues concluded that children need to know common strategies for introducing and expanding themes and that they need to coordinate their ideas with others and produce situationally appropriate verbal and nonverbal behavior. Children who were rejected were unsuccessful in implementing one or a combination of these features.

Clearly, children learn to be socially competent through play. *Social competence* is defined here as children's abilities to communicate, cooperate, interact, and assess social situations and make adjustments to their interactions according to those assessments. In addition to learning social competence, children develop a personal history at school starting from the first day of school. Children develop these in-school personal histories as they conjointly construct both the school and peer cultures (see Kantor et al., 1993, for a complete discussion of this topic). This information is powerful for all ECE teachers, but it takes on more significance for them with regard to their understanding of children with disabilities, who might be at higher risk for school failure than their peers without disabilities because of language or emotional disabilities. If children with disabilities are rejected in their first interactions at school, they may develop a negative personal history at school and thus be continually rejected by their peers.

## PLAY IN INCLUSIONARY ENVIRONMENTS

As already discussed, the significance of play in the ECE environment should not be underestimated; but play is of equal if not more importance in ECE programs serving children with disabilities (Cook, Tessier, & Klein, 1996). Although research on the significance of play for children with disabilities is somewhat limited, the contention that play is an important contributor to their development is becoming widely accepted. Play is not only inherently worthwhile but also provides an important context for intervention (Barnett, Carey, & Hall, 1993; Division for Early Childhood [DEC] Task Force on Recommended Practices, 1993; Fox, Hanline, Vail, & Galant, 1994; Johnson-Martin, Attermeier, & Hacker, 1990; Linder, 1993). Quinn and Rubin (1984) and Rogers (1988) noted that much of the early research on the play of children with disabilities was flawed and provided inconsistent results. However, research (Brooks-Gunn & Lewis, 1982; Hanzlik & Stevenson, 1986; Johnston, 1994) has begun to offer important information. In particular, both the quality and quantity of play of children with disabilities may differ from that of typically developing children.

### Children with Autism

Researchers who studied the play of children with autism (Curcio & Piserchia, 1978; Hammes & Langdell, 1981; Sigman & Ungerer, 1984; Wetherby & Prutting, 1984) reported the existence of delays in the areas of motor and gestural imitation. When compared with groups of children with mental retardation and their peers without mental retardation, children with autism tended to engage in fewer play sequences; exhibited less doll-directed symbolic play; and spent a greater propor-

Here the child's play is linked to cognitive development as he builds. He is learning spatial relations and one-to-one correspondence. He is also engaged in dramatic play through the creation of themes with the people.

tion of time engaging in low-level, or immature, play (Ricks & Wing, 1975; Sigman & Ungerer, 1984).

## Children with Developmental Delays

A number of studies (Hill & McCune-Nicolich, 1981; Motti, Cicchetti, & Stroufe, 1983; Sigman & Ungerer, 1984) demonstrated that children with developmental delays appear to develop symbolic play in the same sequence as their peers without developmental delays do. However, qualitative differences such as reduced attention and engagement, a limited variety of play skills, reduced language use during play episodes, and less sophisticated representational play have also been observed (Krakow & Kopp, 1983; McWilliam & Bailey, 1995). Other studies (Thompson & Berkson, 1985; Wing, Gould, Yeates, & Brierley, 1977) found a high percentage of stereotyped play behaviors of children with mental retardation requiring extensive supports.

## Children with Hearing Impairments

Infants with hearing impairments have been found to demonstrate few atypical play behaviors (Mogford, 1977). However, after the sensorimotor stage of development, children with hearing impairments appear to begin to show delays in the development of representational play (Gregory, 1976) and a decrease in the number of social interactions during play (McKirdy, 1972). A significant factor mitigating these delays appears to be whether the child receives some type of augmentative communication system and/or language therapy (Darbyshire, 1977).

## Children with Language Impairments

Compared with their peers without disabilities, children with language impairments have demonstrated play that is characterized by more solitary play than symbolic play, less organization, and fewer social contacts (Johnston, 1994). However, compared with children matched for language level (i.e., younger children), children with language impairments have been found to demonstrate superior symbolic play abilities in both free- and structured-play conditions (Terrell, Schwartz, Prelock, & Messick, 1984).

## Children with Physical Disabilities

Research on the play of children with physical disabilities (e.g., Brooks-Gunn & Lewis, 1982; Hanzlik & Stevenson, 1986; Jennings, Connors, Stegman, Sankaranarayan, & Mendolsohn, 1985) has produced a variety of findings. Jennings and colleagues found that, when compared with their peers without disabilities, children with physical disabilities appeared to be less involved in their play and less curious, demonstrated more wandering behavior, and engaged in a higher ratio of solitary play to social play. Children with cerebral palsy who were compared with their peers without disabilities were found to demonstrate play with more visual than tactile exploration of toys and to demonstrate fewer play behaviors overall (Brooks-Gunn & Lewis, 1982). However, children with cerebral palsy also demonstrated a higher frequency of social behaviors than their peers with other disabilities (Brooks-Gunn & Lewis, 1982; Hanzlik & Stevenson, 1986).

## Children with Visual Impairments

Given the importance of children's vision to their development of play skills, children with visual impairments unsurprisingly demonstrate both qualitative and quantitative differences in their play patterns compared with their peers without disabilities. Characteristics of the play of children with visual impairments described (Fewell, 1983; Fewell & Kaminski, 1988; Fraiberg, 1977; Rogers & Puchalski, 1984) include repetitive actions, delayed object and symbolic play, and more solitary play than social play.

*Reflection:*  As you read the next section about the teacher's role in play, think about your own experiences in early childhood education (ECE) environments. Have all teachers been involved in children's play processes? Did all teachers seem to understand the importance of play to children's development? What did the teachers do while children were at play?

# THE TEACHER'S ROLE IN PLAY

This section describes the teacher's role in an inclusive ECE environment. The suggestions herein are designed to facilitate children's cognitive and social development and promote all children's successful participation in a play-based classroom. One way to organize the discussion about the teacher's role is to divide children's play into two categories: constructive play and sociodramatic play. *Constructive play* can be described as children interacting with materials and working toward a goal. Two examples are children building a sand castle at the sand table or pouring water into various containers at the water table. *Sociodramatic play* can be defined as several children engaged in pretend-play who adopt roles, "write scripts," and establish themes.

## Teaching Strategies

There are teaching strategies that can be used specifically with the two types of children's play. First, by encouraging and facilitating children's play, teachers demonstrate that they value play and view it as an important part of the ECE curriculum. Through play interactions, teachers can build relationships with children and be afforded access to the children's perspectives. These interactions can also provide important information for teachers' ongoing assessment of children. Second, teachers can also help children expand and elaborate on their play.

Teachers also need to observe some general guiding principles that apply to all types of children's play as they take an active role in children's play:

1. Be sensitive to children's needs. Individual children may have emotional issues that they need to work on in their play.
2. Have respect for children's ideas and chosen themes. Often children choose themes that adults dislike, such as fictional superheroes; but continually changing themes shows disregard for children's ideas.
3. Participate in children's play but follow their lead. Adults' participation should facilitate and support, not control.

## Classroom Environment

In any type of play, one of the important roles that a teacher assumes is that of organizer. How the environment is set up can either support and encourage play or inhibit and discourage it.

### Physical Setup

Jones and Reynolds (1992) suggested that teachers present a logically ordered classroom environment so that children remain focused. They stated that organizing children's play environments is easier if figure–ground relationships are clear. Well-defined play areas help children choose play areas and understand what they can do there. Labeling play areas with lettered, braille, and picture-cued signs helps children identify and locate particular play areas in the classroom. Clear pathways and free-flowing traffic patterns are important so that children can easily gain access to play areas and play there undisturbed. If children have to walk through the block area to get to the dramatic play area, for example, the chances of block structures being knocked down are increased, as are children's frustration levels and subsequently the requirement that the teacher assume the role of mediator and problem solver.

The physical setup of the classroom should remain fairly fixed if the class includes children with visual impairments so that these children can participate fully and successfully. Providing areas that encourage children to play together and cooperate—as well as small spaces that encourage children to spend quiet, reflective time individually—is important. Many children, especially those with emotional disabilities, need a space where they can spend quiet time by themselves because they can become overwhelmed by the active play areas and high noise levels of busy, engaged children. Providing such a safe outlet helps these children regain control of their behaviors and their environments.

### Classroom Schedule

Another concern integral to the arrangement of the classroom environment is the classroom schedule. Allowing time for play demonstrates to children that the teacher values play. Building complex structures with blocks, creating rich themes, negotiating roles, and working cooperatively require time. Christie, Johnson, and Peckover (1988) demonstrated that limiting the time available for children to play in fact limits what children can accomplish in their play. Although some scheduling parameters are imposed, such as shared outdoor space during playtimes and mealtimes, a more flexible attitude regarding time and use of materials can be developed.

---

*Look at the following example illustrating flexibility in classroom scheduling:*

John has spent the entire free-choice time building a Batman structure, and he is disappointed when he has to put his structure away. His teacher suggests a few alternatives: He can save the structure with a note saying "to be continued" attached to it; extend his free-choice time that day; or set up a designated shelf for small, unfinished projects.

---

### Materials Selection

Materials selection is another important aspect of the teacher's role. When choosing materials, teachers need to be mindful of three principles:

1. Materials should have multiple uses. For example, blocks can be used in other ways, not just for building. They can become part of dramatic play as, for example, walkie-talkies or parts of a spaceship.

2. Materials should be failure-proof or open ended.
3. Materials should be usable by children of various ages.

An example of multiuse materials is blocks, which can be used to construct a variety of structures or as a telephone in sociodramatic play. Various sizes of blocks and other construction materials such as Legos, Bristle Blocks, and Duplos can accommodate varying levels of physical development and representational skills. Fluid materials such as water and bubble mixtures with various containers for discovery are appropriate examples of play materials that allow children to create and discover without fear of failure or of not finding the right solution to a play "problem," thus making such materials failure-proof. Providing such play materials allows children to work at their present levels and progress at their own rate, thus fulfilling the third principle, that materials be usable by children of various ages.

## Teachers' Roles as Active Participants and Conversation Partners

As active participants, teachers can adopt the role of co-explorer and conversation partner. In both roles, the teacher can help children focus, reflect, and consolidate their learning. As a co-explorer, teachers can

1. Encourage and support children's explorations and ideas (e.g., "This idea looks interesting, but I'm worried about the water getting on our carpet. How can we use this idea and also keep our carpet dry?")
2. Facilitate problem solving (e.g., "How can we make this sand wheel turn?")
3. Parallel play (e.g., pouring sand through a funnel, building with Legos next to children who are also using Legos)

As conversation partners, teachers can

1. Ask open-ended questions (e.g., "What do you think will happen when you add water to the flour?")
2. Reformulate language and clarify ideas (e.g., "Your idea is to use tape to hold the spaceship together")
3. Use language to promote logical reasoning or explain a process (e.g., "When you added water to the sand, you made mud")

In sociodramatic play, teachers can also adopt the roles of conversation partner and co-explorer; but they may also adopt the roles of player and negotiator or mediator. Negotiating and mediating are roles specific to helping children develop social skills and fostering their successful participation in playgroups. As discussed in the literature review in this chapter, these skills are necessary for sociodramatic play to be successful. Before discussing some specific teaching strategies to use with sociodramatic play, the following general guidelines for teachers engaged in sociodramatic play need to be discussed:

1.  Refrain from insisting or forcing children to play with a child whom they have rejected, because that can lead to children's resentment and further rejection of that child.
2.  Intervene when children's rejection of a particular child is a source of concern and when rejection is a repetitive pattern in the classroom (some rejection is typical of children in a group environment).
3.  Assist by helping children learn a repertoire of sociodramatic play strategies rather than trying to gain entry for the child (i.e., ask, "Can John play?"). Remember that children must fit in with the peer group without adult intervention and that they need to be independent and autonomous to be successful.

Based on the research on social competence (Corsaro, 1985; Kantor et al., 1993; Ross, 1985), the following strategies that children use in sociodramatic play are known to be unsuccessful:

1.  Overuse of particular initiation routines (e.g., adopting firefighter role and continually using that to gain entry, regardless of ongoing theme)
2.  Inappropriate, inflexible initiations (e.g., crying, whining, refusing to adapt behavior to ongoing theme)
3.  Using the same behaviors within roles (e.g., firefighter, always using fire hose, not incorporating other behaviors as needed)
4.  Aggressive behaviors (e.g., children forcing their way into playgroups with either verbal or physical aggression, knocking over play structures, pushing other children)
5.  Atypical or misunderstood strategies (e.g., using inappropriate language, making strange sounds)
6.  Self-serving initiations (e.g., child who asks "Can I play?" draws attention to individual child rather than contributing to group's play)

The teacher can help children who are unsuccessful in entering a playgroup become more successful by using the following strategies:

1.  Help children become aware of their own social goals and those of other children. Children playing together may have incompatible objectives in mind, such as the previous examples of the children's pretend-play involving the pirate ship and doctor's office and the superheroes and firefighter.
2.  Together with the children, reflect on how their behavior affects others. For example, a teacher might say, "Steve, I noticed that your idea was to make a scary face to enter the play; but the other children were afraid of you when you made that face."
3.  Explain and interpret children's behaviors to the other children. For example, a teacher might say, "Steve pushed you because he wanted to play with you. He can't use words to ask you," and "Steve, when you push Jim, he gets angry and afraid, and he may get hurt."

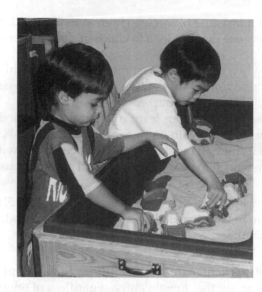

Play provides numerous opportunities to negotiate and problem-solve through sharing
materials.

4. Help children develop social skills necessary for them to enter playgroups
   effectively. A teacher might say, "I see that those children are playing firefight-
   ers. Can you think of something that a firefighter would say?" or "What do you
   think a firefighter would need to put the fire out?" Help children focus on the
   ongoing theme of the other children's play and the objects that are being used,
   and help them understand the importance of entering the playgroup by using
   a strategy that fits that particular theme.

5. The teacher needs to provide opportunities for children who have been
   rejected by the other children to play with children who have been more
   socially successful, and the teacher him- or herself should play with children
   who have been rejected by other children. Children learn by doing, and, as
   they engage in more controlled social interactions, they can build their repertoire of skills.

## Teachers' Roles as Co-players

In sociodramatic play, teachers can be co-players, which is different from being children's playmates. A co-player can adopt a role and interact within the sociodramatic play; but the teacher follows the lead of the child and respects the child's
choice of theme and the script. The play is still created and directed by the children.

*Look at how this child creates and directs the play involving the teacher as a participant:*

[Context: Jewel and the teacher are sitting in the sociodramatic play area.]
*Teacher:* "How can I help?"
*Jewel:* "You can be the sister. I'm the mom."
*Teacher:* "What can the sister do?"
*Jewel:* "She can go to the store to get dinner."
*Teacher:* "Would you like something special?"
*Jewel (smiling):* "Nope, just something yummy."

## CONCLUSIONS

In this chapter, the importance of children's play and some general guidelines for teachers' roles with regard to children's play have been discussed. The role that the teacher adopts is determined by individual children's abilities and interests. Teachers' roles can be thought of as being flexible and involving a range of involvement in children's play along a continuum from minimal involvement to active intervention. Teachers' response to children at play must always be guided by knowledge of children's development as well as an understanding of individual children's needs within a given play context.

## REMEMBER THIS

1. Play and development are linked in young children's lives. Play both contributes to children's development and is linked to various stages in their development.

2. Play contributes to children's social development, promotes their development of social skills, helps them understand another person's perspective, and helps them learn social rules and norms necessary for their successful participation in the adult and peer cultures.

3. Play contributes to children's cognitive development, including creativity, divergent thinking, problem solving, language, and representational thought.

## REFERENCES

Athey, I. (1984). Contributions of play to development. In T.D. Yawkey & A.D. Pellegrini (Eds.), *Child's play: Developmental and applied* (pp. 9–27). Mahwah, NJ: Lawrence Erlbaum Associates.

Barnett, D W., Carey, K.T., & Hall, J.D. (1993). Naturalistic intervention design for young children: Foundations, rationales and strategies. *Topics in Early Childhood Special Education, 13*(4), 430–444.

Berk, L. (1994). Vygotsky's theory: The importance of make-believe play. *Young Children, 50,* 30–39.

Bretherton, I. (1984). *Symbolic play: The development of social understanding.* San Diego: Academic Press.

Brooks-Gunn, J., & Lewis, M. (1982). Development of play behavior in handicapped and normal infants. *Topics in Early Childhood Special Education, 2*(3), 14–27.

Bruner, I. (1974). The growth of representational processes in childhood. In J. Anglin (Ed.), *Beyond the information given* (pp. 152–164). New York: W.W. Norton.

Christie, J., Johnson, E.P., & Peckover, B. (1988). The effects of play period duration on children's play patterns. *Journal of Research in Childhood Education, 3*(2), 123–131.

Connolly, J.A., & Doyle, A. (1984). Relation of social fantasy play to social competence in preschoolers. *Developmental Psychology, 21,* 233–240.

Cook, R.E., Tessier, A., & Klein, M.D. (1996). *Adapting early childhood curricula for children in inclusive settings.* Upper Saddle River, NJ: Prentice-Hall.

Corsaro, W. (1985). *Friendship and peer culture in the early years.* Greenwich, CT: Ablex Publishing Corp.

Curcio, F., & Piserchia, E.A. (1978). Pantomimic representation in psychotic children. *Journal of Autism and Childhood Schizophrenia, 8*(2), 181–189.

Dansky, J. (1980). Make-believe: A mediator of the relationship between play and associative fluency. *Child Development, 51,* 576–579.

Dansky, J., & Silverman, I. (1975). Play: A general facilitator of associative fluency. *Developmental Psychology, 11,* 104.

Darbyshire, J.O. (1977). Play patterns in young children with impaired hearing. *Volta Review, 79*(1), 19–26.

Denzin, N.K. (1977). *Childhood education.* San Francisco: Jossey-Bass.

Division for Early Childhood (DEC) Task Force on Recommended Practices. (1993). *DEC recommended practices: Indicators of quality in programs for infants and young children with special needs and their families.* Reston, VA: Council for Exceptional Children.

Elgas, P., Klein, E.L., Kantor, R., & Fernie, D. (1988). Play and the peer culture: Play styles and object use. *Journal of Research in Childhood Education, 3,* 142–153.

Emihovich, C. (1981). The intimacy of address: Friendship markers in children's social play. *Language in Society, 10,* 189–199.

Erickson, E. (1963). *Childhood and society* (2nd ed.). New York: W.W. Norton.

Fein, G. (1986). The play of children. In G. Fein & M. Rivkin (Eds.), *The young child at play: Reviews of research* (Vol. 4, pp. vii–ix). Washington, DC: National Association for the Education of Young Children.

Fewell, R.R. (1983). Working with sensorially impaired children. In S.G. Garwood (Ed.), *Educating young handicapped children* (2nd ed., pp. 235–280). Rockville, MD: Aspen Publishers.

Fewell, R.R., & Kaminski, R. (1988). Play skills development and instruction for young children with handicaps. In S.L. Odom & M.B. Karnes (Eds.), *Early intervention for infants and children with handicaps: An empirical base* (pp. 145–158). Baltimore: Paul H. Brookes Publishing Co.

Fox, L., Hanline, M.F., Vail, C.O., & Galant, K.R. (1994). Developmentally appropriate practice: Applications for young children with disabilities. *Journal of Early Intervention, 18*(3), 243–257.

Fraiberg, S. (1977). *Insights from the blind: Comparative studies of blind and sighted infants.* New York: Basic Books.

Garvey, C. (1974). Some properties of social play. *Merrill-Palmer Quarterly, 20,* 163–180.

Garvey, C. (1977). *Play.* Cambridge, MA: Harvard University Press.

Garvey, C. (1979). Communication controls in social play. In B. Sutton-Smith (Ed.), *Play and learning* (pp. 109–125). New York: Gardner.

Genishi, C., & Dyson, C. (1984). *Language and assessment in the early years.* Greenwich, CT: Ablex Publishing Corp.

Goncu, A. (1993). Development of intersubjectivity in the dyadic play of preschoolers. *Early Childhood Research Quarterly, 8,* 99–116.

Gregory, F. (1976). *The deaf child and his family.* London: Allen & Unwin.

Hammes, J., & Langdell, T. (1981). Precursors of symbol formation and childhood autism. *Journal of Autism and Developmental Disorders, 11*(3), 331–346.

Hanzlik, J.R., & Stevenson, M.B. (1986). Interactions of mothers with their infants who are mentally retarded, retarded with cerebral palsy, or nonretarded. *American Journal of Mental Deficiency, 9*(5), 513–520.

Hartup, W.W.L. (1983). Peer relations. In E.M. Hetherington (Ed.) & P.H. Mussen (Series Ed.), *Handbook of child psychology: Socialization, personality and social development* (Vol. 4, pp. 103–196). New York: John Wiley & Sons.

Heath, S.B. (1985). Narrative play in second language learning. In L. Galda & A. Pellegrini (Eds.), *Play, language and stories: The development of children's literature behavior* (pp. 147–166). Greenwich, CT: Ablex Publishing Corp.

Hill, P., & McCune-Nicolich, L. (1981). Pretend play and patterns of cognition in Down's syndrome children. *Child Development, 52,* 611–617.

Howes, C. (1988). *The collaborative construction of pretend: Social pretend play functions.* Albany: State University of New York Press.

Isaacs, S. (1933). *Social development in young children.* New York: Schocken Books.

Jennings, K.D., Connors, R.E., Stegman, C.E., Sankaranarayan, P., & Medolsohn, S. (1985). Mastery motivation in young preschoolers. *Journal of the Division for Early Childhood, 9*(2), 162–169.

Johnson, J. (1976). Relations of divergent thinking and intelligence test scores with social and nonsocial make-believe play of preschool children. *Child Development, 47,* 1200–1203.

Johnson-Martin, N.M., Attermeier, S.M., & Hacker, B.J. (1990). *The Carolina Curriculum for Preschoolers with Special Needs.* Baltimore: Paul H. Brookes Publishing Co.

Johnston, J.R. (1994). Cognitive abilities of children with language impairment. In R.V. Watkins & M.L. Rice (Eds.), *Communication and language intervention series: Vol. 4. Specific language impairments in children* (pp. 107–121). Baltimore: Paul H. Brookes Publishing Co.

Jones, E., & Reynolds, G. (1992). *The play's the thing: Teachers' roles in children's play.* New York: Teachers College Press.

Kantor, R., Elgas, P., & Fernie, D. (1993). Cultural knowledge and social competence within a preschool peer culture group. *Early Childhood Research Quarterly, 8,* 125–147.

Krakow, J., & Kopp, C. (1983). The effect of developmental delay on sustained attention in young children. *Child Development, 54,* 1143–1155.

Linder, T.W. (1993). *Transdisciplinary play-based intervention: Guidelines for developing a meaningful curriculum for young children.* Baltimore: Paul H. Brookes Publishing Co.

McKirdy, L.S. (1972). *Play and language in 4–5-year-old deaf and hearing children.* New Brunswick, NJ: Rutgers University. (ERIC Document Reproduction Service No. ED 113220)

McWilliam, R.A., & Bailey, D.B., Jr. (1995). Effects of social structure and disability on engagement. *Topics in Early Childhood Special Education, 15*(2), 123–147.

Mogford, K. (1977). The play of handicapped children. In B. Tizard & D. Harvey (Eds.), *The biology of play* (pp. 170–184). Philadelphia: Lippincott-Raven.

Monighan-Nourot, P., Scales, B., Van Hoorn, J., & Almy, M. (1987). *Looking at children's play: A bridge between theory and practice.* New York: Teachers College Press.

Motti, F., Cicchetti, D., & Stroufe, L.A. (1983). From infant affect expression to symbolic play: The coherence of development in Down Syndrome children. *Child Development, 54,* 1168–1175.

Parten, M.B. (1932). Social participation among preschool children. *Journal of Abnormal and Social Psychology, 27,* 243–269.

Pellegrini, A. (1980). The relationship between kindergarten's play and achievement in pre-reading, language and writing. *Psychology in Schools, 17,* 530–535.

Pepler, D.J., & Ross, H.S. (1981). The effects of play on convergent and divergent problem solving. *Child Development, 52,* 1202–1210.

Piaget, J. (1962). *Play, dreams and imitation in childhood.* New York: W.W. Norton.

Quinn, J.M., & Rubin, K.H. (1984). The play of handicapped children. In T.D. Yawkey & A.D. Pellegrini (Eds.), *Child's play: Developmental and applied* (pp. 63–76). Mahwah, NJ: Lawrence Erlbaum Associates.

Ricks, D., & Wing, L. (1975). Language, communication and the use of symbols in normal and autistic children. *Journal of Autism and Childhood Schizophrenia, 5*(3), 191–221.

Rogers, S.J. (1988). Cognitive characteristics of handicapped children's play: A review. *Journal of the Division for Early Childhood, 12*(2), 161–168.

Rogers, S.J., & Puchalski, C.B. (1984). Development of symbolic play in visually impaired infants. *Topics in Early Childhood Special Education, 3*(4), 57–74.

Ross, D. (1985, April). *Social competence in kindergarten: Applications in symbolic interaction theory.* Paper presented at the annual meeting of the American Educational Research Association, Chicago.

Rubin, K.H., Fein, G., & Vanderberg, B. (1983). Play. In E.M. Hetherington (Ed.) & P.H. Mussen (Series Ed.), *Handbook of child psychology: Socialization, personality and social development* (Vol. 4, pp. 698–774). New York: John Wiley & Sons.

Sigman, M., & Ungerer, J. (1984). Cognitive and language skills in autistic, mentally retarded and normal children. *Developmental Psychology, 20*(2), 293–302.

Singer, J.L. (1973). *The child's world of make believe: Exceptional studies on imaginative play.* New York: John Wiley & Sons.

Singer, J.L., & Singer, D.G. (1985). *Make believe games and activities to foster imaginative play in young children.* Glenview, IL: Scott, Foresman.

Smilansky, S. (1968). The effects of sociodramatic play on disadvantaged preschool children. New York: John Wiley & Sons.

Sylva, K., Bruner, J.S., & Genova, P. (1976). The role of play in the problem solving of children 3–5 years of age. In J.S. Bruner, A. Jolly, & K. Sylva (Eds.), *Play: Its role in development and evolution* (pp. 244–257). New York: Basic Books.

Terrell, B.Y., Schwartz, R.G., Prelock, P.A., & Messick, C.K. (1984). Symbolic play in normal and language impaired children. *Journal of Speech and Hearing Research, 27,* 424–429.

Thompson, T., & Berkson, G. (1985). Stereotyped behavior of severely disabled children in classroom and free-play settings. *American Journal of Mental Deficiency, 89*(6), 580–586.

Vygotsky, L. (1976). Play and its role in the mental development of the child. In J.S. Bruner, A. Jolly, & K. Sylva (Eds.), *Play: Its role in development and evolution* (pp. 536–554). New York: Basic Books.

Wetherby, A., & Prutting, C. (1984). Profiles of communicative and cognitive-social abilities in autistic children. *Journal of Speech and Hearing Research, 27,* 364–377.

Wing, L., Gould, J., Yeates, S., & Brierley, L. (1977). Symbolic play in severely mentally retarded and in autistic children. *Journal of Child Psychology and Psychiatry, 18,* 167–178.

# Activities

1. Observe a play episode in which a child is building with blocks. Discuss what the child is learning or how playing contributes to the child's development.

2. Observe two preschool-age children playing in a classroom for 30 minutes. Using Parten's (1932) social categories for play interaction, classify the children's behavior. Notice whether they remain in the same social category or move in and out of categories over time. Remember to include in your observation the age of the child.

3. Observe a teacher and a child or group of children interacting in a play episode. Describe the teacher's role. What specifically does she or he tell the children to do during this interaction? Focus on the language that the teacher uses.

# Inquiry Learning
# and Child Development

*Peggy M. Elgas, Ellen Lynch,*
*Brenda Hieronymus, and Sally Moomaw*

## CHAPTER ORGANIZER

In this chapter, we explore the following ideas . . .

1. The child as a constructor of knowledge and the principle of active learning

2. Vygotsky's view of learning in a social context and the teacher's role in scaffolding and in the zone of proximal development

3. Classrooms as communicative contexts in which teachers and children co-construct the rules for participation in classroom activities

When considering the needs and behaviors of children in a classroom environment, it is important to begin with a discussion of how individual children develop and learn. Moreover, it is crucial that teachers understand how children interact with their peers and with adults in group environments and how that interaction contributes to their development. Three major sources influence early childhood education (ECE) teachers' classroom approach in these areas:

1. Piaget (1926/1971), for his seminal work on children's thinking and how children learn
2. Vygotsky (1978), for his description of the adult role in education (i.e., the concept of scaffolding) and the social and cultural elements of education
3. Sociocultural researchers, for their descriptions of classrooms as cultures (Green, 1983b; Gumperz, 1982; Mehan, 1979; Philips, 1972)

Also discussed in this chapter are Vygotsky's and Piaget's theories regarding play and its contribution to development. Each of these theories provides important information regarding child development and how children learn. (For detailed discussion of the play research, see Chapter 6.) Each also provides a different but complementary lens through which to view and interpret classroom life. This chapter provides a descriptive summary of the theories propounded by these researchers in terms of how the theories pertain to inquiry learning and child development and inform teachers' practice in the classroom.

**Reflection:**   As you read the next section, make a list of examples from your experiences of concepts that Piaget propounded. Was it easy to think of examples? Was it easier to find examples of some concepts than for others?

## PIAGET

Piaget's (1926/1971) ideas regarding children's thinking and the construction of knowledge have been an important influence in ECE programs. Although the stages of development (i.e., sensorimotor, preoperational, concrete and formal operations), one of Piaget's most cited contributions, are important, the focus here is on children's thinking processes, which guide curriculum planning and influence programs. According to Piaget, two of the most important principles regarding learning are that the child is a constructor of knowledge and that knowledge is constructed and changes over time as the "organism" (i.e., the child) changes and develops.

Piaget (1926/1971) described the preschool-age child as a *preoperational thinker*. Children whose thinking is preoperational tend to understand objects and events in terms of the way the objects and events look; their thought is closely tied to action. Related to the idea of thought and action are Piaget's two types of knowledge: physical and logicomathematical. Physical knowledge is knowledge of an object that can be observed. Children acquire this knowledge by acting on objects (Kamii & DeVries, 1978). Logicomathematical knowledge is created or constructed when we create relationships between objects. The relationship exists only in the mind of the person who puts these objects into the relationship. Kamii and DeVries

This child is physically acting on the materials as he explores and interacts. This activity allows for the child's construction of knowledge.

further illustrated the differences between the two types of knowledge by identifying their sources. With physical knowledge, the source of understanding is partly external; but with logicomathematical knowledge, it is internal. Although the distinction is important, in reality it is impossible to separate the two types of knowledge. Knowing the physical properties of objects is necessary in order to form a relationship between them and thus make them interrelated and dependent on one another. For example, as children poke, squeeze, roll, and pound playdough, they are learning the properties of the material—how it feels, how it smells, how it looks, and what happens when it is acted on. As children continue to have experiences with playdough, they may come to understand that there are, for example, different colors of dough. Children must construct this concept of *difference* (i.e., logicomathematical knowledge), but their construction of it is based on their physical observation and manipulation of the material.

---

*Look at the following example of how physical and logicomathematical knowledge are related:*

Ramps and various sizes of balls are set up in the large-muscle room. Tanisha picks up one of the smaller balls, squeezes it, and places it on the ramp. As the balls quickly roll down the ramp, she squeals, "Look at it go." She repeats this action with the same ball many times. Tanisha then picks up some of the balls of different sizes and examines those before rolling them down the ramp.

Tanisha is actively engaged in constructing both physical and logicomathematical knowledge. By examining the movement of the ball as she plays with it and then observing the results of her actions, Tanisha is learning about the properties of balls, such as that they are round and smooth and that they roll. As she interacts with the balls, she begins to create relationships between balls, such as their different sizes or how far each rolls.

---

How do children create relationships? According to Piaget (1926/1971), it is necessary for young children to act on objects. Kamii and DeVries (1978) suggested that the manipulation of objects helps children think better (i.e., to observe and reflect on their actions). Later in childhood, they are able to think about relationships in an abstract sense, without the use of objects. However, the mindless manipulation of objects is not encouraged. It is in the thinking and subsequent inventing that learning occurs. This process can be facilitated by providing children with objects that encourage exploration and experimentation and through asking thought-provoking, open-ended questions.

Another important aspect of Piaget's theory that helps to illustrate children's learning is the notion that learning begins with understanding. Children approach any situation with some level of understanding and begin by applying their understanding to it. If the new information is consistent with the child's understanding, then the information is assimilated without cognitive disequilibrium. For example, a child may have an understanding that balls are round and that they will roll. Presented with a basketball, baseball, and soccer ball, the child will understand that, though they may be different in size, they are all round and will roll, so the child's previous understanding holds true. If, however, a football is introduced, the child will have to adjust his or her understanding or accommodate his or her schema of balls in order to account for a ball that is not round.

---

*Another example of how a child's physical and logicomathematical knowledge are related is Sean's experience with marbles:*

Sean sat down at the activity table at one of the four places set up with trays. Inside each tray was a large piece of playdough that was flattened out like a pancake. A number of marbles were embedded in the playdough. Sean picked up the right side of his tray, making it higher than the left, and held it there with a look of surprise on his face. He shook the tray several times and then repeated his actions but instead tilted the tray on the left side.

---

Based on his previous experiences, Sean's level of understanding about marbles is that they roll. In the situation just described, they did not, which conse-

quently caused Sean to experience some cognitive conflict and enc...
explore and experiment with marbles under these novel conditions...
exploration, he would then make new discoveries and construct...
standing. Piaget would say that Sean had adapted; that is, he had re...
of equilibrium between himself and his environment.

Adults are often presented with new information that must be accommo-
dated. For example, most adults have some knowledge of microwave ovens,
photocopy machines, and computers; but when confronted with a new machine,
their previous understanding of the concept of machines is challenged. Through
repeated and varied experiences, children manipulate objects, which in turn helps
children mentally construct some understanding of objects and the relationships
between them. With repeated exposure to such experiences over time, children's
understanding is challenged and refined and continues to become more complex
and more complete.

To further illustrate this point, reflect on a common adult experience such as
cooking. When first trying a recipe, adults follow the directions exactly. However,
rarely does the finished product resemble the beautiful illustration in the cookbook
or taste exactly as anticipated. Through talking with others, one might find, for example, that adding 5 more minutes to the baking time than the recipe suggests or
using fewer seasonings than the recipe recommends may bring a more palatable
result. Using this information and with repeated experiences, this particular recipe
may evolve into something quite different from what one used in the first attempt.
In addition, one's whole understanding of the process of cooking expands and is
changed. Recipes often become only general guidelines after one accumulates
knowledge derived from these experiences.

Implicit in Piaget's (1926/1971) theory of learning is the importance of errors
or mistakes. The vignette involving Sean and the marbles illustrates this notion of
children's cognitive errors and how these errors are a part of the learning process.
This thought has challenged the notion of traditional education that correct answers are the goal. Active learning values the process or the "finding out" of the
answer over the product or the right answer. Through their discovery processes,
children learn to make choices, solve problems, and become autonomous learners.
Piaget summarized his idea of appropriate education as follows:

> The goal of intellectual education is not to know how to repeat or retain ready-
> made truths (a truth that is parroted is only a half-truth). It is in the learning
> to master the truth by oneself at the risk of losing a lot of time and going
> through all the roundabout ways that are inherent in real activity. (1948/1973,
> pp. 105–106)

# VYGOTSKY

Vygotsky's (1978) theory is valued for both its sociocultural focus and its elucida-
tion of the teacher's role in the active-learning classroom. In a classroom rooted in
Vygotskian theory, emphasis is placed on classroom discourse because Vygotsky
viewed learning as a sociocultural process. Language in such a classroom is

This child is constructing physical knowledge in his learning. He uses his body in the construction of an understanding of height, width, and inclination as he walks upon the play equipment.

viewed as both a system and a tool for thought and is believed to be both communicative and social in nature. Moreover, adherents of Vygotsky hold that thought processes originate in social interaction.

The Vygotskian classroom is viewed as both a community of learners and a sociocultural system that is created by the teachers and children within it. The classroom environment is viewed as a dynamic, interactive system in which children have an active voice and play an active role. It encompasses both joint construction of learning and individual learning. The teacher is an active participant who works as a facilitator and supporter of children's learning. In terms of the adult role, Vygotsky is probably most closely associated with the terms *scaffolding* (although he did not use that term) and *zone of proximal development*. *Zone of proximal development* refers to the region in which learning and development take place. It is the distance between what children can do independently and what they can do with the help of an adult or a peer who has gained more knowledge or experience (Berk & Winsler, 1995; Vygotsky, 1978).

The process of scaffolding includes many elements (Berk & Winsler, 1995). The social environment is the scaffold or support system that allows children to move forward. Teachers who are effective at scaffolding keep children working in the children's zone of proximal development. This strategy necessitates structuring both the environment and the task at an appropriately challenging level and adjusting the amount of adult participation based on children's abilities. Responsive interaction is a necessary element in the scaffolding process. The teacher allows children to be largely responsible for the problem solving and decision making as he or she asks questions that promote discovery and exploration. Attaching language to the social interaction and attaching language to the physical experience helps children reflect on the discovery that has just occurred. For example, a teacher might comment, "I noticed that when you mixed the red and blue paint, you made a new color."

*In the following example, a teacher scaffolds a child's experience:*

Elliot, a child with a severe language impairment, and Alisha are playing at the water table. Elliot looks at Alisha and says, "I finish." He hangs his smock on the hook and again says, "I finish." Alisha just looks at him. "Hey, you get finish," Elliot says to Alisha. Alisha does not reply. Elliot goes over to the dramatic play area, where he begins playing by himself. The teacher has observed the entire situation. She approaches Elliot and says, "You can ask Alisha to play with you in dramatic play." He runs back to the water table and says to Alisha, "You want to play with me?" as he waves his arm toward himself.

In the situation just described, the teacher scaffolded Elliot's experience as she helped him use language to get his social needs met. Structuring the environment to facilitate children's working together is also an important part of Vygotsky's theory. Negotiation, problem solving, and cooperation lead children to levels of interaction that they could not attain independently (Berk & Winsler, 1995). These aspects of development are often evidenced in children's spontaneous play when one child who is more competent in the developmental area or task at hand helps another child understand and achieve success, as well as facilitates the play episode.

*While reading the following example, think about the concept of scaffolding:*

In the beginning of the school year, Stephen, a child with disabilities and little experience with blocks, was trying to build a tall structure; but he had used smaller blocks at the base than at the top. At a certain point, the structure was going to topple over. Darwin had been watching this and said to Stephen, "No, no, no! You can't do that!" Darwin sorted the blocks according to size, starting with the large blocks. He said to Stephen, "Here, you can help me. Use these big ones first. Don't build it too high, or it will fall over."

**Reflection:** In the next section, you will read about the concept of *frame of reference.* Can you think about times when you and a friend or relative had unique understandings of what you thought was a simple event? Does the concept of *frame of reference* help you understand such misunderstandings?

## CLASSROOMS AS COMMUNICATIVE CONTEXTS

The research on classrooms as microcultures (Green, 1983b; Gumperz, 1982; Mehan, 1979; Philips, 1972) is in keeping with Vygotsky's notion of classrooms as dynamic sociocultural systems. Sociocultural researchers view classrooms as cultures that are developed, enacted, and maintained by their participants (Green, 1983b; Mehan, 1979). A *culture,* more broadly defined, is a system of standards for perceiving, believing, evaluating, and acting. In other words, a culture is whatever one has to know and believe in order to operate in a manner that is acceptable to the members of that culture (Spradley, 1980).

A classroom's culture is constructed over time as its members interact with and react to each other (Gumperz, 1982). This understanding has resulted in a shift in how classroom learning occurs. Classrooms had been viewed as the teacher's domain, where information is a one-way process and learning is transmitted by the teacher to children, who are passive receivers. Based on Gumperz's understanding of classrooms, the view of sociocultural researchers is that the classroom is an interactive, a dynamic, and a reciprocal learning place. Moreover, the sociocultural researchers' perspective is an expansion of the view that learning is constructed by the individual interacting with the environment. In their view, individuals do indeed construct their own knowledge; but learning includes and is interwoven with the social interactions that take place in the classroom and the classroom environment itself (Green, 1983a; Gumperz, 1982).

Just as the classroom environment is constructed through social interactions and becomes patterned over time as routines and rituals are established, so too are common expectations, language, and behavior patterns developed (Bloome, 1989; Wallat & Green, 1979). Spradley (1980) referred to these common expectations and behavior patterns as *the culture of the group.* The classroom culture is developed as the participants interact and establish mutually accepted beliefs, values, and expectations for classroom behavior (Green, 1983a; Kantor, Green, Bradley, & Lichu, 1992). Sociocultural researchers view classrooms as differentiated communicative environments with shifting requirements for participation (Erickson & Schultz, 1981; Green & Harker, 1982). These requirements for participation or participant structures refer to the demands and varying rights, rules, and obligations that occur within that environment (Philips, 1972).

To illustrate the idea of participant structures, think about the large-group time and what it requires to be successful in a large-group time. That is, in which behaviors must participants engage to fit in? Some of these behaviors include gaining attention in an appropriate manner (e.g., by not interrupting anyone, by waiting one's turn) and staying on the topic at hand or suggesting a related topic during classroom discussion (Kantor, Elgas, & Fernie, 1989). If, for example, the topic of discussion is the children's favorite foods, then a child's comment about

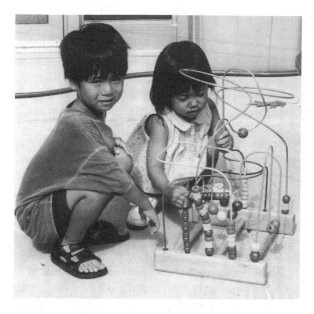

Here the children are experiencing joint construction of learning. The children scaffold each other's learning as they play with the marble track. Each of them may be at a different developmental level, and they may have different ideas about this experience. Through their interaction, they can move to a higher level of understanding.

Grandma's dog would not be appropriate. The student's role, therefore, is viewed as complex and as being an active participant who uses previous social and linguistic information to actively construct social and academic interactions in the classroom (Green & Harker, 1982; Kantor et al., 1989; Kantor et al., 1992).

Along with the idea that classrooms are communicative environments in which participants interact, negotiate, and arrive at shared meanings, bear in mind that each individual brings to the classroom a frame of reference. *Frame of reference* refers to a set of expectations that have developed over time in face-to-face interaction (Green & Harker, 1982; Heap, 1980). This set of expectations guides behavior in similar situations. *Frame of reference* also suggests the idea of *frame clashes* (Green, 1983a), which refers to situations in which two participants with different frames of reference interact in the same situation. Frame clashes can also affect a student's success in the classroom.

*The following example helps to illustrate the idea of frame clashes:*

Carl entered the classroom at midyear after attending a Montessori program. On his first day, the class was working in small groups, measuring various classroom items and recording their findings on a graph. Carl stood up and asked, "Where is my mat? Where are my things?"

---

Carl clearly had a different idea of "how to do school" that was based on his previous experience and participation in a Montessori classroom. The emphasis in Montessori classrooms is on individual development; therefore, Carl and his Montessori classmates had typically been provided with individual places to work and separate materials. Carl had no frame of reference that would help him understand small-group time or help him know how to act in such a situation.

## CONCLUSIONS

After reading these summaries of the Piagetian, Vygotskian, and sociocultural theories, the reader may have questions: How do these three theories work together? How can they inform practice or facilitate an understanding of how children learn? Piaget's work helps one understand how children think in a qualitatively different way and how their thinking is inseparably linked to their actions. This information helps teachers set up the learning environment, choose materials, and design activities that are appropriate for children. In addition, Piagetian theory can guide teachers' observations when they assess children's growth and development. Piaget also affords us great insight into children's perspectives.

Vygotsky's theory acknowledges the active-learning concept, or the constructing of knowledge; but he places this learning in a sociocultural context. Understanding children's families' cultures (i.e., the cultures they bring with them to the classroom) and understanding the demands and expectations of society as a whole help the teacher understand individual children as well as the classroom as a group. The teacher's role, specifically in terms of scaffolding, can be understood in relation to both individual children and the classroom as a group. Assessing individual children's development and working within their zones of proximal development is an important task of the teacher. Related to that task is the social interaction that takes place between individual children and the group and how this interaction, specifically through the use of language, helps to shape children's development.

The sociocultural researchers' views of classrooms are related to Vygotsky's ideas of culture and social interactions in classrooms. Their unique contribution, however, rests with the idea of classrooms as minicultures in which norms of behavior and interaction are constructed by the participants over time. Viewing classrooms from this perspective helps teachers understand the importance of making the rules of participation explicit. This rule-making role does not imply that teachers should be directive, but rather implies that they should help each child uncover the rules and expectations for successful participation in both the school culture and their peer culture. This knowledge also helps teachers identify frame clashes and help children resolve conflicts based on these differing frames of reference in the classroom. The latter is a particularly important goal for teachers of children with disabilities.

Combined, an understanding of these three theories of classroom culture can provide ECE educators with a framework within which to work. These theories address both individual development and the effect of group dynamics on development. Moreover, these theoretical approaches address children's 1) participation in the classroom as they interact with materials and adults, 2) the teacher's role, and 3) the reciprocal nature of child–teacher interaction.

## REMEMBER THIS

1. Piaget described preschoolers as preoperational thinkers who view the world differently and think in ways that are qualitatively different from the ways that adults do.

2. According to Vygotsky and his concept of the zone of proximal development, children are capable of moving to a higher level of cognitive understanding by interacting with adults and more experienced peers.

3. Classrooms can be viewed as minicultures and dynamic systems in which children and teachers co-construct the rules for participation.

## REFERENCES

Berk, L., & Winsler, A. (1995). *Scaffolding children's learning: Vygotsky and early childhood education*. Washington, DC: National Association for the Education of Young Children.

Bloome, D. (1989). *School and literacy*. Greenwich, CT: Ablex Publishing Corp.

Erickson, F., & Schultz, J. (1981). When is a context? Some issues and methods in the analysis of social competence. In J. Green & C. Wallat (Eds.), *Ethnography and language in educational settings* (pp. 147–160). Greenwich, CT: Ablex Publishing Corp.

Green, J. (1983a). Exploring classroom discourse: Linguistic perspectives on the teaching–learning process. *Educational Psychologist, 18*, 180–199.

Green, J. (1983b). Teaching and learning as a linguistic process: A state of the art. *Review of Research in Education, 10*, 151–252.

Green, J., & Harker, J. (1982). Gaining access to learning: Conversational, social and cognitive demands on group participation. In C.L. Wilkinson (Ed.), *Communicating in the classroom* (pp. 183–224). San Diego: Academic Press.

Gumperz, J.J. (1982). *Discourse strategies*. Cambridge, England: Cambridge University Press.

Heap, J. (1980). What counts as reading? Limits to certainty in assessment. *Curriculum Inquiry, 10*(3), 265–292.

Kamii, C., & DeVries, R. (1978). *Physical knowledge in preschool education*. Upper Saddle River, NJ: Prentice-Hall.

Kantor, R., Elgas, P., & Fernie, D. (1989). First the look and the sound: Creating conversations at circle time. *Early Childhood Research Quarterly, 4*(4), 433–448.

Kantor, R., Green, J., Bradley, M., & Lichu, L. (1992). The construction of schooled discourse repertoires: An interactional sociolinguistic perspective on learning to talk in preschool. *Linguistics and Education, 4*, 131–172.

Mehan, H. (1979). *Learning lessons*. Cambridge, MA: Harvard University Press.

Philips, S. (1972). Participant structures and communication: Warm Springs children in community and classroom. In C. Cazden, V. John, & D. Hymes (Eds.), *Functions of language in the classroom* (pp. 370–394). New York: Teachers College Press.

Piaget, J. (1971). *The language and thought of the child.* New York: World Publishing. (Original work published 1926)

Piaget, J. (1973). *To understand is to invent.* New York: Grossman. (Original work published 1948)

Spradley, J.P. (1980). *The ethnographic interview.* Austin, TX: Holt, Rinehart & Winston.

Vygotsky, L. (1978). *Mind in society: The development of higher mental processes* (M. Cole, V. John-Steiner, S. Scribner, & E. Souberman, Eds. & Trans.). Cambridge, MA: Harvard University Press.

Wallat, C., & Green, J. (1979). Social rules and communicative contexts in kindergarten. *Theory into Practice, 18*(4), 275–284.

# Activities

1. Observe preschool-age children engaged in an active learning activity. Record an example of physical knowledge and logico-mathematical knowledge.

2. Observe a teacher and a child interacting. Describe how the teacher scaffolds the child's learning. What specific strategies does the teacher use?

3. Think of an instance in your own life when a frame clash occurred. What were the consequences of this experience?

# Inquiry Learning
# and Curriculum Planning

*Peggy M. Elgas, Kimberli Rioux,*
*Nancy Struewing, and Connie Corkwell*

## CHAPTER ORGANIZER

In this chapter, we explore the following ideas . . .

1.  Quality curriculum programs rooted in solid theoretical and philosophical perspectives

2.  The practices that constitute a quality early childhood education curriculum

3.  How classrooms are organized around the elements of space, materials, and interactions

4.  How goals affect classroom practice

5.  How the curriculum is reflected in each of the classroom areas in terms of materials, setup, and what children learn

One of the most fundamental aspects of any program is the curriculum that undergirds the program. *Curriculum* is a dynamic rather than a static concept that is developed on the basis of particular theoretical and philosophical orientations, the interests of children, family preferences, and the adaptations needed to ensure that all children have the opportunity to be successful. This chapter stresses the importance of strong theoretical and philosophical perspectives; the elements of space, materials, and classroom interactions; how goals affect practice; and how the curriculum is implemented in the classroom.

**Reflection:** As you read the next section, think of specific experiences in which you have observed children in a preschool classroom building with materials in the block area. Visualize children moving through various curriculum areas, making choices regarding the materials and how to use them. Was the program implementing a theoretical and philosophical framework?

## THEORETICAL AND PHILOSOPHICAL BASES OF CURRICULUM

First and foremost, quality programs and curricula are rooted in a sound theoretical and philosophical framework. The curriculum described here is influenced by Piaget, Vygotsky, and sociocultural researchers. The play research that describes all aspects of development also guides exemplary practice. (For a detailed discussion of these theories as they apply to the curriculum, see Chapter 9; for a detailed discussion of play, see Chapter 6.) Combined with the philosophical and theoretical bases of the curriculum are the principles of developmentally appropriate practice (DAP) as outlined by the National Association for the Education of Young Children (Bredekamp & Copple, 1997). In this chapter, individually appropriate practice is subsumed within our definition of DAP. Implicit in DAP is the notion of active learning and a play-based curriculum in which all children can construct what they will learn and can experience success. The curriculum is developed on the basis of children's current interests, ideas, and understandings as well as on teachers' understanding of child development and how children learn. Adaptations for individual children are made through collaborative observation and assessment in the classroom, thus ensuring the successful participation of all children.

---

*The following brief description of a typical school day may help illustrate the general concepts discussed in this chapter so far:*

Lamont arrives at the classroom, kisses his mother good-bye, and hangs the cutout footprint with his name on it on the Who Is Here wallchart. He hangs his jacket in his cubby and runs to the block area to join Joe, who is building a large structure that he calls "the zoo." The children all gather on the floor to play with the small plastic animals in the animals' cages. Lamont goes to another play area, where three children are taking turns playing with a marble track to see who can make the marbles roll the farthest. During this time, Lamont and his friends take turns going to the large-muscle room. The rest of the morning consists of a large-group time, when they sing songs, share free-choice creations, and use interactive charts. There is also outdoor time and lunchtime.

---

An active learning or constructivist classroom encourages children to explore, experiment, make discoveries, make choices, and solve problems. Careful and systematic planning encourages children to be active and independent learners. One way to illustrate that idea is to examine the early childhood education (ECE) program in terms of the physical space, materials, and interactions in the classroom. All classrooms are organized around these three elements; however, the ways in which these elements are implemented distinguish one program from another. The following section provides specific information regarding each of these components and how they are implemented in the classroom.

**Reflection:**   As you read the next section, think about your own classroom or about classrooms that you have observed. Make a list of examples of appropriate and inappropriate uses of space, materials, and interactions in the classroom. How would you modify or change the inappropriate uses to make them more positive? When you look at your list of examples of appropriate and inappropriate uses of space, are there any aspects that consistently differentiate the appropriate and inappropriate uses?

## Space

How the physical space of the classroom is arranged sends a message to children about what they can and should do in it. Because a primary goal is to encourage children's active involvement in the classroom, the classroom environment is set up to be aesthetically pleasing, interesting, and visually well defined. This type of setup invites children to explore the classroom space. Separate areas for common activities such as sociodramatic play, block building, and art should be clearly labeled and visually distinct. Easy access for choice making and autonomous cleanup is an important consideration. The design and arrangement of the classroom, including traffic flow patterns, are also important. Although the play areas are created at the beginning of the year, often they are redesigned after observations of the children's use of them are made. Not only do the groups of children in the classroom change from year to year, but even within a school year children may use the areas in different ways.

---

*The following vignette illustrates how simple changes in the classroom setup can yield positive results:*

At the beginning of the school year, the block and manipulative areas were combined. In this particular class, there were several regular block builders who liked to create large, intricate structures. This resulted in little floor space being left for manipulative play. One day, Steve complained to the teacher that, while he was sitting on the floor, one of the block builders stepped on his hand. The next day, the manipulative play shelf was turned around to create separate work spaces for the block and manipulative play areas. The block building continued to flourish throughout the year, and more manipulative play was also observed after the play areas were separated.

---

Classroom accommodations are also made for children with disabilities. For example, for children with visual impairments, changes in the classroom's physical space should be minimal and infrequent. Larger play areas and pathways in those areas can be constructed to facilitate easy wheelchair movement. Collaboration between families, classroom teachers, and support staff can yield numerous ideas to help facilitate successful participation by all members of the class.

## Materials

Materials are chosen on the basis of their potential to interest children, multiple uses (or open-ended nature), and multilevel appeal (i.e., all children, regardless of ability, can interact with them). Another important criterion for selection of materials is whether that material or object can promote children's physical knowledge. To help determine whether an object promotes physical knowledge, the following questions should be asked:

- Can children act on the object?
- When children act on the object, can they vary their actions?
- Can they observe immediate changes resulting from their actions on the object?

---

*The following vignette illustrates the idea of children's active learning and physical knowledge:*

A marble track is introduced into Sara and Beth's classroom. Sara and Beth are able to act on the marbles and the marble track, vary what they do with the marbles, and observe the results of their actions. Children in the class spend the entire day rolling the marbles and watching them. The next day, Sara and Beth begin manipulating the track and find that they can shoot the marbles in various directions. They predict where they think the marbles will go and place baskets in various places to catch them.

---

Providing an ample variety of materials helps promote choice and decision making. However, careful attention must also be paid to both the quantity and variety of materials that are made available at one time to avoid overwhelming young children and thus making it difficult for them to choose. Quantity and selection are also important considerations for children with disabilities, particularly for those children who are easily overstimulated and have difficulty with self-control. Materials can and should be changed periodically as related to thematic planning and in response to children's interests. Material changes and combinations are also made in response to children's current level of understanding. These variations and combinations are introduced to stimulate further exploration and hypotheses testing.

---

*As illustrated in the following vignette, a teacher could vary the marble play described in the preceding vignette by introducing a different-size track and different-size marbles or a slight change in ramps and balls:*

John approached the ramps in the muscle room; but instead of finding balls as he usually did, there were various wooden shapes, including a cone, a cylinder, and an egg shape. He picked them up and looked at them. After touching these objects for some time, he placed the cylinder on the ramp vertically and gave it a nudge. When it did not roll as he expected, he examined it again and then placed it on its side. As it rolled down the ramp, he excitedly screamed, "Look! Look! It rolls." He continued to experiment with the other shapes.

---

Small changes do yield large results. Children first need time to explore and discover the properties of the materials themselves, and then they can try to figure out what they might do with the materials as the materials are manipulated. Children need time to experience success and to build a knowledge base. They need time to discover the properties of, for example, sand, marbles, chutes, ramps, and balls before proceeding to the next step of their interactions with such materials. Simple modifications of materials in the classroom can lead them to new discoveries that they must absorb into their consciousness.

## Interactions Among Children

Interactions among children in the classroom can be facilitated in many ways. Structuring the physical space in the classroom can promote interactions among peers. For example, planning a large block-building space encourages a number of children to collaborate to create large structures. Limiting the amount of play-dough or the implements to use with the dough encourages children to negotiate and problem-solve sharing of materials.

The teacher can also verbally facilitate interactions among children. She can refer children to each other for assistance and the sharing of individual discoveries. For example, the teacher might say, "John, you can ask Eliza how she made that purple paint, since you were interested in using some on your paper," or, "I noticed that Rob has built a large tower with those little blocks. Let's ask him how he did that." Along with individual problem solving, group problem solving can be encouraged. For example, the teacher might say, "Maybe if you and Jason work together, you can figure out how to build your tower higher, even though you have already used all of the large blocks." Helping children to recognize each other's work or to work together may be especially important for children with disabilities who have limited communication skills.

Interactions between the teacher and the children in the classroom are as important as children's peer interactions. The teacher can make comments or ask questions that encourage exploration and experimentation. The teacher can use language that helps children predict, hypothesize, discover causes and effects, and problem-solve. For example, the teacher might say, "I wonder what will happen when you add the water to the flour, sugar, and spices"; "I noticed that when you added that long block your tower fell over"; or, "How do you think you can make it reach?" By attaching language to children's experiences, the teacher allows children to reflect on their discoveries and begin to make connections between their actions and what happened as a result of their actions. The particular conversational or interactional strategies that the teacher decides to use are dependent on the situation at hand and individual children's interests and needs.

---

*In the following example, a teacher helps a child with disabilities move from a frustrating situation in which he has almost no involvement to one in which he is highly involved. Using only a few words, the teacher helps the child make an important discovery that leads to further exploration:*

Jason is sitting on the floor, surrounded by Duplos. He begins kicking his feet and throwing the Duplos after several unsuccessful attempts to put them together. Jason's teacher sits down beside him and guides Jason's hand as she says, "Push." Jason locks the Duplos together. The teacher says, "See, you put them together by pushing." Jason continues to work on the other Duplos for an extended period of time.

---

## Goals that Guide and Influence Practice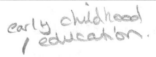

This section describes the goals that guide the ECE program. The goal statements are followed by specific examples of how they can be achieved in the curriculum. The goals that guide and influence practice are that all children will:

1.  Become autonomous, independent learners
2.  Become a member of a community of learners
3.  Become problem solvers and decision makers who feel confident in their ability to choose and approach new situations
4.  Develop a fuller understanding of their world
5.  Become producers and consumers of print and feel comfortable interacting with and using print

In addition to the three organizational components of space, materials, and interactions, curricula are also guided by specific goals that ECE teachers have for the children in their classrooms. Strategies that teachers can use to promote children's becoming autonomous, independent learners include encouragement versus praise and child-focused versus teacher-directed learning. Encouragement builds children's self-concepts and fosters their independence as they focus on their work instead of on praise they receive. Encouragement focuses on children's attempts rather than on their accomplishments so that they can feel successful while they are in the process of acquiring skills. In a child-focused classroom, children's ideas are valued and become a part of the classroom. Children in such a classroom feel capable and competent and begin to develop ownership of the classroom.

Becoming a member of a learning community requires that children learn how to interact in socially acceptable ways and how to make friends. Providing children with opportunities to work with their peers in extended free-choice periods and in group environments with the teacher's facilitation helps children to develop social skills and form stable friendships. Problem-solving and decision-making skills can be developed by providing children with numerous opportunities to choose play areas, materials, and partners. Teacher-planned activities that engage children in problem-solving situations are also important. Children gain confidence in their abilities to make choices and problem-solve, and consequently they eagerly approach new situations. Children who are provided with activities that are relevant and meaningful to them are able to develop a fuller understanding of the world around them and gain a greater understanding of everyday life. Children who are exposed to print-rich environments and have numerous opportunities to interact with print in meaningful ways begin to understand some concepts about print, such as that print can communicate and carry meaning over time. These two concepts are important in forming the foundation for reading and writing.

## CLASSROOM AREAS

The descriptions of curriculum areas presented in this section are meant as a guide to, not as a prescription of, what should happen in the classroom. Specific decisions with regard to each aspect of the curriculum need to be guided by the interests, needs, and abilities of the children in the class. Curriculum planning in practice is more integrated than the way it is described in this section; separate planning of each curriculum area is described herein for ease of presentation only.

### Art Area

---

*Look at how the teacher in the following vignette reacts to a child's discovery:*

Jim was painting at the easel, using a large brush to make long, wide strokes. There were three containers of paint in front of him, each holding a different color of paint.

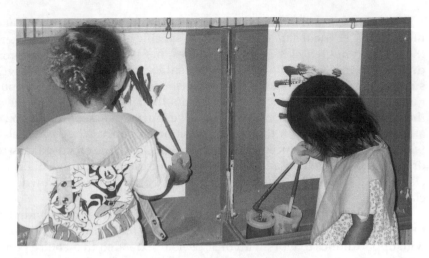

Children are provided with opportunities to explore and gain experience with paint as they build a repertoire of knowledge about the medium. They might observe what changes occur if they use a large brush or mix the paints.

Up until now, Jim had used each color separately. This time, however, he dipped his brush in each of the paint containers before making a stroke across his paper. When he brushed the paint on his paper, he gasped and a look of surprise spread over his face. "Chocolate!" he exclaimed. He called a teacher over to the art area and pointed excitedly to the easel in front of him. "Chocolate," he said, pointing to his paper. "No chocolate here," he said, pointing to the containers, "but chocolate here," he continued, gesturing to his painting. "I see you've made the new color by mixing these paints together," the teacher replied.

---

When examining the connection between children's art and their learning, an important aspect to consider is the process of creating versus the product that is created. Although both are important, children enjoy and need numerous experiences in which they can freely explore and experiment with different media. Their exploration and experimentation with art are the essential first steps in building their repertoire of understandings related to art and self-expression. Children need many opportunities to explore and manipulate media before they are consistently able to represent ideas in a recognizable way. They must first learn the properties of paint, clay, and collage, and then they must learn what will happen if certain utensils are used in conjunction with a particular medium (e.g., what changes can be observed if a large brush is used instead of a small one). Repeated as well as varied experiences over time are an essential part of the art curriculum. In addition, building on children's previous experiences and already-acquired learning is important (e.g., using additives with paint, such as sand or condensed milk, after children have discovered the properties of tempera paint).

Art can promote children's physical, perceptual, cognitive, social, and emotional development. For example, children can develop eye–hand coordination and fine motor control as they learn to use small brushes and drawing implements. Perceptual abilities such as visual and spatial awareness are enhanced as children cover part or all of their painting surfaces. Children are also provided with numerous opportunities to explore shape, size, color, and form. They can learn about cause and effect as well as practice their skills in decision making (e.g., which colors and brushes to use when painting) and problem solving (e.g., how to combine paints to make the color purple, how to stick collage materials to a base). Through the use of various media, children are able to represent and communicate their ideas nonverbally and can also benefit socially and emotionally. Children's sense of identity emerges as they freely create and express themselves; their sense of autonomy develops as they work independently and make decisions about their work. Children's cooperation can also be fostered as they share materials or collaborate in group projects. Table 1 presents ideas for arranging materials and developing thematic connections in the art area.

## Block Area

---

*Look at the development of cooperative play with blocks that may promote children's social skills:*

Joe had made several unsuccessful attempts at entering the block area, where the building had become increasingly interesting. In general, his techniques had been somewhat self-serving (e.g., making unauthorized changes, dismantling classmates' work). He even tried making signs to hang on the buildings as the other children had done; however, his fine motor skills did not lend themselves to readable letter formation, and, besides, others had already assumed the sign-making role. As Joe watched one of the children build an impressive replica of a high-rise office building, he noticed a set of building toys that had been placed in the area. He began to form several small but distinct tools, which he carefully placed beside the building. "I made tools!" he announced. "This is the sander, and you use it like this," Joe said. Other children asked to use the toy sander as well as the toy hammer and nail gun. Soon the entire group was working together to repair and expand the building.

---

The block area provides experiences that can enhance children's cognitive, physical, social, and emotional development. Children develop spatial relationships as they build various structures. They also learn mathematical concepts as they gain experience in measuring, one-to-one correspondence, and patterning. Their understanding of scientific concepts develops as they explore and manipulate the properties of ramps and objects that roll on ramps. The block area is a rich avenue for teaching writing. Children often want to make signs to identify their building or to send a message such as "Danger: Keep Out." Block building often

Table 1.   Art area

| Levels of curriculum | Setup | Materials | Thematic connections |
|---|---|---|---|
| Art shelf | Shelves that have labels, pictures, and container cutout shapes for the basics that remain on the shelf<br>A place nearby to work | Different drawing utensils (e.g., markers, pencils, chalk)<br>Different kinds of paper<br>Glue, stapler, tape<br>Hole punch, scissors<br>Collage materials (e.g., yarn, cotton balls, tissue paper) | Babies: Pastel paints and cotton balls<br>Fall: Collage made of outdoor fall gatherings |
| Planned activities | Tables and chairs for working | Introduce new materials<br>Move from simple to complex<br>Different painting surfaces and utensils<br>Different drawing surfaces and utensils<br>Different collage bases and materials<br>Clay and other sculpting and molding materials | |
| Easel | Linoleum floor<br>Easy access to a sink<br>A drying rack and specified drying area | | |

encourages social problem solving as children introduce different ideas and negotiate which ideas will be used. Often roles are created and assigned in conjunction with the theme at hand. Because of the materials and the limited size of the block area, cooperative play often results. Teamwork is needed to build large, interesting, complex structures; thus, the block area provides one of the most natural avenues for sociodramatic play, which is discussed next. Table 2 presents ideas for arranging materials and developing thematic connections in the block area.

## Dramatic Play Area

*In the following vignette, notice how the child incorporates what she knows about her environment into her play, which promotes her learning about herself, her family, and her community:*

Mei-Ling is busy in the pretend housekeeping area, neatly reorganizing the food that others have left out and pretending to wash the dishes. She sets a table for three for a meal she has prepared. On the table she places three plates, three cups, three small bowls, and a wok and attempts to distribute the four available chopsticks among the three settings. She sets the first place with a pair of chopsticks and then sets each of the second and third places with a single chopstick. She then proceeds to move a chopstick from the first setting to the second setting, then to the third setting, and then back to the first setting. She continues in this pattern for several minutes. She then pauses for a moment; steps back to look at the table with her hands on her hips; and, with a heavy sigh, turns and leaves the area.

Children enjoy imitating important people in their lives; as they play, they adopt various adult roles. As children act out these roles, they learn about themselves, their families, and their communities. An effectively designed dramatic play area enhances children's language and cognitive development, supports their emotional development, and fosters their development of social skills and social relationships. In the preceding vignette, Mei-Ling developed math concepts such as one-to-one correspondence as well as social and cultural concepts related to family traditions. Through role playing, children learn to ask and answer questions, experiment with solutions, and solve both cognitive and social problems. The dramatic play area also offers a place where children can act out their fears and reenact some of their life experiences. Initially, children may role-play simply for the enjoyment of self-expression or to anticipate how to act in new situations. Gradually, as children interact with each other more frequently and regularly, they begin to demonstrate self-initiated sharing and empathy for others.

Table 2.   Block area

| Setup | Materials | Thematic connections |
|---|---|---|
| Area without cut-through traffic (i.e., make less distracting) | Standard unit blocks | Construction: Tools, construction helmets |
| Surface flat enough to build on or provide flat wooden slabs | Two school shelves fully stocked and well marked | Farm: Small animals, farm buildings |
| Flexible limits and guidelines | Large numbers of standard units | |
| Clean up area or save what was built for the next day | Small numbers of interesting and unusual shapes | |
| How high structures can be built (e.g., provide chairs to stand on) | Props related to a unit (or in response to children's current interests) | |
| Number of children in area at one time | Changing materials periodically to extend play and provide opportunities for other children to enter | |
| Teacher's attitude expresses appreciation of the learning that takes place, demonstrates value and interest in blocks, and respects process and product | | |
| Wall hangings, pictures related to materials (e.g., vehicles, buildings) | | |
| Space for individual work | | |
| Extension of children's ideas in other parts of curriculum (e.g., small blocks with rice in sensory table) | | |

When children identify, plan, and act out themes, they develop the ability to think creatively, express ideas and feelings, and work cooperatively with others. They learn to listen to and share with one another and to become more flexible in negotiating roles and scripts. They learn to understand and deal with their world. Table 3 presents ideas for arranging materials and developing thematic connections in the dramatic play area.

## Literacy Area

*Look at the following vignette, which demonstrates the natural way in which children acquire literacy skills through interacting with each other:*

During the entire free-choice time, Ben and Kyle work together constructing a Batman house. The Batman house is a very elaborate and intricate structure with tunnels and rooms of interesting shapes. Many of the rooms are labeled with small signs that the boys have made. At cleanup time, Ben and Kyle are distraught. "We want to keep this for tomorrow," they explain to their teacher. "We need to write a note," they say. The teacher replies, "Okay, what will your note say?" As Ben begins writing his note

Table 3.   Dramatic play area

| Setup | Materials | Thematic connections |
|---|---|---|
| Realistic (for younger children) <br><br> Safe and usable by younger children <br><br> Open ended and multiuse <br><br> Arranged attractively <br><br> Placed in a well-defined area <br><br> Organized for easy cleanup (e.g., labels, special baskets or shelves, and hooks for specific materials) <br><br> Allow room for groups of children to play comfortably together | Child-size kitchen equipment such as a kitchen sink, stove or oven, refrigerator, microwave oven, dish cabinet, small table and chairs <br><br> Dishes (e.g., plates, cups, silverware) <br><br> Pots and pans, wok, chopsticks (other cookware common in different cultures) <br><br> Dolls and doll clothing <br><br> Doll furniture (e.g., bed, highchair) <br><br> Doll accessories (e.g., bottles, blankets, rattles) <br><br> Child-size rocking chairs and living room furniture | Bakery: Chef's hats; aprons; oven mitts; cookie sheets; rolling pins; pretend bakery food such as cookies, pies, various breads (cultural variety) <br><br> Dance: Tap shoes, ballet slippers, tutus, scarves, vests, native costumes from other cultures, sequined top hats, white gloves, ribbon streamers, large mirrors, cassettes of various types of dance music, a stage with chairs for an audience <br><br> Post office: Mailboxes for individual children, men's blue workshirts, canvas bags (to be used as mailbags), postal hats, assortment of paper, pencils, lick stamps (from junk mailings offering videos or magazines), envelopes, rubber "Canceled" stamps <br><br> Camping: Child-size tent, small grill, pretend cookout food, mess kits, binoculars, cameras, picnic blanket or small picnic table, picnic baskets, pond set up with fishing poles and magnetic fish, small logs for a campfire |

on construction paper, he and Kyle say, "Nobody can touch this Batman house. It is for us. Do not clean it up or put the blocks away. Somebody lives here." "Where would you like to hang this sign?" the teacher asks. "On the front door," the boys reply.

Children acquire literacy skills in much the same way that they learn to talk. They learn to speak and communicate through interacting with others rather than by direct instruction from adults. How children learn to become readers and writers involves more than their "breaking the code" or learning letters and sounds. Literacy involves broader concepts such as knowing that print can be used for social purposes and to meet personal needs (e.g., to inform by means of labels and signs, to aid memory by writing, to express personal feelings, as substitutes for spoken words). In the preceding vignette, Ben and Kyle would certainly have stayed overnight and guarded their Batman house from the school's cleaning staff or from intruders; however, that was not possible. They also knew from their previous experiences in the classroom that leaving a note for someone who was not present at the time would communicate their wishes.

Because the United States is a literate society, children arrive at school with some preformed ideas about language and print. Most children have a rudimentary command of language when they start school and are already reading print in their environments (e.g., a McDonald's sign, the backs of the boxes of their favorite cereals). Provided with meaningful experiences, children can broaden their understanding of print. For example, children learn about books and the process of reading when they are exposed to quality literature and have opportunities to read to each other. Interactive charts can be used to introduce new vocabulary to children and provide them with experiences in voice–print pairing as the words on the chart are read aloud. Children can learn about the forms and functions of print as they are provided with various writing implements and opportunities to use these in meaningful ways. Table 4 presents ideas for arranging material and developing thematic connections in the literacy area.

## Manipulative Play Area

*Look at how children use manipulative toys in an open-ended manner in the following vignette, promoting the abilities of children of different developmental levels and allowing for choice:*

In the manipulative play area, David and Darrell are stacking large pegs. Each of them is making a peg tower. They have anchored the towers in separate pegboards. As their towers get taller and begin to lean, their activity attracts Nikki to the manipulative play area. David looks at Darrell, points to the top of his peg tower, and says, "Can you put that on there?" Darrell brings his pegs and puts his tower in a differ-

Table 4.  Literacy area

| Levels of curriculum | Setup | Materials | Thematic connections |
|---|---|---|---|
| Literacy center | Shelves, table, and chairs for writing<br>Bulletin board or homosote board that can be used as a story wall to display notes, other writing, and books created by the children | Blank books<br>Various types of paper and writing utensils<br>Various types of fasteners to make their own books<br>Interactive charts | Post office: Set up a post office with a mailbox and various letter-writing materials, stamps, and envelopes (include a math post office game) |
| Book area | Shelves to display books<br>Comfortable chair, pillows, quiet space away from louder areas such as block area | A variety of books that span various age levels, reading abilities, and interests | |
| Literacy events throughout the day | | Writing materials placed in every area to facilitate sign making and notes<br>During group times, writing ideas for songs or problem-solving situations<br>During small-group time or free-choice time, writing out a recipe for whatever was accomplished, such as how they built their structures at the woodworking table, what they discovered while dissecting pumpkins, or what happened at the water table with tubes and food coloring | |

ent hole on David's pegboard. David again points to the top of his tower as he looks to Nikki for assistance. Nikki moves in to become the stabilizer for the tower as David and Darrell continue to shuffle peg sections back and forth in an attempt to extend the height of the tower. Paul enters the manipulative area, circles the group a few times as he observes, and then moves to another area of the classroom. Esther joins in and begins to attach her own stack of eight or nine pegs. David, still intent on his own goal and determined to make the tower reach the ceiling, looks to the teacher, who is observing nearby, and asks her, "Can you put high? I can't get it." The teacher suggests that David ask Esther for her ideas on how to extend the tower. David walks over to Esther, hands her the section of pegs that he wants to place on top of the tower, and says, "Esther, how do you get that up there?" Nikki is silently holding the original tower, which is still anchored in the pegboard. Esther quickly puts her peg tower down, takes the section that David handed her, and says, "Oh, yeah. Okay!" Esther looks at Nikki and nonverbally indicates to her to continue holding the tower

Math games can be constructed to promote concepts. These children are exploring math concepts such as one-to-one correspondence and counting.

as she separates the tower just above her eye level, adds the section that David handed her, and reattaches the top section. As the tower nears the ceiling, Esther stands back and smiles while the others cheer.

Manipulative play area activities should be open ended. They should allow children of different ages and abilities opportunities to use the same materials in a variety of ways. Children are thus able to make choices and learn basic concepts (e.g., shapes, colors). Simple activities such as using pegboards can be quickly and easily adapted by having children use only particular colors or shapes for patterning skills or by adding a second pegboard and a die to create a simple math game. The manipulative play area not only lends itself to a variety of functioning levels but also provides children with opportunities for solitary play or cooperative, interactive play with their peers.

In the preceding vignette, the children involved in building the peg tower all entered the play by "doing their own thing." The children were quickly able to move into a cooperative play situation in which they were able to problem-solve and work together collaboratively to reach a common goal. The manipulative play area thus provides children with many problem-solving opportunities in their interactions with materials and with their peers and the teacher. Table 5 presents ideas for arranging materials and developing thematic connections in the manipulative play area.

Table 5    Manipulative play area

| Setup | Materials | Thematic connections |
|---|---|---|
| Ample floor space and shelf space<br><br>Begin with duplicate materials: Move to sharing of materials | Divided shelves for display of materials<br>Pegboard activity<br>Stringing activity<br>Construction materials: An array from simple to complex (i.e., Bristle Blocks, magnetic blocks, Duplos, snap blocks, Legos, marble works)<br>Puzzles<br>Math manipulatives (i.e., collections, grid games)<br>Sorting activity | Babies: Pegboard with baby bottles (e.g., cake toppers), pastel and alphabet beads to string, collection of baby items (e.g., cake toppers), pastel Legos<br>Fall: Natural collections (e.g., assortments of nuts, acorns, pine cones, buckeyes, leaves) for sorting or with ice cube trays and tongs, pegboard with small plastic carrots |

## Math Area

*Look at how play activities can promote children's learning of math and math-related concepts:*

Ian and Bryant are playing in the block area, building separate buildings. Bryant stops suddenly, exclaiming, "Hey, I don't have as many blocks! I need more blocks. I can't do the office building." Ian looks at him and then at the blocks and says, "I know. I know." Ian starts counting the blocks out loud, "Two for you, and two for me," and, as he counts, he divides them into two piles until all of the blocks are separated. Bryant watches carefully, and, as the piles grow and begin to look equal, he smiles and says, "Okay, okay!"

Through their daily interactions with materials and people, young children develop math-related concepts. Specifically, they are learning about classification as, for example, they sort the counting bears by color or they group blocks by size and shape. As they interact with small blocks and manipulative toys, children often create patterns. As children set a lunch table with silverware, plates, and napkins, they gain an understanding of one-to-one correspondence when they place one item at each place setting. In the block area, while children play by themselves or with their peers, many meaningful experiences with counting can occur. For example, they might want to count the blocks left on the shelves to determine whether they have enough blocks to finish their project, or they may need to know how many blocks are there because there are not enough materials for everyone playing. Children also begin to develop an understanding of the four mathematical operations: addition, subtraction, multiplication, and division. Ian and Bryant needed to divide the blocks so that their play could continue. Ian was able to verbalize his strategies while Bryant observed the results, and he was able to understand because the piles had the appearance of being equal. Math games can also be

Table 6.   Math area

| Levels of curriculum | Setup | Materials | Thematic connections |
|---|---|---|---|
| Math games<br>Group time math<br>Math events throughout the day | Provide materials and games of varying levels of difficulty that allow all children to participate<br>Observe and comment on children's discoveries, but avoid correcting their mistakes<br>Provide materials and experiences that allow children to test their ideas and challenge their mistakes, facilitating their movement to a higher level of understanding | Graphs, counting songs<br>Lunch, waiting lists, blocks, manipulatives, dividing playdough) | Zoo: Graphing favorite zoo animal after a field trip<br>Babies: Math game with miniature baby bottles for markers |

constructed to promote children's understanding of the concepts discussed during the games. (For a detailed discussion of appropriate math games, see Moomaw & Hieronymus, 1995.) Table 6 presents ideas for arranging materials and developing thematic connections in the math area.

## Music Area

*Look at how music provides children with opportunities for self-expression and promotes their learning:*

Molly and Ayanna are sitting on the floor in the area where group time is typically held, singing a song in which the teacher frequently includes the names of children in the class. Each girl holds her own stack of classmates' name cards that they have retrieved from two different interactive charts in the room and takes turns singing a verse of the song: "Oh, I wish I had a little red box to put [*insert child's name*] in. . . ." Ayanna looks down at the name cards, pulls one out, and holds it up. Ayanna finishes the first verse and looks at Molly. Molly finds She-Yuan's name in the stack of cards, holds up the card for all to see, and takes her cue to continue the song: "Oh, I wish I had a little red box to put She-Yuan in. I'd take her out and give her a hug and put her back again. . . ."

When children are exposed to music, they are provided with opportunities for singing, responding physically to different rhythms, participating in creative expression, playing instruments, and listening. Music, whether quiet and soothing or quick and lively, helps to set a mood and provides social activities that help children feel that they are a part of the group. Music activities can be enjoyable ways to improve children's cognitive and motor skills, as well as providing an outlet for children's energy and high spirits.

Music is naturally enchanting to children and can occur in all areas of the classroom in a number of ways. There is typically a music area set aside for exploration and experimentation with different musical instruments. The instruments placed in the area may be commercially manufactured or handmade but should be durable enough for young children's developing physical coordination. If the instruments are handmade, they should be made neatly and attractively to entice children to use them. Children's experimentation with the instruments encourages their awareness of cause-and-effect relationships and develops their listening skills as they compare, for example, sounds made by similar instruments of different sizes. In their free exploration of instruments and songs, children learn to enjoy singing, which encourages their creative expression as they invent new songs or put new twists to familiar ones. If a song or rhythmic poem is posted in the music area, children often sing or chant the words while playing a musical instrument. This type of activity improves children's fine motor coordination and encourages their literacy through voice–print pairing, thus enhancing the value of meaningful print as the children learn new words and concepts.

Group time or circle time is common in many preschools and is an enjoyable way to develop children's gross and fine motor skills (e.g., through movement songs, fingerplays); improve children's balance, coordination, and rhythm; and build children's group participation skills. Teachers can select songs that require children to follow directions or work with a partner, thus supporting and enhancing the children's social interactions with their peers. In a group situation, children are often positioned close to other children and are therefore developing and increasing their body awareness skills as they simultaneously perform various physical movements and try not to bump into others. Children enjoy repeating familiar songs independently, as Molly and Ayanna did in the preceding vignette. They experience growing confidence in their musical abilities when music is presented as a regular, fun, nonthreatening activity.

Music should be an integral part of each day in ECE programs because research (Begley, 1996) has suggested that children's early exposure to music enhances their cognitive development. Music played in the classroom while open activities are taking place exposes children to various cultures and can set the mood of the classroom. Table 7 presents ideas for arranging materials and developing thematic connections in the music area.

## Outside Play Area

*Outside play is a wonderful way for children to develop socially, emotionally, and cognitively while they are physically active:*

Jack is climbing to the top of the climber. He says to his teacher, "Watch me climb to the top. I can do it!" He climbs to the top of the climber and waves to the teacher. Steve climbs up next to him and says, "Let's be pirates. This can be our ship. I'll be the Captain. Help me drive."

Table 7.   Music area

| Setup | Materials | Thematic connections |
|---|---|---|
| Designated area for display and use<br><br>Low bench or accessible, inviting area for displaying instruments<br><br>Variations of strikers or mallets, if used, such as rubber mallets, felt mallets, wood mallets, wood or metal strikers<br><br>Pictures related to the instrument (if native to a different culture, pictures of the instrument in use; or general pictures of people/children interacting with the instrument)<br><br>Possibilities to consider in setting up a group time music activity:<br><br>• Teacher can demonstrate fragile instruments, inappropriate for free exploration, and monitor the children as they study the instrument.<br><br>• A new instrument to be used by the group as a whole or later placed in the music area can be introduced with appropriate guidelines (e.g., strike the clave gently).<br><br>• There should be enough instruments for each child and the teacher or other adults who are assisting to use for a large-group activity.<br><br>• Guidelines for use of the instrument for a large-group activity should be given before the instruments are distributed so that the attention of the children is maintained. | Song or rhythmic poem may be posted on a chart or in large print<br><br>Recordings of a variety of cultural music<br><br>Listening station: Tape recorder with attached headphones (usually a small number of these)<br><br>Simple instruments:<br>• Autoharps or zithers<br>• Bells or bell collection (vary by size, type, culture)<br>• Chinese temple blocks<br>• Claves or African tongue drums<br>• Various drums<br>• Various maracas or shakers (handmade or commercial)<br>• Rhythm sticks<br>• Sand blocks<br>• Tambourines<br>• Tone blocks<br>• Triangles<br>• Wind chimes made of various materials (e.g., tuned and nontuned metal, plastic)<br>• Xylophones | Zoo or rainforest: Rainsticks of various sizes<br><br>Farm: Cowbells of various sizes, bell collection<br><br>Firefighters: Triangles<br><br>Dance: Commercial maracas or shakers made with clear drinking bottles and various fillers (e.g., sand, pasta, colored rice, colored water with glitter) |

Although playgrounds and outdoor playtime are most often regarded as a time and place where children can develop physically, outdoor playtime can also provide numerous opportunities for children's social, emotional, and cognitive development. Playgrounds provide children with opportunities for negotiating, sharing, and taking turns on, for example, the climber, slide, and swings. In addition, children learn to play cooperatively as they dig and create structures in the large, shared sandbox. While children play in the sand, their cognitive development can also be enhanced. Pouring, sifting, and measuring sand lead children to discoveries regarding weight, quantity, and measurement, and they learn how to fill containers without spilling most of the sand.

Sensory experiences present themselves to children continually in the form of sights (e.g., light, shade), fragrances (e.g., flowers, grass), and sounds (e.g., birds, insects). Children can make other discoveries about the outdoors by digging in dirt; planting and caring for flowers; and exploring trees, grass, and bushes. Outdoor play presents children with opportunities for physical challenge and mild risk taking (e.g., Jack's experience in the vignette on page 166). Children are able to exercise their large muscles outdoors because they have greater freedom of move-

The water table may be set up for a science experience. This child is interacting with the boats and basters to observe and make discoveries as she moves to objects and begins to formulate questions and ideas.

ment. Children's muscle precision is advanced through their repeated experiences of running, jumping, and climbing. Finally, numerous opportunities for sociodramatic play present themselves (e.g., the previous vignette involving Jack and Steve's pirate play). In those types of activities, children learn how to interact with each other, express their opinions, negotiate, and problem-solve. Table 8 presents ideas for arranging materials and developing thematic connections in the outside play area.

## Science Area

*Children may be encouraged to experiment with their environment when teachers design the classroom environment to promote children's curiosity and enthusiasm. Look at one child's investigation and play in a science area:*

Bryant, a child with autism in an inclusive preschool classroom, is one of the first children to approach the incline. He places a disk on its flat side at the top of a ramp and gently shoves it with his finger, watching it scoot downward about an inch. He

Table 8. Outside play area

| Setup | Materials | Thematic connections |
|---|---|---|
| Enough space and equipment that encourages action and active participation | Variety and complexity | Fall: Child-size rakes |
| | Large motor equipment (e.g., slide, climber, swings) | |
| Large-group areas and smaller areas with more individual space | Fine motor equipment (e.g., tools for digging, sifting, pouring) | |
| Areas well defined (e.g., concrete areas for riding tricycles and other equipment; grassy areas for running, resting, picnicking) | Materials that extend indoor curricular areas | |
| | Art (e.g., large projects such as painting murals with large brushes, messy projects such as bottle spray painting) | |
| Adequate, well-marked pathways | | |
| Areas of sun and shade | Literacy (e.g., books related to the outdoors) | |
| Places for uninterrupted gardening and nature projects | Science (e.g., gutters, large balls) | |
| A large sandbox area | | |

taps the disk again, and it moves another inch. He repeatedly taps the disk, watching the disk gradually slide until it reaches the bottom of the ramp. Bryant replaces the disk at the top of the ramp and repeats his tapping motions, watching the disk go down the ramp inch by inch in a scooting motion, time after time. After several attempts, he looks over the disk carefully and attempts to set it down once again at the top of the ramp, this time, however, on its side. As he lets go of the disk, it briskly rolls to the bottom of the incline and across the floor of the room, stopping several feet beyond the edge of the science area. Bryant's eyes grow wide, he smiles broadly, and he laughs aloud as he retrieves the disk and begins to set it at the top of the incline again.

Children are naturally curious and are, in their own ways, like scientists who predict, experiment, observe, compare, classify, measure, draw conclusions, infer, communicate, and record results. A science activity that is open ended and attractively displayed promotes children's curiosity and fosters in them an experimental attitude. Children's interest in and enthusiasm for their discoveries encourages them to become active, self-directed learners who share their observations and ideas.

The science area is most often intended to develop children's knowledge of physical properties, through either the movement of objects or the changes in the properties of objects. Although the science area may occasionally be set up for observation only (e.g., an ant farm, magnifying glasses with fossils), activities that are interactive tend to draw children's interests and develop their problem-solving skills. Children have the opportunity to make intentional actions to produce a desired effect, which in turn allows them to gain scientific information and acquire knowledge. Science area activities can promote children's skills and habits outside of the classroom, such as respect for wildlife and the environment and taking care

Table 9.   Science area

| Setup | Materials | Thematic connections |
|---|---|---|
| If the area is set up so that the activity is dictated, children never hypothesize. Set it up so that they must figure out through exploration. Grade activities from simple to complex, adding variations after ample time for exploration with initial materials. Include pictures of people using the material, of the environment where the material is typically used, or of people doing motions similar to those required to produce an effect. | Inclines<br>Balance scale<br>Tops<br>Magnifying glasses<br>Pendulum<br>Sink and float<br>Kaleidoscopes<br>Planting<br>Gears and simple machines<br>Labyrinth (marble to guide through a wooden maze with pitfalls, using a tilting motion)<br>Pinwheels with billows, fans, etc.<br>Pets (e.g., fish, gerbils, rabbits, mice, turtles, hermit crabs)<br>Incubator (hatching live eggs)<br>Insects (e.g., ant farm)<br>Nature collections (e.g., shells, nuts, pine cones, nests) | The science area may relate to a theme or specifically to other areas of the classroom<br><br>Winter: Inclines (e.g., pictures of sledding)<br>Construction: Pendulum (e.g., wrecking ball with colored blocks)<br>Bakery: Balance scale (e.g., ingredients, vinyl cookies)<br>Farm: Grain mill (e.g., grinding wheat, corn)<br>Incubator (e.g., duck and chicken eggs) |

of plants and pets. Table 9 presents ideas for arranging materials and developing thematic connections in the science area.

## CONCLUSIONS

An appropriate ECE curriculum is developed from philosophical and theoretical bases, DAP, the goals that teachers have for children, and the children's interests and ideas. It is a collaborative effort by all of the adults (e.g., classroom teacher, speech-language pathologist, psychologist, social worker) involved in caring for the children in the program, with successful participation for all of the children being the primary goal. A knowledge of child development principles as well as individual children guides the curriculum development process. Curriculum planning is a dynamic, reciprocal process between children and adults as children suggest ideas and teachers act on those ideas and the children's current understanding.

## REMEMBER THIS

1. Curriculum planning is a collaborative process that involves all of the adults caring for the children as well as the children's ideas and interests.

2. Curriculum can be thought of as a dynamic process that is adapted according to children's changing interests, abilities, and understandings.

3.  Curriculum planning is an integrated process. Although plans are made for individual classroom areas, integration of those areas is always considered.

## REFERENCES

Begley, S. (1996, February 19). Your child's brain. *Newsweek,* 55–62.

Bredekamp, S., & Copple, C. (Eds.). (1997). *Developmentally appropriate practice in early childhood programs* (Rev. ed.). Washington, DC: National Association for the Education of Young Children.

Moomaw, S., & Hieronymus, B. (1995). *More than counting: Whole math activities for preschool and kindergarten.* St. Paul, MN: Red Leaf Press.

# Activities

1. Observe a preschool classroom during free-choice time. Choose two classroom areas, such as the sociodramatic play and block areas. List the materials located in and describe the setup of each area.

2. Observe two different preschool classrooms. Compare and contrast how the classrooms are organized around the elements of space, materials, and children's peer interactions.

3. Interview a preschool classroom teacher about his or her goals for the children. Ask him or her specifically how the classroom is organized to support those goals.

c  h  a  p  t  e  r

9

# Developing an
# Inclusive, Prosocial Curriculum

*Iris R. Daigre, Lawrence J. Johnson,*
*Anne M. Bauer, and Deborah Anania Smith*

## CHAPTER ORGANIZER

In this chapter, we explore the following ideas . . .

1. The characteristics of classrooms in which prosocial skills are emphasized

2. The following methods and strategies for facilitating prosocial behaviors in children:
   a. Natural, prosocial interactions
   b. Modeling and attachment
   c. Prompts
   d. Problem solving and conflict resolution
   e. Group interactions
   f. Physical environment
   g. Teacher–family interactions

One of the most important skills that a child develops is the ability to interact with others successfully in a social environment. Although it is difficult to identify a precise set of skills that enable a child to be successful in social environments, it is clear that some behaviors can be characterized as prosocial. Typically, prosocial behaviors promote harmonious relationships among peers (Hay, 1994). They are important because they often determine how happy and fulfilled people are as adults. Some prosocial behaviors are showing sympathy or kindness to someone, helping someone, gift giving, accepting a gift, sharing, cooperating, comforting someone in distress, showing concern for someone, taking into account the perspective of another person, and other behaviors that promote harmony within a group (Wittmer & Honig, 1994). Children incorporate these behaviors into their repertoire of behaviors at an early age, and it is imperative that early childhood education (ECE) teachers understand how to and have the ability to nurture prosocial behaviors in the children they teach. This chapter identifies characteristics of classrooms in which prosocial skills are valued and discusses strategies for nurturing the development of children's prosocial skills.

**Reflection:**  As you read the next section, think about prosocial behaviors and your own philosophy of how children learn. Is the development of prosocial behavior an important part of your philosophy? How can an emphasis on prosocial behavior enhance a child's ability to learn?

## CHARACTERISTICS OF A PROSOCIAL CURRICULUM

Good ECE programs strive to meet the developmental needs of all children and their families. There is a commitment to respecting the dignity, worth, and uniqueness of individual children and helping children achieve their full potential in the context of classroom relationships that are based on mutual trust, respect, and positive regard (Feeney & Kipnis, 1992). In the early 1980s, many early childhood programs shifted away from emphasizing social interactions and placed more emphasis on cognitive development in the curriculum (Bredekamp & Rosegrant, 1992). The focus is shifting, almost full circle, to include social development as the key component of curriculum in ECE programs.

*Curriculum* is everything that occurs in the classroom. It should incorporate what, how, and when children learn best. Everything that happens affects and shapes the curriculum. Among other things, individual differences among children such as age; diverse cultural backgrounds; and different interests and variations in growth, development, and learning styles must be considered when making decisions regarding curriculum. By focusing on social development in the curriculum, prosocial behaviors will be emphasized throughout the classroom. Taking a prosocial stance dramatically changes the look of classrooms, which traditionally have focused on cognitive development. An observer in a classroom employing a prosocial curriculum might see children engaged in activities designed to promote sharing, empathy, or helping. Emphasis is placed on helping children incorporate behaviors that encourage harmonious social interactions.

Children may play cooperatively to ensure that all have a turn in the sociodramatic play area. The teacher may facilitate prosocial behaviors by supplying sufficient manipulatives at the water table to encourage several children to play together. As children play together, they can be encouraged to cooperate on a specific task (e.g., filling a pitcher with water) or to share manipulatives and engage in turn taking. Children may be encouraged through modeling to take the perspective of another person.

All children, through interaction with others, learn empathy and compassion in a prosocial environment. Their self-esteem may increase as they perform acts of altruism and caring for others. All children are given an opportunity to learn about and be sensitive to others who may be different from themselves. They can learn to be tolerant and more accepting of others. However, children who have difficulty with prosocial behaviors may have several problems with social interactions (Odom & Brown, 1993). Some children may have difficulty with entry-level skills for engaging in social situations, which restricts the amount of time that they have to experience the benefits of prosocial behavior. Other children engage in aggressive or negative behaviors, which alienates peers and limits the experiences that these children have with more positive social behavior. Finally, some children attempt to engage in social interactions but have limited social skills, so the reactions of their peers are nonexistent or negative.

These children need help to learn social behaviors that will allow them to engage in an increasing number of social interactions with positive outcomes. As the positive outcomes become more frequent, the likelihood that children will repeat the behaviors that produced the positive outcomes increases. As a result, classrooms that promote positive social interactions naturally nurture the prosocial behavior of the children in the classroom. The next section describes strategies that can be used to facilitate positive social interactions that facilitate the development of prosocial behaviors in children. However, before moving to this next section, a series of suggestions that can help ensure that the curriculum and classroom promote prosocial behavior in children follows. This list has been compiled from the recommendations of Cook, Tessier, and Klein (1992) and Wittmer and Honig (1994). In the next section, some of these suggestions are elaborated.

1. Adults in preschool environments can encourage prosocial behaviors in children by valuing and modeling prosocial behaviors (Wittmer & Honig, 1994). These adults must be committed to respecting the dignity, worth, and uniqueness of all children, family members, and colleagues within the preschool program. Relationships among children, family members, and professionals are based on trust, respect, and positive regard (Feeney & Kipnis, 1992).

2. Label and encourage prosocial behaviors as they occur. As we have asserted before, all children experience and display prosocial behaviors in their natural interactions in the classroom. When children display these behaviors, it is important that teachers acknowledge and encourage them by expressing positive regard for them. The teacher can give children a hug, a wink, a smile, or a comment or respond with any other behavior that will indicate the teacher's

Prosocial skills are acquired by young children as they problem-solve together as they play. Each child learns to negotiate his or her roles, themes, and use of materials.

positive regard for the prosocial behavior. As previously stated, it is difficult to define a precise set of behaviors that are prosocial behaviors. However, some examples of prosocial behaviors are

a. Showing sympathy or kindness to another individual
b. Helping an individual
c. Giving something to another individual
d. Accepting something that has been given
e. Sharing
f. Cooperating
g. Comforting another individual in distress
h. Showing concern for another individual
i. Taking the perspective of another person
j. Other behaviors that promote the harmony of the group (Wittmer & Honig, 1994)

Plan activities that promote cooperation. Activities that require two or more children to cooperate to achieve a specific goal will increase social interactions between the children. As a result, there will be expanded opportunities for children to practice prosocial behaviors (Cook et al., 1992).

3. Provide sufficient materials for several children to play together. Having enough manipulatives or toys encourages children to play together in the same area. When children are playing in the same area, the possibility of their sharing and cooperating is enhanced (Cook et al., 1992).

*Reflection:*   The next section addresses methods and strategies that both children and adults can use to foster children's prosocial skills. As you read about these strategies, make a list of times when you have seen these strategies implemented in the classroom. Are some strategies used more frequently than others? What are some reasons why some strategies are used more often than others?

## METHODS AND STRATEGIES THAT FACILITATE PROSOCIAL SKILLS IN CHILDREN

As emphasized in the previous section, it is important that adults in preschool environments focus on prosocial behaviors. In order to learn about the needs and interests of each child, a teacher must become both an observer and a participant in the classroom. In particular, the teacher must be responsive to the needs of each child and each child's verbal and nonverbal initiations of interaction or requests for communication (Howes, Hamilton, & Matheson, 1994). Teachers facilitate children's prosocial behaviors by valuing and emphasizing them, developing early positive socialization with children and children's families, encouraging children to interact with their peers, helping children enhance their social interaction skills, and forming positive social relationships with children's families. The strategies described in the following sections illustrate actions that can help foster and facilitate prosocial skills of children in a preschool environment.

### Encouraging Natural Prosocial Interactions

In developmentally appropriate practices (DAP) classrooms in which prosocial skills are valued and emphasized, teachers and staff respect the dignity, worth, and uniqueness of each individual, including each child, each member of the staff, each family member, and each other. Honig and Wittmer (1996) recommended that educators precisely label and encourage children's prosocial behaviors when they naturally occur. Encouraging prosocial behaviors that occur naturally is the most powerful way to help a child incorporate these behaviors into their repertoire of behavior (Kostelnik, Stein, Whiren, & Soderman, 1988; Wolery & Bredekamp, 1994). Naturalistic strategies involve brief interactions between adults and children throughout the typical school day that encourage behaviors that promote group harmony. It is important that the teacher be a good observer and be aware of the likes of the children in the class. Some children like a big hug, whereas others prefer a subtle smile or a wink. Typically, all children respond well to specific comments that indicate that they have helped another child.

---

*Consider the following interaction:*

Keena tries two times to build a tower with large wooden blocks. She builds the tower to a height of approximately 2 feet, and then it falls over. Seth has been watch-

ing Keena and asks if he can play with her. Keena says, "Okay," and the two children begin to work together to build a third tower. This time, Seth grabs the larger
square blocks and puts them on the bottom of the tower. With the large blocks at the
bottom, Keena and Seth are able to build a tower that is as tall as they are. Jamie,
the teacher, has been observing this interaction and adroitly moves toward the two
children and, with a big smile, says, "Look at what the two of you were able to do
together. By helping each other, you built a super-high tower."

---

In the interaction described in the preceding vignette, the teacher labeled the
prosocial behavior and indicated her positive regard for the prosocial behavior.
The children experienced a natural sense of accomplishment by succeeding in
building a tall tower and were further encouraged by the teacher's expression of
positive regard for their behavior and achievement. It is important that teachers be
aware of responses that encourage children and indicate to children that they have
positive regard for their prosocial behaviors. Such encouragement should be
immediate and expressed as naturally as possible. Furthermore, the teacher's positive statement should be specific and designed to label the prosocial behavior and
indicate how the behavior helped the situation.

**Reflection:**   As you read the next section, think about the following questions.
Why is attachment important in promoting prosocial skills? How can appropriate
prosocial behaviors be modeled for children? Think of a scenario in which you can
model prosocial behaviors in a natural manner.

## Modeling and Attachment

Strategies of modeling prosocial skills include being aware of and accepting the
need of children to form attachments with their teachers. Early childhood educators, through their caregiving and modeling of social roles throughout the process of establishing secure attachment with children, facilitate children in forming
trusting relationships with adults (Howes, Phillips, & Whitelock, 1992). Once established, children's trusting relationship with adults aids them in forming relationships with their peers. In a study of teacher–child relationships, Howes and
colleagues (1992) observed that the more emotionally secure children are with
their teachers, the more competent they are both with their peers and in general.
This result was most evident in preschool classrooms. Young children who seemed
insecurely attached tended to be dependent; withdrew from their peers; clung to
adults in immature, fearful ways; and were unable to rely on adults in exploring
their environments. In addition, 4-year-old children who had fewer experiences
with other children had fewer opportunities for successful autonomous problem
solving, were thought to have misinterpreted their peers' friendly overtures, and
responded aggressively to their peers (Howes et al., 1994; Howes et al., 1992).
   Some children whose cultural background is different from those of the classroom teacher, their peers, and the school community may arrive at school feeling

The physical environment promotes social interaction among children. The tire swing is interesting to the children and an appropriate part of the play curriculum as children engage in conversation and turn taking.

overwhelmed by the classroom environment. Culture shock, a phenomenon once thought to occur only in adults, paired with their inability to comprehend or to speak the native language of their peers, may impair children's ability to interact socially. Professional caregivers and ECE educators must successfully impart knowledge of American culture to children and their families from different cultural backgrounds and develop awareness and sensitivity to the cultural contexts in which these children and their families live.

By being sensitive and empathetic to the needs of children to form secure attachments with teachers, ECE educators promote prosocial skills development in young children (Bowlby, 1988). Once children become securely attached to their teachers, they may simply check in with, or touch base with, or seek help briefly from their teachers, returning to discover and explore with their peers (Hay, 1994).

## Prompts

Strategies that facilitate prosocial skills in children include using effective prompts and scaffolding teacher–child interactions and child–child interactions. Effective prompts result when the educator furnishes only as much help as is absolutely necessary. They are given before or during a child's learning of a new skill. Prompts are verbal or physical cues that encourage a child to engage in an interaction and tend to be used at more informal times such as playtime, snack time, and outside playtime. For example, a teacher may use a gesture paired with her voiced "Hello!" as he or she greets the child in the morning, thus encouraging children to respond with a pleasant "Hello!" in return.

Prompts are best used in a supportive and instructive manner and then withdrawn as the skills are being taught. For example, the teacher might provide a child with the words necessary for him or her to ask another child whether he or she can play with the manipulative with which that child is playing. At first, the teacher might say, "Ask Jimmy if you can play firehouse." As the child learns to make requests on her or his own, the teacher might gradually withdraw the prompt or expand on the child's language by changing the prompt.

## Problem Solving and Conflict Resolution

In DAP classrooms, children play peacefully and cooperatively (Bredekamp & Rosegrant, 1992). Conflicts between peers can be resolved through processes of conflict resolution and problem solving that support their cognitive development. Chapter 2 discusses the teachers' and other service providers' use of problem-solving techniques. These techniques can also be used with children to help children resolve and understand conflicts. Helping children at an early age to understand and resolve conflicts can help them acquire skills that they can use throughout their lives. Six basic steps to use in conflict resolution follow:

1. *Initiate mediation:* Maintaining a neutral stance, approach children in conflict and make a statement to them. If necessary, stop their aggressive behaviors.
2. *Gather data:* Find out the feelings of the victim and the needs and wants of the aggressor.
3. *Define the problem:* Rephrase the children's statements about their feelings or restate the issue of contention in a manner with which the children agree.
4. *Generate alternative solutions:* Entertain suggestions for resolution of the problem from the children involved in the conflict as well as from observers of it.
5. *Agree on a solution:* Work with each child to reach agreement to one of the alternative suggestions. Restate the solution that both children have accepted.
6. *Follow through:* Monitor the children's behavior to be sure that they are participating in the agreed-on solution and, when appropriate, bring closure by announcing that the problem is resolved (Wittmer & Honig, 1994).

In order for the problem-solving process to occur, four conditions need to be established:

1. Children need to trust the facilitator.
2. Enough time needs to be taken with the children; rushing through the process is not effective.

3. Adults and children have sufficient energy to engage in problem solving; when any member of the process is tired, hungry, or sick, the process is unlikely to work.
4. Basic communication skills are needed; simple words or signs such as "Mine" and "Help me" and nonverbal communications such as gestures paired with facial expressions relieve the immediate stress of misunderstanding.

After practicing conflict resolution a few times, children tend to learn to move quickly to solve problems. When caught in a struggle over an object, children who are familiar with conflict resolution procedures look at the teacher across the room and solve the problem themselves. The use of additional means of communicating messages such as role-plays, props, gestures, drawings, and other types of visual demonstration may be necessary in helping children with disabilities learn to use problem-solving strategies (Wolery & Wilbert, 1994).

## Group Interactions

Group time is an ideal opportunity to facilitate children's interactions with each other, emphasizing their development of prosocial skills. As the teacher engages children in singing, storytelling, rhymes, and poetry, she or he aids children in their collaborations and interactions. The class may work together in drawing or writing a story related to a shared experience (e.g., a trip to the zoo) that can be made into a big book to be read during group time. Making and sending a large thank-you card to a special friend of the class or a get-well card to an absent classmate teaches children empathy and caring. Within group time and on the playground, teachers can organize games and activities that encourage children's cooperative play. Some examples of these activities are children digging holes together, making small mountains in the sandbox, building dramatization, and engaging other activities that require them to cooperate. Such activities should help children engage in and sustain conversation with their peers, persist in communication with each other, and play together.

## Physical Environment

The space allocation within the classroom has a profound effect on children's opportunities for socialization. Enough room needs to be provided so that everyone, including children and adults in wheelchairs, can move about easily in the classroom. All areas and materials must be safe. Adults must be able to see all parts of the room from every area of the room. Areas for noisy activities need to be separated from quiet activity spaces. Classrooms designed with space for groups of different sizes and age-appropriate materials for children of various levels of development facilitate children's prosocial peer interactions. Be mindful that changing the layout of the classroom affects children's socialization patterns.

Prosocial goals in the curriculum include socially appropriate behaviors. These children are learning to share
and cooperate in play. They also demonstrate positive
communication skills while in the baby pool.

*Look at Willa's classroom:*

In the fall, Willa, an early childhood teacher, made few changes in her classroom
setup. During the previous year, it had been a kindergarten classroom. It was large,
with narrow areas on two sides of the room resembling long halls. The staff could
walk quickly from area to area. Once her preschoolers found it, however, they treated
it as a running track. The children in her class, who were not yet acquainted with
classroom culture, literally ran in circles around the room. Also, shelves, tables, and
chairs were situated in small spaces at the center of the room. Some were too small
for an adult, so adults could not sit down and participate with the children in their
activities. Willa rearranged her classroom and made changes in the pathways from
one area to another, creating larger spaces for centers and materials, obstructing the
children's "running track," placing shelves of blocks next to the wall, and creating
more areas for play. These changes in the physical setup of the classroom had a positive impact on children's opportunities for socialization. Adults, once peering over
shelves and screens, looking down on children, were now sitting next to the children
and could still see all parts of the room from any location in the room. Running was
reserved for children's outside play. Now, more children could sit together, play together, and interact with each other.

In designing the physical environment of the classroom, the teacher can create
a playhouse area that includes a table and four chairs. When it is time to purchase
materials, choose items that allow more than two children to play at a time. Instead
of purchasing, for example, a single-person tricycle, purchase a small toy bus that
seats four children; a two-seat tricycle; a small seesaw; or large, foam outdoor
blocks that encourage two children to arrange them and build with them. Fur-

nishings inside the classroom that promote prosocial behavior include soft cushions and chairs placed in comfortable areas that permit children to have quiet "alone" time or that facilitate one-to-one quiet conversations between children and their peers or between children and adults.

It is important that early childhood teachers select or adapt materials that are interesting and appropriate to the developmental level of the children in the class. Materials that facilitate development of children with disabilities are often also of interest to children without disabilities. Examples of such materials are light boards and light tables for children with reduced vision, manipulatives of various sizes to accommodate children's differing skill levels, toys of different shapes and textures (e.g., a collection of teddy bears of different colors, sizes, and textures), tape recorders with earphones, and toys that respond to verbal speech and make noises. Early childhood teachers should consider children's needs and interests in choosing classroom toys and materials so that children are engaged and supported in achieving their goals.

If necessary, early childhood educators can introduce a new material, scaffold its use, and explore with children how to play with it. It is helpful to notice which materials in the classroom facilitate children's social interaction and then use those materials to sustain children's peer conversations. These materials are frequently ones that promote children's imaginary play (e.g., dress-up clothes, dishes) and joint motor play or a combination of both (e.g., balls, wagons, seesaws, blocks, toy trucks and cars).

Attention needs to be paid to color coordination and decoration in the classroom (Wittmer & Honig, 1994). It is important to design classrooms that are aesthetically pleasing and uncluttered in which care is taken to reduce aspects of the classroom that induce distraction and promote disorganized stimulation in the children (Bredekamp & Copple, 1997).

## Teacher–Family Interactions

Collaborative relationships among parents and school personnel can begin with the first contact between them. A cohesive, inclusive plan to involve families in which all members of the community collaborate facilitates the social success of all children in the classroom, builds positive relationships, and encourages children's prosocial behaviors. Collaboration among families and staff provides an opportunity to emphasize the importance of children's learning prosocial skills in relation to their development of more traditional skills related to self-help and readiness.

As teachers work to acquire greater competence in communicating with children and their families, they must recognize that their own cultural backgrounds and experiences affect how they teach. Cultural differences within the classroom should be explored and understood. These differences should be celebrated because they enhance the school experience for all (Lynch & Hanson, 1998). The first step is to establish positive relationships with families. Prior to the 1990s, this was not always the practice of ECE educators; families from different cultural backgrounds were expected to assimilate to American society.

Early childhood educators must acquire cultural sensitivity; that is, they must be able to see the world from the viewpoint of children and their families. It is important that early childhood teachers learn as much as possible about the cultures of the families in the communities that they serve. Which ethnic and cultural groups are represented? How recently have they arrived in the United States? What are their primary languages? What are their beliefs regarding, for example, child rearing, health, healing, and the causes of disabilities? In ECE programs in which there are children from different cultural backgrounds, collaborative relationships between families and professionals become significant. It is important to make use of cultural interpreters for ease in communication and to take time to explore families' concerns, priorities, and resources in the community. Some families from diverse cultures may choose to be involved in their children's education. Culturally competent early childhood educators seek to develop a bias-free curriculum (Bredekamp & Copple, 1997) and classroom practices that are sensitive to the cultures of the children in their class and the children's families. Understanding children from a cultural perspective helps put their prosocial behaviors into an important context that cannot be overlooked.

**Reflection:**   Now that you have read about various strategies that can be implemented to promote children's prosocial skills, which classroom strategies do you feel will be successful? Which ones might be more difficult to implement? Can you think of any other strategies not mentioned in this chapter that would work to promote prosocial skills in young children?

## CONCLUSIONS

Good ECE programs use a variety of interventions and strategies to promote prosocial skills in children. ECE educators focus on facilitating both verbal and nonverbal conversations among adults and children. A curriculum that emphasizes prosocial skills differs from one that includes discipline and child management plans. In programs that promote prosocial development, professionals work collaboratively with children's families. Children's prosocial skills are valued, modeled, and emphasized. Finally, such programs respect the dignity, worth, and uniqueness of each individual, and ECE teachers' efforts are directed toward helping children and adults achieve their full potential.

## REMEMBER THIS

1.   Prosocial skills are valued, modeled, and acknowledged in a classroom that emphasizes prosocial behavior.

2.   Through their sensitivity, cultural awareness, and cross-cultural competence, ECE educators can make classroom experiences meaningful for children from different cultures and their families.

3.  Various methods and strategies can be used to promote children's prosocial behaviors in and out of the classroom.

# REFERENCES

Bowlby, J. (1988). Developmental psychiatry comes of age. *American Journal of Psychiatry, 145*(1), 1–10.

Bredekamp, S., & Copple, C. (Eds.). (1997). *Developmentally appropriate practice in early childhood programs* (Rev. ed.). Washington, DC: National Association for the Education of Young Children.

Bredekamp, S., & Rosegrant, T. (Eds.). (1992). *Reaching potentials: Appropriate curriculum and assessment for young children* (Vol. 1). Washington, DC: National Association for the Education of Young Children.

Cook, R., Tessier, A., & Klein, M.D. (1992). *Adapting early childhood curricula for children with special needs.* New York: Macmillan.

Feeney, S., & Kipnis, K. (1992). *Code of ethical conduct and statement of commitment.* Washington, DC: National Association for the Education of Young Children.

Hay, D.F. (1994). Prosocial development. *Journal of Child Psychology and Psychiatry, 35*(1), 29–71.

Honig, A.S., & Wittmer, D.S. (1996). Helping children become more prosocial: Ideas for classrooms, families, schools, and communities. *Young Children, 51*(2), 62–70.

Howes, C., Hamilton, C.E., & Matheson, C.C. (1994). Children's relationships with peers: Differential associations with aspects of the teacher–child relationship. *Child Development, 65*, 253–263.

Howes, C., Phillips, D.A., & Whitelock, M. (1992). Thresholds of quality: Implications for the social development of children in center-based child care. *Child Development, 63*(2), 449–460.

Kostelnik, M.J., Stein, L.C., Whiren, A.P., & Soderman, A.K. (1988). *Guiding children's social development.* Cincinnati, OH: South-Western Publishing Co.

Lynch, E.W., & Hanson, M.J. (Eds.). (1998). *Developing cross-cultural competence: A guide for working with children and their families* (2nd ed.). Baltimore: Paul H. Brookes Publishing Co.

Odom, S.L., & Brown, W.H. (1993). Social interaction skills interventions for young children with disabilities in integrated settings. In C.A. Peck, S.L. Odom, & D.D. Bricker (Eds.), *Integrating young children with disabilities into community programs: Ecological perspectives on research and implementation* (pp. 39–64). Baltimore: Paul H. Brookes Publishing Co.

Wittmer, D.S., & Honig, A.S. (1994). Encouraging positive social development in young children. *Young Children, 49*, 4–24.

Wolery, M., & Bredekamp, S. (1994). Designing inclusive environments for young children with special needs. In M. Wolery & J.S. Wilbert (Eds.), *Including children with special needs in early childhood programs: Vol. 6. Research Monograph of the National Association for the Education of Young Children* (pp. 97–118). Washington, DC: National Association for the Education of Young Children.

Wolery, M., & Wilbert, J.S. (Eds.). (1994). *Including children with special needs in early childhood programs: Vol. 6. Research Monograph of the National Association for the Education of Young Children.* Washington, DC: National Association for the Education of Young Children.

# Activities

1.  Observe and note children's prosocial behaviors in an inclusive preschool environment. What actions of the staff promote children's prosocial skills?

2.  Observe a conflict between children, and identify the strategies that the staff use to intervene and resolve the conflict.

3.  During your observations in preschool environments, take notes regarding facilitative interactions between children of differing cultures.

4.  Interview an adult from another culture or an adult or child with a disability as well as the parents of a child without disabilities from the majority culture. Talk to them about their hopes and dreams for their children. How similar were the hopes and dreams for their children of parents from these groups? How important were children's prosocial skills to the realization of their parents' hopes and dreams?

5.  Talk to your family, and learn about your cultural heritage. Were any members of your family from another culture? What was it like for them as newcomers to the United States or as children entering school for the first time?

6.  Observe two or more people interacting. Record as many prosocial behaviors in which they engage as you can.

## chapter 10

# Group Structures

*Peggy M. Elgas and Ellen Lynch*

## CHAPTER ORGANIZER

In this chapter, we explore the following ideas . . .

1. The benefits of small-group time
2. Important classroom management strategies to help manage small-group time
3. The various ways to implement small-group time
4. The teacher's role in structuring and facilitating small-group time
5. General guidelines and specific suggestions to help you maximize small-group time

Small-group activity is one of the defining features of early childhood education (ECE). If one were to observe ECE, early childhood special education (ECSE), and Head Start classrooms, one curriculum strategy likely to be common to all three would be the use of small-group activities. This chapter highlights the benefits of small-group time, presents management strategies that will help teachers be successful, discusses small-group options and the teacher's role in facilitating and structuring small groups, and presents guidelines to help teachers maximize small-group time.

***Reflection:***  As you read the first section of this chapter, think of specific experiences that you have had with small groups of children interacting with each other. What were some of the benefits of small-group activity for the children? Were important lessons learned?

## BENEFITS OF SMALL-GROUP TIME

The benefits of children's social interaction with peers and their learning are well documented (Corsaro, 1985; Malaguzzi, 1993; Piaget, 1926/1971; Vygotsky, 1993). Both Piaget and Vygotsky discussed the importance of children's peer interactions in their learning processes. Piaget suggested that children's interaction with other children provides numerous opportunities for encountering differing viewpoints, which consequently produce cognitive conflict. Through these repeated changes of viewpoints, children begin to accommodate their thinking to fit discrepant information (Tudge & Rogoff, 1987).

Vygotsky (1993) suggested that children's cognitive development results from their collaboration with peers. He, like Piaget (1926/1971), saw value in peer conflict; however, Vygotsky suggested that heightened understanding would result only if the partners in the collaboration resolved their conflicts and moved toward a joint view of whatever was at issue.

Fostering children's social interaction can be accomplished in many ways, such as during free-choice time, when children choose play partners and form friendships and social groups. Social interaction can also be promoted by providing children with regular opportunities to work collaboratively. Although preschool-age children need a great deal of time to engage in free-choice activities and individual activities, small-group work is an important part of these children's learning process.

Dewey (1900) was one of the first U.S. educators to describe the classroom as a microcosm of the larger society. He suggested that educators facilitate children's individual development as well as interdependence and develop a classroom based on those goals (i.e., by fostering cooperation and collaboration). Therefore, various opportunities for children to work together were integrated into the ECE curriculum shortly after the turn of the 20th century.

In her study of a Japanese preschool, Kotloff (1993) suggested that cooperative small-group experiences can help develop children's abilities to resolve conflicts and make decisions with peers as they provide repeated opportunities for negotiating and problem solving. Gandini (1993), Malaguzzi (1993), and Rinaldi (1993), all representatives of the Reggio Emilia approach to ECE, supported that idea. Reggio Emilia educators have been instrumental in bringing small-group work to the forefront of ECE in the 1990s. They have articulated the benefits of small-group work as an integral part of their curriculum and philosophy.

Children first need to establish trusting relationships before becoming members of a group.

One of the main philosophical bases of the Reggio Emilia program is the belief that education is based on social relationships (Malaguzzi, 1993). In Reggio Emilia programs, social interaction is viewed as a fundamental experience for children, and the small-group classroom format is viewed as the most desirable venue for allowing the maximum amount of communication (Malaguzzi, 1993; Rinaldi, 1993). Reggio Emilia educators see the group work as a necessity, which is rooted in their belief that children develop a positive sense of self and acquire their identities in the context of their group, not in isolation from other people (New, 1993). Through social communication with their peers and adults in the Reggio Emilia classroom, children gain recognition, which reinforces and strengthens their sense of identity. The small-group format facilitates communication and provides the opportunity for fruitful interactions (Rinaldi, 1993). Children negotiate and problem-solve as they try to describe their ideas to others as well as clarify and reformulate their initial hypotheses. Through this type of exchange, children can move to a higher level of understanding that they could not achieve on their own (Rankin, 1993). In addition, Kohlberg and Lickona (1978) described the emotional benefits of small-group work for children. They suggested that children feel a sense of connection and positive self-worth as a member of the small group. Through group work, children develop a sense of responsibility for the welfare of the group and develop empathy toward others as they identify with each other.

Selman and Schultz (1990) found that when power and autonomy issues were resolved, children's social interactions moved into what they described as a shared connection between individuals. Intimacy occurred only after a common ground had been established. Shared connections that are based on emotions and that are truly interpersonal were found to be most likely to involve extended interaction times.

Cannella (1993) suggested structuring the classroom environment to support children's social interactions. The suggestions included helping children feel socially and intellectually comfortable in expressing ideas and opinions, even if their ideas are different from others', and creating situations in which children can explore freely while interacting with adults and their peers.

Stafford and Green (1996) suggested that cooperative learning activities are a necessary component of successful integrated preschool classrooms. They found that planned, cooperative activities such as parachute play and balloon and ball tossing helped children to establish rapport with and support for each other. Children spontaneously offered assistance while participating in these activities. To extend these social behaviors, during free-choice time teachers encouraged and recognized children's accomplishments as well as their attempts to play together. Teachers also helped children recognize their shared interests and facilitated their interactive play.

Small-group work can provide numerous benefits to children. Certainly, social interaction is an important part of learning and development and may be more significant in inclusive ECE environments. Children in inclusive environments have the opportunity to develop prosocial feelings toward each other and can learn to cooperate with each other (Stafford & Green, 1996). However, children with disabilities may not be as competent at building relationships and sustaining interactions, for various reasons (e.g., language delays; hearing impairments; impulsive, aggressive behaviors). Vygotsky suggested that "underdevelopment springs from the isolation of the abnormal child from his collective. . . . Any given [impairment] in a child produces a series of characteristics which impede the normal development of collective relations, cooperation and interaction with others" (1993, p. 83). Berk and Winsler (1995) further contributed to this idea by discussing specific disabilities and their effects on children's success or lack thereof in the classroom. As an example, they suggested that children with attention-deficit/hyperactivity disorder may exhibit maladaptive interaction patterns and need mediation from adults to be productive, interactive members of the classroom.

Elgas and Barber-Peltier (in press) also found that the small-group format was helpful for children with disabilities, especially one of the children with a language delay in their study. Because of the child's language delay and his inability to have his needs met by making verbal requests, this child (referred to here as Jimmy) often resorted to physical means of expressing his needs. Because of his behavior, other children often rejected him and extended to him fewer opportunities to play and engage in social interaction. Regular meetings provided Jimmy with opportunities to interact, negotiate, and problem-solve with the support of the teacher, who could interpret Jimmy's ideas for the other children. Much to the initial surprise of the other group members, Jimmy's ideas were often the most creative and consequently were well received by the group. Prior to this experience, the children in the classroom had not often had positive experiences with Jimmy.

---

*The following two examples describe Jimmy's interactions in the classroom:*

It is free-choice time, and several children are building in the block area. Jimmy is working on a small, enclosed structure. Michael and Corry are building tall structures side by side. Jimmy looks around for more of the small, rectangular blocks. He sees that Michael has a pile sitting next to him. Jimmy runs over to Michael, points to the blocks, and says something like, "Have some." Michael looks at him confusedly and does not say anything. Jimmy asks Michael again, using the same phrase, which is again difficult for Michael to understand. Michael just looks at Jimmy, puzzled. Jimmy stamps his feet and grabs a handful of blocks. As he does, Michael tries to grab them out of Jimmy's hands, screaming, "Hey! Those are mine!" Jimmy drops some of the blocks as he pushes Michael to the ground.

During one of the group times, the children become interested in building a large car. They pursue this interest for many weeks, and, to encourage the children's planning process, a day is spent exploring the teacher's car in the parking lot outside the school. When they return to the classroom, the children share with the group what they observed and how they would like to add to the car that they are constructing. Many of the children say that they would like to add mirrors and different windows. Jimmy, however, remembers that the teacher's car was a hatchback model. He says he has an idea. The teacher interprets Jimmy's message so that all of the children can understand and helps gather the materials that Jimmy says they need. Jimmy demonstrates how the class can make a hatchback with some cardboard and string to open the hatchback door. The children excitedly help Jimmy implement his idea.

---

The small-group times also provided a physical area with boundaries within which children were motivated to resolve disputes rather than walking away to play individually or with someone else (Elgas & Barber-Peltier, in press). As the children met on a regular basis, teachers noted several changes in their behavior. They began to know each other as individuals, learned some of the benefits of working with someone else, and began to create a sense of belonging and identity as a group. As the children contributed unique ideas, they began to appreciate each other. Most important, through repeated, facilitated interactions, the children developed a sense of mutual trust. Through teacher facilitation, the children were able to communicate successfully, and through problem solving all children were able to have their needs met, regardless of whether they had disabilities. Small-group times evolved into a positive experience for everyone in the classroom.

**Reflection:** As you read the next section, think about classrooms that you have been in as either a student or a teacher. Think about a challenging experience and a cooperative experience. Are there strategies discussed in the next section that might have contributed to the challenging behavior or to the cooperation that you witnessed?

## Classroom Management Strategies

Before discussing guidelines for implementing small-group times, a few classroom management strategies need to be presented. In the study by Elgas and Barber-Peltier (in press), when regularly scheduled group times began, a great deal of time was spent on problem solving as children learned to work together. As in any other social environment with young children, some challenging situations may arise that necessitate problem solving.

---

*Look at the following example, and note how the teacher facilitates problem solving:*

During a group time, two children may have difficulty sitting next to each other. Another difficulty may be that the carpet square on which a child is seated may not be of the specific color on which she wanted to sit; further complicating the situation, someone may already be sitting on the one blue carpet square that is her favorite. Problem solving in this type of situation supports and is consistent with the overall classroom management goals of children's autonomy and independence. Helping the children arrive at a mutually agreed-on decision is the ultimate goal, rather than having the teacher tell the children what to do, in such a situation. The teacher in the carpet square dilemma, for example, begins by stating the problem so that both children understand the nature of the conflict: "It seems that both of you want the blue carpet square, but we only have one. What can we do to solve this problem?" The teacher would then have the children generate solutions. Depending on the age and experience levels of the children, the teacher either may have to suggest ideas or may need only to facilitate the discussion. After the children involved agree on one idea, they test the solution by implementing it. The teacher helps the children assess the idea they have implemented, and, if both children believe that it is a successful one, the teacher can comment on their ability to solve the problem: "I see you have both worked out a solution that you like for sharing the blue carpet square." If the children do not believe that their idea is successful, then the teacher helps them generate additional solutions. In this particular case, the suggestion might be that the children will take turns sitting on the blue carpet square: One of them will sit on the carpet square today, and tomorrow the other will have a turn. As a reminder and to promote the children's literacy, the teacher has them write a note with a place where their names can be checked off when they take their respective turns. While the teacher is helping to facilitate this process, it is important that the other children in the class are kept actively involved. This can be accomplished, for example, by the teacher's making available a variety of books to be read before small-group times officially begin and if children finish their small-group tasks early or an unexpected

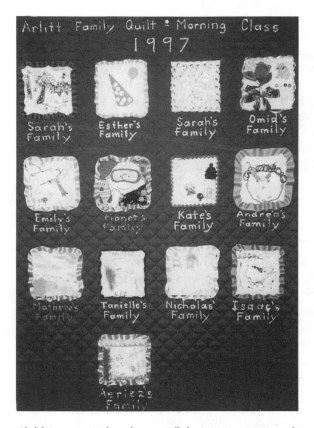

Children are ready to begin collaborative projects such as this quilt design after numerous opportunities to work alone and together. Each family's square became a part of a larger quilt that included all of the families in the Arlitt Center. Unity and community in the classroom can also enhance the entire child development center.

event occurs, such as the carpet square dispute. Children can also begin working on another activity, or, if appropriate, they too may participate in the problem-solving discussion.

Another important factor to consider is children's understanding of explicit expectations for their behavior in the classroom. Generally, in all classroom situations, explicit expectations help make children aware of what is appropriate behavior. In the case of small-group time, explicit behavioral expectations help facilitate children's understanding of what it means to be a small-group member. Facilitating children's understanding of the expectations in each classroom situation helps them know what they *can* do as opposed to their being told only what they cannot do. It is especially important in small-group situations because expectations for children's behavior are different in small-group times than in any other curricular area. For example, children have to share space with other children. They are expected to stay in the designated small-group space and work with the materials rather than playing for awhile and then moving to another area as they do during free-choice time. When a problem arises, walking away is not an option. In terms of interactions, children wait their turn for talking with the teacher. Because of these behavior requirements, it is especially important that the teacher provide children with the information necessary for their successful participation.

---

*Explicit expectations can be transmitted through discussion and numerous reminders, as illustrated by the following example:*

"Today we have water and different sizes of tubes. Let's see what we can find out about these. We will be working in this space instead of on our carpet squares, so, if the floor gets wet, we can clean it up easily. Remember, if you finish with your discovery before everyone else, you can help a friend, read one of the books, or draw with one of the markers. Those are your choices. We will wait for everyone to finish so that we can clean up and go to snacktime."

---

Another important management strategy that also applies here is providing choices so that children are empowered and involved in the decision-making process. Although some rules are nonnegotiable, such as those involving safety issues and cleanup, choices can be provided in all other situations. The preceding vignette illustrates this point in that cleanup and remaining with the group were expected behaviors; however, children who finished early were provided with options from which they could choose. Likewise, on a particular day, the teacher might select the materials to be used in small-group time; but there might be a wide variety of materials available and possible outcomes so that children would still have choices within the teacher-planned activity. In addition, small-group activities can and do move in new directions as children make choices, provide input, make discoveries, and generate ideas. Besides allowing children to feel empowered, the opportunity to make choices gives children a feeling of ownership of the classroom and curriculum. Facilitating children's feelings of ownership of the classroom and curriculum are especially important in small-group time, when the goal is to build a sense of community and feel connected to each other.

**Reflection:**   As you read the next section, think of an exemplary teacher and try to visualize how he or she implemented small-group time. Describe which of the strategies described in the next section that teacher implemented. Did that teacher do anything that is not described in the next section?

## Implementing Small-Group Time

There are different ways of incorporating small-group time into the curriculum. Reggio Emilia schools provide continuous opportunities for small-group work, and the children themselves select small-group projects in those programs. Another way of incorporating small-group times is to schedule a regular daily time when the same group members will meet in the same place. This tactic may be helpful for children who have never experienced group work and need to develop a sense of trust in others. The following are some important aspects of instituting this curriculum component:

- Be explicit, not directive, about expectations for the children's behavior and what it means to be a group member. For example, talk with the children about the idea that they are part of a group and that the group gathers at the same time daily, and identify who the regular members of the group are. Comment on children's work, and refer them to each other for ideas and problem solving.
- Facilitate children's problem solving individually and with other children. For example, the teacher might say, "Dave had the idea to use wood pieces for his building, but he is having a hard time. Does anyone have any ideas that will help him?" Alternatively, the teacher might say, "You can ask Kisha how she got her pieces of paper to stick together."
- Develop the role of co-explorer. Demonstrate interest in and curiosity about the materials and the children's ideas. For example, the teacher might say, "I wonder what will happen if we add blue food coloring to the red food coloring."
- Facilitate respect for individual children's work and their unique contributions. For example, the teacher might say, "Jesse had the idea to add water, and your mixing idea was different; but you both solved your problems."

Small-group time should reflect developmentally appropriate practice (DAP) (Bredekamp, 1987) as well as be consistent with and support overall curriculum goals, which should include

- Active learning through exploration and experimentation
- Divergent thinking and problem solving creative work
- Autonomous work
- Conversation

In addition, small-group time should promote children's social interaction with other children and with adults. To help facilitate these interactions, topics chosen should be related to children's experiences and interests (Katz & Chard, 1993). Children should be included as active members of the group by being encouraged to contribute ideas, questions, and activities. In addition to the general goals just described, specific goals to remember when planning include the following:

- Children's experience of working in a group
- The teacher's establishing ground rules for the children's group work
- Children's opportunities to make unique contributions to the group
- Children's becoming members of and feeling that they have ownership of the group
- Children's opportunities to cooperate and collaborate with others

To accomplish the preceding goals, systematic planning for small-group time is necessary. Because many children first need time to establish trusting relationships and become members of a group, starting off a group with a collaborative project may be problematic. A more appropriate place to start is having each child work side by side with identical materials. This type of activity minimizes concerns that may arise over children's having to share physical space and materials. During this first phase of group work, teachers can help make explicit the ideas of small-group time (e.g., the regular meeting place with the same members), which will promote the children's awareness of each other and help them understand that small-group time has a predictable structure. In addition, teachers can state their expectations regarding children's participation, such as that children will work together with materials and share their ideas with each other (Williams & Kantor, in press).

As children become accustomed to meeting and sharing ideas with each other and begin to form an identity, the group can progress to incorporating collaborative projects in small-group time. These projects can encompass various curriculum areas (e.g., art, by working on multimedia murals; science, by engaging in a small water table experiment in which children explore and experiment together). During these collaborative projects, the teacher continues to facilitate children's cooperation and collaboration while referring children to each other, commenting on individual and group work, and promoting group problem solving.

Some specific ideas for projects on which children can work individually and collaboratively are described in the list that follows. This list presents just a small sample of what can be done; most activities introduced into the classroom can also be made appropriate for small-group work. Working with children's ideas is an important part of small-group time. As children become more comfortable in the small-group environment, they will provide interesting ideas.

*Individual side-by-side work with identical materials*
- Individual art projects, such as painting, drawing, or weaving with a variety of materials
- Manipulative explorations, such as constructing a small building with Bristle Blocks or stringing various materials together
- Literacy activities, such as writing in blank books or keeping personal journals
- Science activities, such as dissections of apples or of small pumpkins
- Math activities, such as geoboards and patterning with small blocks

Here children work collaboratively on a science project. The children explore and work together as they make discoveries.

*Collaborative work*

- Art activities, such as creating murals or sculptures
- Manipulative activities, such as working on wire sculptures or building with blocks
- Literacy activities, such as making books or stories about a shared experience of the children made up of photographs of an event and children's dictation of the story
- Science activities, such as cooking or water experiments with tubes and funnels
- Math activities, such as graphs and charts representing children's interests and ideas (e.g., favorite foods)

## CONCLUSIONS

The benefits of small-group time experiences for all children have been well documented in the literature. Adding this curricular experience may further enhance all children's social participation in the classroom. This enhancement of children's participation may be especially true for those children who have difficulty in communicating with others or developing and maintaining social interactions and relationships. The format of small-group time provides unique opportunities for children and adults to interact and develop trusting relationships. Moreover, the small-group environment provides an arena in which children representing a variety of learning abilities are able to be successful and demonstrate competence.

# REMEMBER THIS

1. Preschool-age children can benefit from both individual, spontaneous work and small-group work because each provides different but necessary experiences.

2. Small-group time provides children with opportunities to work collaboratively with their peers as trusting relationships are developed.

3. The teacher's role in small-group time is that of facilitator and co-explorer as the teacher helps children question, explore, experiment, and reflect during active learning experiences with their peers.

## REFERENCES

Berk, L., & Winsler, A. (1995). *Scaffolding children's learning: Vygotsky and early childhood education.* Washington, DC: National Association for the Education of Young Children.

Bredekamp, S. (Ed.). (1987). *Developmentally appropriate practice in early childhood programs serving children from birth through age 8.* Washington, DC: National Association for the Education of Young Children.

Cannella, G. (1993). Learning through social interaction: Shared cognitive experience, negotiation, strategies, and joint conception for young children. *Early Childhood Research Quarterly, 8,* 427–444.

Corsaro, W. (1985). *Friendship and the peer culture.* Greenwich, CT: Ablex Publishing Corp.

Dewey, J. (1900). *The school and society.* Chicago: University of Chicago Press.

Elgas, P., & Barber-Peltier, M. (in press). Building a sense of community and self-worth through small-group work. *Young Children.*

Gandini, L. (1993). Fundamentals of the Reggio Emilia approach to early childhood education. *Young Children, 49*(1), 4–8.

Katz, L., & Chard, S. (1993). *Engaging children's minds: The project approach.* Greenwich, CT: Ablex Publishing Corp.

Kohlberg, L., & Lickona, T. (1978). Moral discussion and the class meeting. In R. DeVries & L. Kohlberg (Eds.), *Constructivist and early education: Overview and comparison with other programs* (pp. 142–181). Washington, DC: National Association for the Education of Young Children.

Kotloff, L.J. (1993). Fostering cooperative group spirit and individuality: Examples from a Japanese preschool. *Young Children, 48*(3), 17–23.

Malaguzzi, L. (1993). An education based on relationships. *Young Children, 49*(1), 9–12.

New, R. (1993). Cultural variations on developmentally appropriate practice: Challenges to theory and practice. In C. Edwards, L. Gandini, & G. Forman (Eds.), *The hundred languages of children* (pp. 215–231). Greenwich, CT: Ablex Publishing Corp.

Piaget, J. (1971). *The language and thought of the child.* New York: World Publishing. (Original work published 1926)

Rankin, B. (1993). Curriculum development in Reggio Emilia: A long-term curriculum project about dinosaurs. In C. Edwards, L. Gandini, & G. Forman (Eds.), *The hundred languages of children* (pp. 189–211). Greenwich, CT: Ablex Publishing Corp.

Rinaldi, C. (1993). The emergent curriculum and social constructivism. In C. Edwards, L. Gandini, & G. Forman (Eds.), *The hundred languages of children* (pp. 101–111). Greenwich, CT: Ablex Publishing Corp.

Selman, R.L., & Schultz, L.H. (1990). *Making a friend in youth.* Chicago: University of Chicago Press.

Stafford, S., & Green, V. (1996). Preschool integration: Strategies for teachers. *Childhood Education, 72*(4), 214–218.

Tudge, J.R.H., & Rogoff, B. (1987). Peer influences in human development: Piagetian and Vygotskian perspectives. In M.H. Bernstein & J.S. Bruner (Eds.), *Interaction in human development* (pp. 17–40). Mahwah, NJ: Lawrence Erlbaum Associates.

Vygotsky, L.S. (1993). In R.W. Reiber & A.S. Carton (Eds.) & J.E. Knox & C.B. Stevens (Trans.), *The collected works of L.S. Vygotsky: Vol. 2. The fundamentals of defectology.* New York: Plenum.

Williams, D., & Kantor, R. (in press). Learning to how to do group. In R. Kantor & D. Fernie (Eds.), *The early childhood classroom through an ethnographic lens.* Cresskill, NJ: Hampton Press.

# Activities

1. Observe a small-group time and free-choice time in a preschool classroom. Describe how they are different experiences for the children. (For example, What are the goals? What are the children doing?)

2. Compare and contrast the teacher's role in a small-group environment and a free-choice time.

3. List and describe three specific activities from three different curricular areas that you might introduce as the teacher of a small-group time for preschool-age children.

## chapter 11

# Informal and Formal Assessment

*M.J. LaMontagne and Gwen Wheeler Russell*

## CHAPTER ORGANIZER

In this chapter, we explore the following ideas . . .

1.  In early childhood education programs, the purpose of assessment is to gather information to be used to develop individualized programs for all young children.

2.  The assessment process, although focusing on one child and one family at a time, still requires a collaborative effort among professionals and families to ensure the collection of valid information.

3.  For young children with disabilities, assessment takes on new dimensions in relation to early childhood special education criteria and procedural safeguards.

4.  Transdisciplinary assessment is the preferred practice in early childhood education.

5.  Families remain a central component in the early childhood education assessment process.

6.  Wide variance among instruments requires careful review to determine their appropriateness for use with young children and their families.

7.  Program evaluation is an important part of early childhood evaluation and as-
    sessment procedures but is the least likely evaluation to be implemented consis-
    tently in early childhood education programs.

Early childhood education (ECE) has grown dramatically in size and scope since
the late 1980s. Early childhood program enrollment has evolved from homogenous
populations to heterogeneous groups of young children. The diversity and developmental ranges of these young children include gifted children, children with
developmental delays, children at risk for learning problems, children for whom
English is a second language, and children from many different cultural backgrounds. The complexity of implementing developmentally appropriate practice
(DAP) for such diverse groups of children requires the accumulation of information regarding children's current developmental status and the children's families'
priorities, concerns, and resources for supporting the development of their children. In order to accomplish the immense challenge of meeting the needs of all
young children in an ECE program, program staff must have the knowledge and
skills to design and implement valid evaluation and assessment policies, procedures, and instruments.

---

*Look at the following example of a team meeting to address a child's special cir-
cumstances:*

Kiesha and her family have recently arrived in the United States from South Africa.
At 4 years of age, she is the oldest of three siblings and the first in her family to attend
an ECE program. Her parents report that English is the language spoken at their
home, but they are worried because Kiesha seems to be very fearful of her new home
and the preschool program. At a parent–teacher conference, Kiesha's parents and
teachers discuss how to fit the ECE program to meet Kiesha's unique needs.

---

In the preceding example, the teachers and parents as a team explore the types
of information (e.g., child's skill levels, family's priorities, child's personality characteristics and learning styles) that will be needed in order to design a developmentally and individually appropriate program for Kiesha. Once this information
is identified, the team can select the most appropriate method (e.g., standardized
tests, observations, family interviews, informal assessment inventories) to use with
this child. This chapter presents relevant legislation, implementing theory in practice, the purposes of evaluation and the assessment of approaches to evaluation and
assessment, and assessment instruments for program evaluation.

**Reflection:**   Throughout this book, references have been made to the influence of
legislation on early childhood special education (ECSE). As you read the next section, think about why legislation has played such a prominent role in ECSE but not
in ECE.

## LEGISLATION

For young children with disabilities, evaluation and assessment are inherent aspects of their individualized family service plans (IFSPs) and individualized education programs (IEPs). From the initial federal mandate regarding the education of children with disabilities, the Education for All Handicapped Children Act of 1975 (PL 94-142), to its amendment, the Education of the Handicapped Act Amendments of 1986 (PL 99-457), services for young children with disabilities and their families have begun with an evaluation of the child's abilities and the family's concerns, priorities, and resources. The Individuals with Disabilities Education Act (IDEA) of 1990 (PL 101-476) and the Individuals with Disabilities Education Act (IDEA) Amendments of 1991 (PL 102-119) require that education agencies identify young children who may have disabilities. ECE programs have the responsibility of not only identifying young children who may have developmental delays but also identifying discrepancies or delays in skill development of all children so that learning opportunities are created to support all children's developmental growth.

IDEA and the IDEA Amendments outline specific procedural safeguards that apply to the evaluation and assessment of young children with disabilities and their families. The purposes of these safeguards are to protect children and families from the negative effects of misidentification of children as having or not having disabilities and to provide a framework for the assessment process. Participation in evaluations that significantly affect their children's educational futures is a stressful event for families. It is critical that evaluation accuracy be ensured and that children in need of educational services be matched with the services and supports for which they are eligible. IDEA specifically states that evaluations must be multifactored and administered by a multidisciplinary team. The intent of these procedures is to ensure that all developmental domains are assessed and that the information is gathered by more than a single professional. In addition, all evaluations and assessments must be culturally sensitive, unbiased, and administered in the child's native language. Due process procedures are designed to provide families and professionals with a written guide to negotiating disagreements over evaluation or assessment results. Included in IDEA are precise time frames for referral, evaluation, eligibility, and placement. These time lines support children's and families' timely access to services for which they qualify.

Section 504 of the Rehabilitation Act of 1973 (PL 93-112) is another piece of federal legislation that supports educational services for children with disabilities. Section 504 prohibits discrimination against students with disabilities and is increasingly being applied to educational environments by the U.S. Office of Civil Rights (McLean, 1996). Under this statute, the definition of *handicapped* is broader and more inclusive than the eligibility requirements set forth in IDEA. Section 504 defines someone who is *handicapped* as anyone having any mental or physical impairment that significantly affects one or more of the major life areas, including learning. If a child is eligible for a Section 504 education plan, then the school district is responsible for ensuring that the necessary accommodations or services in the general education environment are provided. With regard to children in kindergarten and Grades 1–12, the provisions of Section 504 are easily followed. For early childhood programs, however, the application of the Section 504 provisions is more nebulous (McLean, 1996). Until public preschool education exists, it is difficult to establish discrimination against young children with disabilities in general education environments. Therefore, owing to the financial costs, schools and education agencies are less inclined to identify young children as being eligible for a Section 504 plan (e.g., children with attention-deficit/hyperactivity disorder, children with health or medical concerns) and provide the additional services and accommodations outlined in Section 504.

## IMPLEMENTING THEORY IN EARLY CHILDHOOD EDUCATION PRACTICE

When working with young children and their families, consideration must be given to recommended and preferred practices. A framework can be provided that guides the selection of evaluation and assessment practices to use with young children and their families. The National Association for the Education of Young Children (NAEYC) developed a set of DAP guidelines that included a section on assessment (Bredekamp, 1987). As services for young children with disabilities and their families have expanded, the nature of practices employed in ECSE has been brought to the forefront (Odom, McLean, Johnson, & LaMontagne, 1995). In 1991, the Division for Early Childhood (DEC) of the Council for Exceptional Children (CEC) established its Task Force on Recommended Practices and identified components of recommended practices for young children with disabilities and their families. Among the components of recommended practices was a strand related to evaluation and assessment procedures, techniques, and methods.

Hanson and Carta (1996) pointed out that in the 1990s, a family-centered model has emerged to replace more traditional models of ECE program delivery. This philosophy was formally implemented in the passage of IDEA and is clearly articulated in DAP for young children. In addition to individual states' efforts to develop family-centered services systems in compliance with federal mandates, professional organizations have taken the initiative to develop guidelines for family-centered practice (e.g., Bredekamp, 1987; DEC Task Force on Recommended Practices, 1991). From a family-centered perspective, the family is at the center of the process (Mahoney & Weller, 1980; Turnbull & Turnbull, 1990). A family-centered framework for ECE stresses the dynamic interplay between the family and their sociocultural environment as the vehicle that creates change in both (Patterson & Moore, 1979). That is, the child's learning does not occur in an isolated environment but rather through transactions among the child, the family, and the sociocultural environment (Thurman & Widerstrom, 1985). It has been suggested that the early intervention field will shift its emphasis toward functional independence in natural environments rather than maintaining a focus on demonstrating skills in the average range on an assessment instrument (Craig & Haggart, 1994). It will be the collaboration among families and professionals that supports the exchange of information that will allow ECE to meet these goals.

Embracing a family-centered perspective requires that early childhood professionals select evaluation and assessment instruments that reflect the sociocultural environment of children and their families. An important consideration in this process is the understanding of the social ecology of the family. This approach requires that the early childhood educator examine the family within their sociocultural context from a socioecological perspective (Vincent, Salisbury, Strain, McCormic, & Tessier, 1990). Only through this understanding can the ECE professional successfully match the purpose of the evaluation or assessment and the resulting education programming with the needs, priorities, and preferences of families in the program (Strain, 1987).

---

*Look at one example of how communication between families and educators may provide valuable information about children and their families' cultures:*

The Demarais family had provided Eduardo's early childhood teachers with a great deal of information related to their family preferences, rules, and cultural traditions. With this family input, the early childhood educators provided an education environment that was sensitive to Eduardo's ethnic and religious background and his family's values. The early childhood educators also were able to design learning opportunities for Eduardo that reflected the expectations and needs of the multitude of community environments in which he participated (e.g., home, church, his grandmother's house, the family's business office).

---

The Demarais family had specific ideas related to Eduardo's education. Through family interviews, the early childhood staff were able to gain valuable information that led to an acceptable and appropriate preschool program for Eduardo. Recognizing the unique socioecological context of Eduardo's family, these professionals gathered the necessary data for a developmentally and individually appropriate program for this boy. Working as a collaborative unit, this family and Eduardo's early childhood program staff developed a learning environment that took into account Eduardo's family's sociocultural context in the preschool environment.

Learning information specific to a culture and working with a mediator or guide can help lay the foundation in developing a collaborative relationship with families (Lynch & Hanson, 1998). Such a partnership with the family provides the basis of an assessment that addresses their concerns. Although it is still common for assessments to be protocol driven, there are changes (e.g., family interviews with cultural elders present) that can tailor the assessments to the child's needs and the family's concerns and priorities, which helps to ensure that their cultural perspective is honored (Johnson, McGonigal, & Kaufmann, 1989; Hanson & Lynch, 1992).

Within evaluation and assessment, several theoretical perspectives drive the development of instruments and support the match between evaluation or assessment and program philosophy. Table 1 provides an overview of the theoretical perspectives and examples of instruments representing each perspective. Understanding the underlying theoretical framework of an evaluation or assessment instrument allows early childhood educators to make certain decisions related to the nature of the assessment. Early childhood educators must use test instruments that are congruent with their program's philosophy. If the program is constructivist, using a behavioral instrument does not support programming or intervention activities. A program embracing a developmental approach is likely to be more comfortable using the Battelle Developmental Inventory (BDI) (Newborg, Stock, Wnek, Guidubaldi, & Svinicki, 1988) instead of the Infant Psychological Development Scales (Uzgiris & Hunt, 1975). In addition, the purpose of the assessment guides the selection of evaluation or assessment instruments.

**Reflection:** Think about the last time you played with young children. Are there unique characteristics of young children that make it difficult to assess them? How do children's ages affect assessment of them?

Table 1.  Theoretical perspectives in evaluation and assessment

| Approach | Description | Instruments |
|---|---|---|
| Developmental | Uses maturational theory of child development and normal sequence of development<br>Maturation of the nervous system guides physical, psychological, cognitive, and social development<br>Compares development of individual child to age norms | Gesell Developmental Schedules (Gesell, 1925)<br>Battelle Developmental Inventory (Newborg, Stock, Wnek, Guidubaldi, & Svinicki, 1988)<br>Bayley Scales of Infant Development (Bayley, 1969)<br>Carolina Curriculum for Preschoolers with Special Needs (Johnson-Martin, Attermeier, & Hacker, 1990) |
| Cognitive | Hierarchical stages of cognitive development<br>Piagetian sequence of stages and associated cognitive processes<br>Intelligence viewed as result of social learning experiences<br>Child's interactions with environment influence cognitive maturation | Infant Psychological Development Scales (Uzgiris & Hunt, 1975)<br>Stanford-Binet Intelligence Scale (4th edition) (Thorndike, Hagen, & Sattles, 1985)<br>Kaufman Assessment Battery for Children (Kaufman & Kaufman, 1983) |
| Behavioral | Uses behavioral learning theory<br>All behavior is learned<br>Behavior is reinforced by consequences<br>Emphasis on acquired skills and new skills to be learned<br>Age not significant factor in learning<br>Functional approach<br>Task analysis and applied behavior analysis | BRIGANCE® Diagnostic Inventory of Early Development[a] (Brigance, 1978) |

[a]BRIGANCE® is a registered trademark of Curriculum Associates, Inc.

## PURPOSES OF EVALUATION AND ASSESSMENT

IDEA identifies several core dimensions of the assessment process, including screening, eligibility, and programming (Cohen & Spenciner, 1994). Each of these processes has a specific purpose and outcome; therefore, the processes cannot be mixed and matched without violating the rationale for choosing and the validity of the decision to use a particular assessment process.

The purpose of screening, the first step in the assessment process, is not to identify children for services; rather, screening is a process by which children are measured, usually in large numbers, to find which ones may require further evaluation. Screening assists early childhood staff in identifying those children who need further assessment to determine whether they have developmental delays or are at risk for experiencing developmental delays in the future. The focus of inquiry for screening is "Does this child need to be referred for a diagnostic assessment?" (Cohen & Spenciner, 1994; Wolery, 1989). A potential difficulty with screening instruments is their accuracy in answering the preceding question and thus in meeting the stated purpose of screening. In some instances, assessment may produce a false positive result: Children may fail screening tests and then be referred for eligibility evaluation, but then the eligibility evaluation test results indicate that they do not qualify for ECSE services. In other cases, an assessment may produce a false negative result: Children may pass the screening process but at a later point may be identified as eligible for ECSE services. In either scenario, the screening instrument does not meet its stated purpose, and children and their families pay the price.

---

*Look at the following example of a mother's concerns for her son:*

Houtari's mother was concerned about his development, so she brought him to the neighborhood school where the teachers were testing kids. Even though she was very worried about her son, Houtari's mom knew that he could get help at the preschool program in this elementary school. Houtari and his mom waited for an hour to see the tester, and, while Houtari worked with the tester, his mom sat nervously outside the door. After a half hour, the tester came out with Houtari and said, "He's just fine! Nothing to worry about." Houtari's mom did not know what to say. She knew that Houtari could not do the things other boys his age were doing. Houtari and his mom went home, and she continued to worry.

---

The second step in the assessment process is determination of eligibility. The extent to which a child meets state and federal criteria determines whether that child is eligible for ECSE services and which type of services will be provided (Bailey, 1989). Eligibility criteria vary according to children's ages. Children from birth through age 2 are eligible for early intervention services if they have a developmental delay or an established disability. In those states that recognize at-risk status (see Table 2 for at-risk categories), those infants and toddlers may also be eligible for early intervention services. Preschoolers are eligible for ECSE services if they meet the federal definition of *disability* in IDEA or, in states utilizing developmental delay criteria, the state's criteria for developmental delays. In order to be eligible for ECSE programs under IDEA definitions, preschoolers must be diagnosed as having one of the following conditions:

- Autism
- Deafblindness
- Deafness
- Hearing impairment
- Mental retardation
- Multiple disabilities
- Orthopedic impairment
- Other health impairment
- Serious emotional disturbance
- Specific learning disability
- Speech or language impairment
- Traumatic brain injury
- Visual impairment, including blindness

The third step in the assessment process, programming, involves collecting information from multiple sources to assist the family and the professionals who are going to work with children and children's families. If collaboration is an important part of screening and eligibility steps, it is a critical part of programming assessment. In the third step, parents and professionals form a partnership whose primary purpose is the design, implementation, and evaluation of a developmentally and individually appropriate education plan. As a team, these individuals collect information related to 1) children's developmental status; 2) families' priorities, concerns, and resources; 3) children's personal characteristics (e.g., temperament, interests, motivational attributes, social interaction style); 4) programs' resources and materials; and 5) teaching methods and strategies. Working to-

Table 2.    At-risk categories for infants and toddlers

| Category | Definition | Examples |
|---|---|---|
| Established risk | Medical disorders whose known etiology and pattern of development are associated with developmental delay | Down syndrome<br>Fragile X syndrome |
| Biological risk | History of complications in perinatal, neonatal, or early development that suggests an insult to the central nervous system | Premature infants<br>Small for gestational age infants<br>Prenatal exposure to substance abuse<br>Fetal alcohol syndrome |
| Environmental risk | Child lives in environment that interferes with physical, social, cognitive, language, and emotional development | Poverty<br>Teenage parents<br>Neglectful or abusive environment |

*Source:* Tjossem (1976).

Teachers can use anecdotal recordings to capture children's accomplishments or current levels of understanding.

gether, the team discusses the collection of information and brainstorms possible uses and outcomes of this information and then comes to a consensus with regard to the program plan. It is the comprehensiveness and richness of the information acquired through assessment (e.g., standardized tests, play-based assessments, family interviews, observational data) that directly affects the quality, utilization, and socioecological soundness of the program plan.

## Issues in Early Childhood Assessment

Since the mid-1980s, the view that young children are capable individuals who have competencies that can be demonstrated in perceptual and learning events has been gaining influence (Lamb & Bornstein, 1987; Rosenblith & Sims-Knight, 1985). Early childhood professionals also recognize that the interdependence of developmental systems is a major characteristic of young children that must be addressed if a complete understanding of functioning is to be obtained (Teti & Gibbs, 1990). Campbell (1991) asserted that the primary purpose of assessment is to identify the unique needs of young children with disabilities, with the understanding that in young children these needs constantly change. The multidimensional characteristics of this population necessitate an assessment process that is reflective of these children's ages and their developmental uniqueness.

Young children can be distractible, can tire easily, are often unable to maintain their attention for extended times, and may be afraid of strangers and unfamiliar situations (Peterson, 1988). None of these characteristics can be described as being conducive to the assessment process. In addition, the evaluation process for young children has been expanded to include observations of their level of interest in dyadic exchanges and social behaviors, degree of reactivity to perceptual-cognitive events, states of arousal, habit patterns, temperaments, play behavior, and attentional behavior (Fewell, 1983; Linder, 1993; McLean, 1996). Recommended practices in assessment have evolved from a single event planned for a single child to a multidimensional process including the young child, the child's family, and the coordinated efforts of a transdisciplinary professional team.

**Reflection:**   As you read about teaming models in the next section, think about the ECE programs with which you have had experience. Which teaming model did they use?

## Approaches to Evaluating and Assessing Young Children

Evaluating and assessing young children encompasses many different models and approaches. Whether to select an individual approach or use a combination of approaches is directly related to the purpose of the assessment and the concerns, resources, and priorities of the child's family and the early childhood program. Early childhood educators must remember that, for young children with disabilities, IDEA mandates a multidisciplinary approach that uses family information as a basis for the IFSP and IEP outcomes and goals. For young children without developmental delays, the early childhood educator has a broader range of choice. Regardless of whether a particular child has a disability, the professional should consider the strengths and concerns of each model prior to adopting a specific assessment approach.

### Unidisciplinary Model

The unidisciplinary model is derived from a biological frame of reference referred to as a *medical model* (Foley, 1990). This approach is based on the belief that a single discipline has the skills and knowledge to diagnose and treat individuals with mental health or developmental problems. This particular viewpoint has permeated service delivery for individuals with developmental disabilities since the 1960s and can be seen when a practitioner of one discipline acts as the expert and assumes primary responsibility for the identification and recommended interventions for the young child. Although valid in some of its intentions, the unidisciplinary approach ignores the multidimensional characteristics of young children and the sociocultural context of the children and their families. From the viewpoint used in this model, young children's health and medical problems are often assessed without the added dimensions of their impact on children's social, communicative, and cognitive behaviors within and across socioecological contexts.

*Look at how the following professional's recommendations may be too narrow in dimension:*

It is time for Rita's 36-month checkup with her pediatrician. During her appointment, the nurse administers the Denver Developmental Profile II (Frankenburg et al., 1992) and tells Rita's mom that Rita is behind in her motor skills. The nurse tells Rita's mom to take Rita to the playground and make her climb on the jungle gyms for an hour each day. Rita's mom is instructed to get out crayons and a coloring book at home at night so that Rita can practice coloring.

## Multidisciplinary Model

In the 1940s, a concept of multidisciplinary teaming was developed that was characterized by division of labor by specialization (Ackerly, 1947). Within that framework, professionals from different disciplines coordinated their assessments with minimal exchange of information and interaction (Foley, 1990). In the multidisciplinary model, young children are viewed from multiple dimensions according to professional disciplines. The information gathered is provided to the family in written or oral form by an individual professional. Assessments and interventions are conducted in isolated contexts and usually in environments unfamiliar to young children and their families. Although comprehensive in its information collection efforts, this model does not account for the natural characteristics of young children and thus has the potential to produce questionable results.

*The following example illustrates a variety of assessment conditions and components. Notice the time involved and the possible intricacy of interpretations of the various professionals:*

Lucinda and her family have an appointment at their local school district offices for evaluation of Lucinda's readiness for kindergarten. The appointment starts at 9:00 A.M. with Lucinda working with a teacher. After the meeting with the teacher, Lucinda continues to work for about an hour each with a psychologist, a speech-language pathologist, an occupational therapist, and a school counselor. Each of the five professionals writes an evaluation report summarizing their findings. At a conference with Lucinda's parents, the school counselor reviews with the family the findings contained in each report.

## Interdisciplinary Model

The interdisciplinary model evolved from the multidisciplinary approach described in the preceding section. It moved toward a notion of cooperative cohesion among team members (Hutt, Menninger, & O'Keefe, 1947). In this model of assessment, the infant or toddler with disabilities is assessed individually by team members, and the team members come together to discuss findings and generate recommendations. This model of assessment incorporates the multidimensional nature of young children and professionals. However, like the multidisciplinary approach, it places children in an assessment context that may be unfamiliar and in which task performance is demanded in a limited time frame. Again, the characteristics of young children naturally inhibit them from successfully demonstrating their strengths and abilities.

---

*The following is an example of a complex assessment that involves many professionals and requires that multiple evaluation reports be reviewed:*

A research and education center provides interdisciplinary assessments for the local region. Sini and his family are referred to this center for a complete assessment battery. Throughout the day, Sini and his parents meet individually with a series of professionals (e.g., educational specialist, speech-language pathologist, psychologist, physical therapist, nutritionist, pediatric neurologist). After the assessments, all of the professionals meet to discuss their individual findings and observations. During their meeting, these professionals generate suggestions and recommendations based on the integration of all disciplinary assessment results. Later, each professional generates an evaluation report that reflects the interdisciplinary findings.

---

### Transdisciplinary Model

The transdisciplinary model of teaming has been described as a conscious pooling and sharing of information, knowledge, and skills with the accepted practice of team members' crossing discipline-specific boundaries (United Cerebral Palsy Associations, 1976). This model recognizes the interrelatedness of developmental domains and acknowledges the constant changes that occur during the dynamic period of young childhood (Foley, 1990).

The use of transdisciplinary assessment methods is supported in the literature as one of the most appropriate and effective means of evaluating infants, toddlers, and young children with disabilities (Fewell, 1984, 1991; Katz, 1989; Linder, 1993; McLean & Crais, 1996; Mori & Olive, 1980). Mori and Olive (1980) described the transdisciplinary assessment approach as the collaborative accumulation of extensive information about young children from a variety of disciplines that include medicine, allied and community health, psychology, and education and the careful integration of these data into a comprehensive, holistic profile of children. This model can expand the team's membership to include the families of young children so that families can become active participants in both the assessment process and the intervention plan development, as recommended by IDEA. With a transdisciplinary approach, families become more of a primary player in the process as they are a part of assessment from initial intake to assessment staffing and generation of the IFSP or IEP.

---

*Look at the following example, which demonstrates the primary involvement of families throughout the entire assessment process:*

The teachers in Kamiko's preschool program were concerned with Kamiko's language development. They contacted the program's speech-language pathologist and its occupational therapist (in case Kamiko was having oral-motor problems). One afternoon, Kamiko stayed after school for a transdisciplinary evaluation. While her teacher played and worked with Kamiko, Kamiko's other teacher, the speech-language pathologist, the occupational therapist, and Kamiko's mom watched. The professionals took notes on their observations and protocol sheets while Kamiko's mom made comments and provided information related to Kamiko's communication skills at home and in the community. After the evaluation was finished, the team discussed what they saw and brainstormed ideas for education programming and work to be done at home with Kamiko. From this conference, a single transdisciplinary report was generated.

### *Family-Driven Approach*

One distinct approach to early childhood assessment is the family-driven perspective. According to Section 677(a)(2) of the 1991 amendments to IDEA, a family-directed assessment involves consideration of the "resources, priorities, and concerns of the family and the identification of the supports and services to enhance the family's capacity to meet the developmental needs of their infant or toddler with a disability." IDEA further states that assessments are to be conducted by personnel trained to use appropriate procedures and methods; to be based on information that the family provides in a personal interview; and to incorporate the family's description of their resources, priorities, and concerns related to enhancing the child's development. Part C of the Individuals with Disabilities Education Act (IDEA) Amendments of 1997 (PL 105-17) calls for a family assessment to be used if the family concurs. The law explicitly states that measures are to be family directed in that the family decides whether and to what extent to participate.

The literature on family-centered assessment is consistent with the early childhood perspective, with a focus on the socioecology of the family. Assessment of families should focus on the characteristics of their environment (Bradley, Rock, Caldwell, & Brisby, 1989; Bricker & Littman, 1982; Fewell & Vadasy, 1987; Krauss & Jacobs, 1990; Sameroff, Seifer, & Zax, 1982). An important characteristic within the family environment is the family's culture. As a component of the assessment approach, Bowe (1995) pointed out that cultural competence in testing is good practice. Such practice requires culture-specific knowledge that may affect the administration and interpretation of tests with children and families. This information can be addressed through a process that accommodates the language and culture of the young child. Another means by which to ensure that the cultural perspective of the family is honored is to use assessments that are tailored to the young child's needs and the family's concerns and priorities (Hanson & Lynch, 1992; Johnson et al., 1989). Incorporating these variables is vital to ECE practice. In addition, Neisworth (1993) stated that multiple perspectives are key in assessing young children and their families. A wide variety of measures should be included, particularly those that incorporate the views of family members (e.g., Bailey & Simeonsson, 1990; Child Development Resources, 1989; Dunst, Cooper, Weeldreyer, Snyder, & Chase, 1988).

## Individual Approach

Appropriate measures for assessing young children and families can include techniques and strategies that focus on individual children or their families. Most often used are tests and measurement instruments that are administered to children individually. These measures provide quantitative information that characterizes a child's developmental skills in a specific domain or in overall scores. Individual observations furnish data related to the number of times a young child uses centers or materials or interacts with peers or adults. For families, these individual measurements identify the number and types of concerns, resources, information, or assistance that they need. Individual surveys gather family members' ratings of programs with regard to goals, services, and satisfaction.

Individual assessments can include information that is more qualitative in nature. Individual semistructured interviews are used to obtain an understanding of families' or educators' perceptions of a specific issue. Semistructured interviews allow the interviewer to request additional information from families or educators or to probe their responses to obtain a more in-depth understanding of the issues. Qualitative information obtained through interviewing gives the ECE educator a greater breadth and richness of information related to the point of interest. Systematic analysis of the responses yield a broader picture of the issue and can identify unexpected but related concerns of families and professionals.

---

*The following example demonstrates how communicating with families by using tools such as a family interview may provide valuable information about the families' strengths and possible needs:*

Susie and her family have been enrolled in the Happy Trails Early Childhood Program for more than a year. During the past few months, Susie has been coming to school without her lunch or her lunch money. Her teachers are concerned not only because of the immediate issue of Susie's forgetfulness but also because they learned several months ago that Susie's parents had divorced and that her father, the source of the family's primary income, had moved out of town. Several family needs surveys had been sent home in the hope of discovering whether Susie's mom needed financial assistance from a local human services agency, but so far none of them had been returned to the school. The preschool teacher was scheduled for a home visit and decided to complete a family interview developed by the ECE program. During the interview, when asked about the family's financial needs, Susie's mom stated that she was getting child support and had no real concerns at that time. The preschool teacher continued the interview process, and, in responding to a question related to time, resources, and support, Susie's mom replied that she just did not have the time to do all the "mom things" that she used to do. Susie's mom said that, for example, she used to be able to make Susie's lunch every day because she knew that Susie did not like the foods served at school and is a picky eater. But being a single mom of four kids just wiped out the time Susie's mom needed to make her kids' lunches in the morning, so she was giving Susie lunch money and making her favorite meals at breakfast and dinnertime to ensure that Susie had plenty to eat.

---

In the preceding vignette, the preschool teacher acquired vital information through an unrelated interview question rather than through the target question dealing with financial needs. The teacher also gained insight about why lunch was not an important meal for Susie; that is, she learned that Susie was having her nutritional needs met at breakfast and dinner. Interviewing allows the exploration of issues without depending on whether the right question is asked. Although interviews are an important source of information, they can become biased if systematic procedures are not used for ensuring the validity of recording responses, unbiased interviewing techniques, and integrity of data analysis and interpretation. (For more in-depth information related to interviewing techniques, response recording, and analysis, see Johnson & LaMontagne, 1994.)

Portfolio assessment is another technique for collecting individual information related to children's skills growth and development. Portfolio assessment is a simple technique in which the ECE educator collects products created by young children through work and play during the program year (Arter & Spandel, 1991; Meyer, Schuman, & Angello, 1990). These permanent products can be artworks, pictures, papers, tape-recorded stories, videotaped activities, or written work completed by the child. Portfolio collections should be systematically filed, with dates of creation recorded on the work. Notebooks may be used to organize young children's work in a sequence that shows the developmental progression of children's skills.

### Group Approach

In ECE programs, observations of children as a group are the primary means of assessment. The early childhood educator may record the number of children who use centers or materials to determine whether it is time to create a new center or introduce new materials into the classroom. Group observations may be used to determine the percentage of the class that is engaged in an activity related to a specific curriculum theme. Standardized group assessments are not appropriate for young children because of the uniqueness of this developmental time and the challenges that young children bring to the assessment context.

For families and professionals, a variation of the interview process is appropriate for gathering insight and information related to specific interests of groups of children. Focus group interviews are designed to elicit information from individuals in a group environment (e.g., parents' group, program advisory board, community professionals, education program staff) so that one individual's response can build and elaborate on a response provided by another participant. With the focus group technique, the richness of the information is increased substantially because some participants articulate points, concerns, and issues on

Observation is an assessment method that allows social interactions and current levels of understanding without being intrusive or disrupting children's interactions throughout the day.

which others find they have a perspective to share once the issues are raised but otherwise might not have. The challenge for early childhood educators is developing their skills and abilities in recording themes from the participants' dialogues and facilitating the process without biasing responses or creating an atmosphere that does not support honest expression of opinions (For complete guidelines and precautions with regard to conducting focus group interviews, see Johnson & LaMontagne, 1994.)

## Assessment Instruments

There are a variety of assessment instruments that can be used with young children and their families. The wide variance among instruments requires that the ECE educator review each test and determine its appropriateness for use within his or her early childhood program. When reviewing assessment instruments, the early childhood educator will find important information in the manual related to test item development, descriptions of sample populations on which the instrument was validated, and procedures and adaptations for administration with special populations. This information contributes to the early childhood educator's degree of confidence that the assessment tool will accurately and comprehensively gather the information needed to design and implement an IEP.

### Standardized Instruments

Standardization in testing implies that there are uniform procedures for administering and scoring a test (Anastasi, 1988). In order to compare test scores of different people, testing conditions must be the same and conditions must be controlled. Attention to detailed directions is a major component in the standardization of a new test.

Another important piece of the standardization process is the establishment of norms. In order to standardize a test, the test is administered to a large, representative sample of the type of people for whom it is designed. This representative group serves to establish the norms for the test, and the individual's test performance is compared with the age-appropriate norm sample (Anastasi, 1988). The National Association for the Education of Young Children (NAEYC) (1988) recognized that standardized tests may have a role in assessing the needs of young children. If the standardized tests are objective, accurate, and appropriate, they may provide early childhood teachers with information to help them plan instruction. The most important qualifier for the use of standardized tests is that the test must be useful in helping to improve services and outcomes for young children and their families. Some commonly used standardized tests are the BRIGANCE® Diagnostic Inventory of Basic Skills (Brigance, 1978) and the Kaufman Test of Educational Achievement (Kaufman & Kaufman, 1985).

### Criterion-Referenced Instruments

Measuring children's performance against some prespecified criteria is the basis of criterion-referenced instruments. Criterion-based assessment evaluates children's performance in relation to a stated standard (Bagnato, Neisworth, & Munson, 1989). The focus is on which specific skills children have mastered rather than group or norm comparisons (Benner, 1992). The standards that are chosen should be clear enough to allow agreement among observers. The criteria chosen should not be so cumbersome and time-consuming that they will not be used in a home or classroom environment.

Criterion-referenced tests can be informal instruments such as teacher-created checklists. If formal, commercially available tests are chosen, teachers should exercise caution. The instrument used must reflect children's experiences to ensure appropriate IEP planning. Again, consideration of children's socioecological contexts is an important variable in gaining valid results.

### Developmental Instruments

The developmental approach to assessing children emphasizes the process of growth and development. Children progress through typical hierarchical stages with some individual variations in the amount of time spent at certain stages (Cohen & Spenciner, 1994). Gesell (1925), an early development theorist, identified the ages at which children typically reach developmental milestones based on his extensive observations of young children. Many of these developmental milestones are reflected in instruments used today.

Teachers must be sure to examine the developmental areas covered when selecting an evaluation instrument. The instrument should address the domains specified by the federal definition of *developmental delay*: cognitive development, fine and gross motor physical development, communication development, social and emotional development, and adaptive development. Coverage of these areas ensures a match between the assessment and the curriculum-planning decisions to be made. Obtaining information about a child and the child's family from the family and professionals prior to use of a developmental instrument helps teachers make the best choice of assessment instruments. Developmental instruments can be standardized, such as the Neonatal Behavioral Assessment Scales (Brazelton, 1973), the Bayley Scales of Infant Development (Bayley, 1969), and the BDI. The Assessment, Evaluation, and Programming System (AEPS) (Bricker, 1993) is a developmental test that includes items sequenced and grouped by domain and skill.

### Observation Techniques

*Observation* is defined in the *American Heritage Dictionary* as "to perceive, notice; to watch attentively; to make a systematic or scientific observation of" (1983, p. 474). Bentzen (1993) expanded the concept of observation by suggesting that the organization of concepts defines the processing of facts, which is in turn guided by developmental and behavioral theories and personal viewpoints. Both of these definitions indicate that observation should be perceived as more than the act of seeing. In the context of the present discussion, *observation* is the rigorous act of examining a specific behavior of interest in the context of daily routines. Observation in ECE is based on procedures that provide a structure for ECE educators to record observed behaviors in an authentic and reliable manner that fosters confidence in the accuracy and validity of the information collected.

Observation has many purposes (Bentzen, 1993). It is an assessment method that allows ECE educators to measure what is often deemed unmeasurable: young children's interests, friendships, interaction patterns, motivational characteristics, and learning styles and approaches. Observation is more appropriate for young children because it does not impose contrived situations and items to which children respond within specific time frames. Observation allows children to do what they naturally do in the course of their days. Observational data can provide initial information regarding young children's developmental progression, or they can be used to monitor children's progress toward learning objectives described in an IEP. Observation is a low-cost, efficient technique for documenting skills acquisition in children with or without disabilities and for identifying next steps in children's developmental sequence to be addressed at the next learning opportunity.

There are several types of observation techniques. *Direct observation* refers to recording occurrences of a specific behavior that has been targeted for observation. The recording system may be a frequency count or a checklist. During direct observation, the early childhood educator records a mark each time the young child performs the specified behavior. Behaviors that have a beginning and an end are most appropriate for this type of observation technique (e.g., number of verbal interactions with peers, how many times a young child plays at the sand table, number of times a young child gets angry and throws an object across the room). Although an easy technique to use with relevant information appropriate for programming, direct observation has several limitations. Because the observer is looking for a specific behavior to occur, information regarding the context in which the behavior occurs is lost. Environmental, interactional, and individual information is not recorded, and it is that vital information that gives meaning to the behavior demonstrated by the young child. Without knowing the context in which a behavior occurred, it becomes difficult for the early childhood educator to decide which behaviors are developmentally and individually appropriate for a particular child and which are not representative of the developmental status of the child.

Another form of observation is referred to as *running observations*. Running observations use a descriptive narrative format to record information during a fixed time period. During this time frame, the observer is challenged with recording as much information as possible about a child's skills or behaviors as they occur. This technique is more time- and staff-intensive than other techniques because it requires an individual's direct attention during the predetermined time frame. The early childhood educator must describe the sequence of events, the child's peer and/or adult interactions, the child's use of materials and the child's environment, and the time frame in which the behavioral components (e.g., multiple behaviors, multiple events) of the narrative occurred. In recording their observations, observers must be careful to record objectively what they observe rather than recording their interpretations of the events that they witness. Running observations are based on the sequence of facts underlying the narrative describing the young child's behaviors. Subjective interpretations can invalidate the running observation and create serious problems when teachers try to use such observational information in developing ECE programs.

The richness of the information collected during running observations may offset the time and labor required in this style of observation. Running observations are useful in gaining a comprehensive understanding of a child's behavior in a natural environment. Running observations provide an insight into a child's interaction patterns with adults or peers that may contribute to the child's performance of a behavior or skill. Running observations also allow for the recording of unexpected events, behaviors, or skills. This observation technique is completely adaptable to all situations, environments, and children.

A less intensive form of narrative observation is anecdotal note taking. By using this technique, early childhood educators may record written observations, comments, or concise notes related to a young child's behaviors, interactions, or skills during the day. Anecdotal notes are written shortly following the observation and are brief and focused. Anecdotal observations include the details relating to the context of the behavior, with as complete a description of what actually occurred as possible. An inherent limitation of anecdotal note taking is its reliance on the memory of the adult observer and his or her accuracy in recording events. However, anecdotal notes may provide a sequential history of events and a child's development over a period of time that creates a comprehensive portrayal of the young child's development. Some early childhood educators use anecdotal note taking to record successes and achievements of young children and include these short notes in their portfolio assessments.

## Play-Based Assessment

Play-based assessment is an approach that has emerged from the arena assessment process developed by the United Cerebral Palsy Associations (UCPA) (1976). In UCPA's assessment process, professionals observe a young child with cerebral palsy interact with a single individual, and, using their observations, they record and document developmental milestones as well as descriptive information related to the process by which the child demonstrates skills and abilities. This transdisciplinary approach transforms the assessment process by incorporating the unique characteristics of children into the assessment procedures and allowing children to lead activities; complete tasks at their own pace; and choose interactions with adults, materials, or their peers. In this approach, young children are able to demonstrate their competencies, and observers can identify young children's needs. An important addition is the involvement of the child's family in the assessment process. Parents may choose to be the play facilitator and interact with their child, or they may choose to be an active team observer and record their child's skills and abilities on developmental protocols or informal developmental checklists. Parents also may choose to be quiet observers, commenting and elaborating on their child's demonstration of abilities or responding to inquiries from other team members participating in the play-based assessment. Play-based assessment is a process wherein a single individual interacts with the young child while professionals and members of the child's family observe the child's performance of skills (Linder, 1993). The observers become active participants as they request the elicitation of specific child behaviors during the play session. Play-based assessment is a systematic method of viewing a young child's skills and abilities through the medium of play (Blasco & LaMontagne, 1996; Lifter, 1996; Linder, 1993; Woodruff, 1980).

Five general components define the play-based assessment process (Blasco & LaMontagne, 1996; Linder, 1993; Woodruff, 1980) (see Table 3). Each of these components may be refined, revised, or altered to meet the unique diversity requirements of the early childhood program. Two of the most valuable traits of play-based assessment are its flexibility and its responsiveness with regard to the unique characteristics of young children and their families. Because play-based assessment is a process rather than a product, it can be molded to fit the temperaments, activity levels, and abilities of children and their families. The process of play-based assessment can be lengthened to include more activities and observation opportunities, or it can be shortened to fit the scheduling needs of families and professionals or young children's degree of engagement or interest.

Table 3.    Play-based assessment components

| Components | Actions |
|---|---|
| Team selection based on child and family characteristics | Identify and assign roles<br>    Facilitator<br>    Play facilitator<br>    Team members (inclusive of parents if they so choose)<br>Define purpose of assessment |
| Information disseminated to team members | Gather information related to child and family background, priorities, resources, and concerns<br>Review previous test results |
| Selection of appropriate assessment materials | Identify written observation format<br>Identify and develop activities to support demonstration of skills by young child |
| Conduct assessment | Structure environment in child- and family-friendly manner<br>Review assessment purpose<br>Review team member roles<br>Play facilitator presents activities to the child and/or allows the child to lead the interactions<br>Facilitator supports family members during the assessment and/or gathers additional information from family<br>Team members make suggestions for additional activities<br>Team members record descriptive information on observation forms and record demonstration of behaviors on developmental checklists |
| Assessment staffing | Include family as team member<br>Review past assessment data<br>Review information gathered during play-based assessment<br>Brainstorm insights and recommendations<br>Develop consensus in relation to IEP goals<br>Generate IEP/assessment report |

*Source:* Blasco and LaMontagne (1996).

    The play-based assessment process allows professionals to view a young child's demonstration of skills and abilities and the integration of these skills across developmental domains. Because play is the work of young children, play-based assessment provides assessment items at which the child can succeed. It is important for the early childhood educator to understand the stages and categories of play that the young child uses in the assessment process. Parten (1932) identified categories of social play, and Belsky and Most (1981) used the manner in which a young child manipulates objects and materials to form categories of play activities. Blasco and LaMontagne (1996) summarized young children's play behaviors, their play-associated activities, and the ages at which to use a simpler format to describe typical behaviors of young children as they progress through the various stages of play (see Table 4).

    As with any assessment approach, play-based assessment has disadvantages and advantages. The limitations of play-based assessment center on time and

Table 4.    Categories of play behavior

| Age | Play behavior | Activities |
|-----|---------------|------------|
| Birth–12 months | Sensorimotor/perceptual | Mouthing, looking, banging, locating, localizing |
| 12–24 months | Sensorimotor/exploratory | Simple manipulation, stacking, imitating simple gestures |
| 24–36 months | Exploration | Simple pretend-play, becomes integrated, substitutes objects with constructive play and dramatics |
| 36–48 months | Familiar fantasy themes | Role-play, planned play activities |
| 48–60 months | Complex themes | Multiple planned sequences, substitutions, simple board games |

scheduling issues for professionals and families. Play-based assessment can be an intensive, time-consuming activity for professionals and families. Arranging an assessment appointment that lasts 1–2 hours and is convenient for several different people is a significant disadvantage for some ECE programs. Creative scheduling and team efficiency help support ECE programs in addressing these issues. Another identified concern with play-based assessment is the observation method of data collection related to children's skills and abilities. Observational data have the potential to be biased if the play-based assessment team member interprets that data prior to recording it. Training in observational techniques is a must for individuals participating in play-based assessment. Skills in accurate recording of observed behavior contribute to the validity of the observations. Triangulation of observational information is another factor in the validation process of play-based assessment. When three or more team members observe the same behavior and record the same skill demonstration, the observation is deemed to have been validated. Triangulation increases confidence in the objectivity of observations during play-based assessment. Early childhood programs may choose to videotape play-based assessments in order to address the issue of subjective observations.

Play-based assessment also has many advantages. The adaptability of play-based assessment for all populations of young children, regardless of cultural diversity or disability, is apparent in its flexibility and responsiveness with regard to the uniqueness of children and their families. The transdisciplinary approach used in play-based assessment provides a format for integration of knowledge and skills across disciplines, which naturally leads to a transdisciplinary IEP and transdisciplinary program implementation. With play as the basis for assessment, information can be gathered without any child or family "flunking" the assessment. The play-based assessment process reduces redundancy in testing by using one play facilitator and team members representing the disciplines that the child's family requests to observe the child's developmental performance.

Use of play-based assessment is gaining momentum in designing individualized education programming outcomes. Several states are beginning to examine the potential use of play-based assessment in relation to ECSE eligibility requirements for infants and toddlers with disabilities. As the research base for this approach continues to grow, programs and agencies will be able to make data-based judgments about its appropriateness for use within their ECE programs.

## Program Evaluation

Often when early childhood practitioners design and implement the evaluation component of their programs, the focus of evaluation efforts is placed on outcomes for children and their families. Unfortunately, a critical element, program evaluation, is often overlooked or placed at the bottom of the priority list. Program evaluation is the means by which early childhood practitioners collect information to make informed judgments and decisions (Cohen & Spenciner, 1994; Johnson & LaMontagne, 1994). These data-based decisions serve to 1) guide the design and implementation of individual children's programs, 2) acquire feedback from consumers (e.g., children, families, program administrators, teachers, related-services professionals, community agency personnel) related to program outcomes, 3) monitor progress toward identified goals and objectives, 4) influence policy and procedures within the program and the community, and 5) provide measures of accountability (Bricker & Littman, 1982; Harrison, 1995; Johnson & LaMontagne, 1994; Wolery & Bailey, 1984).

*The following is a situation in which program design and support is contingent on evaluation of the program's effectiveness:*

A local early childhood program decides to begin providing full inclusion opportunities for young children and their families in the community. To accomplish this task, the local board of education has provided funding for 1 year to support two new classrooms at a community center. To continue to receive money in support of the inclusive environment, the early childhood program must provide the local board of education with information at the end of the school year that documents parents' and teachers' satisfaction with the inclusive classrooms, children's developmental gains, and efficient and effective use of program personnel and fiscal resources. The early childhood program staff work together with community personnel to design a program evaluation plan that addresses the requirements of the board of education and supports the inclusive classrooms as they try to implement developmentally and individually appropriate practices in the community.

An effective evaluation plan must consider information from an input, process, and outcome perspective (Johnson & LaMontagne, 1994). During the input stage, identifying the needs and concerns of the consumers is paramount. Gaining access to this information provides the program or agency with direction in planning their goals and objectives for the upcoming year. At the process stage, the focus shifts to monitoring strategies and activities being used to support the

Play-based assessment is a method of viewing young children's skills and abilities through the medium of play. It is flexible and responsive to the unique individual needs of children and their families.

acquisition of stated goals developed during the input phase. Determining the degree to which the program is following its plan of action toward goals helps to keep program staff focused on the steps necessary to achieve their objective. In addition, the process stage allows for refinement of goals and objectives as program circumstances change (e.g., funding revenues decrease, enrollment characteristics change, staffing patterns vary). In the final stage of program evaluation, outcome, the program's impact becomes the primary concern and thus efforts are directed toward determining consumers' degree of satisfaction, children's growth, and staff's development that have occurred. Table 5 summarizes the stages of program evaluation with examples of questions that might be used to guide agencies in designing program evaluation efforts.

Program evaluation design encompasses four basic steps, which are outlined in Table 6. (For a more extensive perspective on program evaluation design, see Johnson & LaMontagne, 1994.) When designing and implementing program evaluation, it is important to consider several factors to ensure the reliability of the information gathered and its relationship to the goals of the ECE program (Joint Committee on Standards for Educational Evaluation, 1981). The key factor is obtaining information that is useful for the ECE program and its stakeholders. The

Table 5. Triphase approach to program evaluation

| Stage | Focus | Questions |
|-------|-------|-----------|
| Input | Assess the needs of the consumers and develop a program to address identified needs | What are the needs of the consumers who use our services?<br><br>Is our program consistent with preferred practice guidelines? |
| Process | Monitor and refine the program evaluation as it is being implemented | Are we following our plan?<br><br>Are we attending to the needs of our consumers?<br><br>Are there any new circumstances to which we should attend? |
| Outcome | Determine the impact of the program on consumers | Are consumers satisfied with our program?<br><br>What impact does our program have on consumers? |

ECE program's stakeholders are the individuals who are invested in its successful implementation. Stakeholders can be educators, staff, administrators, family members, children, or community agencies. The *feasibility factor* refers to the plausibility of implementing the evaluation plan. Every ECE program has parameters defined by staffing and time resources, fiscal support, and guiding policies and procedures. It is better to successfully implement a simple program evaluation that identifies, monitors, and gauges the impact of one goal rather than unsuccessfully implementing a complex program evaluation that examines multiple program goals. Another factor to consider is propriety, which deals with the ethical and equitable components of the evaluation plan. Components of a program evaluation plan must be ethically sound and protect the rights of the individuals who have agreed to participate. Confidentiality of data is critical in establishing an atmosphere in which consumers feel safe to provide honest responses without fear of retribution. The final factor, accuracy, is associated with the degree of confidence that the information and interpretations of it are representative, correct, and consistent. In order for program evaluation to be effective, there must be a high degree of faith that the information gathered was collected from consumers with their appropriate knowledge related to the goals of the ECE program and that the data were collected, analyzed, and interpreted using procedures and methods to ensure objectivity.

## CONCLUSIONS

One of the primary purposes of program assessment is to gather information in order to make an informed decision (McLean, 1996). One of the primary purposes of ECE programs is to provide children with learning opportunities that address their individual uniqueness while engaging children in activities that support their development of skills and abilities across developmental domains. Assessment provides the exact information needed to design IEPs for all young children. Comprehensive and socioecologically sound assessment data provide ECE educators

Table 6.    Steps to program evaluation

| Steps | Description | Focus |
|---|---|---|
| I | Identify the purpose and issues: Program evaluation must have an articulated purpose in order to be systematically implemented in a rigorous manner. | What are the goals of your program? Who are the stakeholders? Primary consumers? Secondary consumers? What are the needs of the stakeholders? What are the key features that make your program unique? |
| II | Identify the best way to collect information: Keep it simple and manageable. | Unobtrusive measures? Existing data such as test scores, IFSP/IEP goals, parent–teacher conference notes Observations? Child, staff, interactions Interviews? Professionals, family members, community staff Tests? Pre–post measurements Questionnaires? Rating scales for consumers and stakeholders |
| III | Design your plan: Program evaluation is a "team sport" and needs all of its members to be successful. | What are you going to do (i.e., action plan)? Rationale for doing it as designed Who is responsible for what part of the action plan? Time line for accomplishing each part of the action plan |
| IV | Implement, evaluate, and reimplement: Program evaluation is cyclical and builds on past efforts and information. | Implement action plan Identify expected outcomes and unintended outcomes Identify problems and solutions Refine the action plan as needed |

with knowledge about children's interests; their interaction patterns with peers, adults, and materials; and their problem-solving styles. Valid and reliable assessment information provides ECE educators with each child's current status of developmental skills and important family information that influences young children's daily educational performance. Continuous assessment documents children's growth and the ECE program's accountability while allowing flexibility as children or the ECE program as a whole demonstrates changing needs. Assessment is strongly linked to programming in ECE and is considered a component of developmentally and individually appropriate practices. Assessment is not just part of the initial stage of an ECE program's eligibility. It includes young children's total ECE program and reflects the program's commitment to providing an individualized education program for young children and their families.

## REMEMBER THIS

1.  For young children with disabilities, evaluation and assessment are inherent aspects of their IFSPs and IEPs.

2. IDEA requires that young children with disabilities receive multifactored evaluations from a multidisciplinary team.

3. Play-based assessment is an extension of the transdisciplinary model of gathering timely and accurate information regarding young children's developmental status.

4. Competence in testing requires culture-specific knowledge that may affect the administration and interpretation of tests involving children and their families.

5. Assessment is the basis of individualized programming for all young children.

# REFERENCES

Ackerly, S. (1947). The clinic team. *American Journal of Orthopsychiatry, 17,* 191–195.

*American Heritage Dictionary.* (1983). New York: Dell.

Anastasi, A. (1988). *Psychological testing* (5th ed.). New York: Macmillan.

Arter, J.A., & Spandel, V. (1991). *Using portfolios of student work in instruction and assessment.* Portland, OR: Northwest Regional Educational Laboratory.

Bagnato, S.T., Neisworth, J.T., & Munson, S.M. (1989). *Linking developmental assessment and early intervention: Curriculum-based prescriptions.* Rockville, MD: Aspen Publishers.

Bailey, D.B., Jr. (1989). Case management in early intervention. *Journal of Early Intervention, 13*(2), 120–134.

Bailey, D.B., Jr., & Simeonsson, R.J. (1990). *Family needs survey.* Chapel Hill: University of North Carolina, Frank Porter Graham Child Development Center.

Bayley, N. (1969). *Bayley Scales of Infant Development: Birth to 2 years.* San Antonio, TX: The Psychological Corporation.

Belsky, J., & Most, R.K. (1981). From exploration to play: A cross-sectional study of infant free play behavior. *Developmental Psychology, 17,* 630–639.

Benner, S.M. (1992). *Assessing young children with special needs.* Reading, MA: Addison Wesley Longman.

Bentzen, W.R. (1993). *A guide to observing and recording behavior.* Albany, NY: Delmar Publishers.

Blasco, P., & LaMontagne, M.J. (1996, September). *Play based assessment.* Paper presented at American Academy of Cerebral Palsy and Developmental Medicine Conference, Minneapolis, MN.

Bowe, F.G. (1995). *Birth to five: Early childhood special education.* Albany, NY: Delmar Publishers.

Bradley, R.H., Rock, S.L., Caldwell, B.M., & Brisby, J.A. (1989). Uses of the HOME Inventory for families with handicapped children. *American Journal on Mental Retardation, 94*(3), 313–330.

Brazelton, T.B. (1973). *Neonatal Behavioral Assessment Scales.* Philadelphia: Lippincott-Raven.

Bredekamp, S. (Ed.). (1987). *Developmentally appropriate practice in early childhood programs serving children from birth through age 8.* Washington, DC: National Association for the Education of Young Children.

Bricker, D. (Ed.). (1993). *Assessment, evaluation, and programming system (AEPS) for infants and children: Vol. 1. AEPS measurement for birth to three years.* Baltimore: Paul H. Brookes Publishing Co.

Bricker, D., & Littman, D. (1982). Intervention and education: The inseparable mix. *Topics in Early Childhood Special Education, 1,* 23–33.

Brigance, A. (1978). *BRIGANCE® Diagnostic Inventory of Basic Skills.* North Billerica, MA: Curriculum Associates.

Campbell, P.I.I. (1991). Evaluation and assessment in early intervention for infants and toddlers. *Journal of Early Intervention, 15*(1), 36–45.

Child Development Resources. (1989). *How can we help?* Lightfoot, VA: Author.

Cohen, L.G., & Spenciner, L.J. (1994). *Assessment of young children.* Reading, MA: Addison Wesley Longman.

Craig, S.E., & Haggart, A.G. (1994). Including all children: The ADA's challenge to early intervention. *Infants and Young Children, 7*(2), 15–19.

Division for Early Childhood (DEC) Task Force on Recommended Practices. (1991). *Recommended practices in early intervention and early childhood special education.* Reston, VA: Council for Exceptional Children.

Dunst, C.J., Cooper, C.S., Weeldreyer, J.C., Snyder, K.D., & Chase, J.H. (1988). Family needs scale. In C.J. Dunst, C.M. Trivette, & A.G. Deal (Eds.), *Enabling and empowering families: Principles and guidelines for practice* (p. 151). Cambridge, MA: Brookline Books.

Education for All Handicapped Children Act of 1975, PL 94-142, 20 U.S.C. §§ 1400 *et seq.*

Education of the Handicapped Act Amendments of 1986, PL 99-457, 20 U.S.C. §§ 1400 *et seq.*

Fewell, R.R. (1983). Assessing handicapped infants. In S. Garwood & R. Fewell (Eds.), *Educating handicapped infants.* Rockville, MD: Aspen Publishers.

Fewell, R.R. (1984). Assessment of preschool handicapped children. *Educational Psychologist, 19*(3), 172–179.

Fewell, R.R. (1991). Trends in the assessment of infants and toddlers with disabilities. *Exceptional Children, 58*(2), 166–173.

Fewell, R.R., & Vadasy, P.F. (1987). Measurement issues in studies of efficacy. *Topics in Early Childhood Special Education, 7,* 85–96.

Foley, G.M. (1990). Portrait of the arena evaluation: Assessment in the transdisciplinary approach. In E.D. Gibbs & D.M. Teti (Eds.), *Interdisciplinary assessment of infants: A guide for early intervention professionals* (pp. 271–286). Baltimore: Paul H. Brookes Publishing Co.

Frankenburg, W.K., Dodds, J.B., Archer, P., Bresnick, B., Maschka, P., Edelman, N., & Shapiro, H. (1992). *The Denver Developmental Screening Test* (2nd ed.) (Denver II). Denver: Denver Developmental Materials.

Gesell, A. (1925). *The mental growth of the preschool child.* New York: Macmillan.

Hanson, M.J., & Carta, J.J. (1996). Addressing the challenges of families with multiple risks. *Exceptional Children, 62*(3), 201–212.

Hanson, M.J., & Lynch, E.W. (1992). Family diversity: Implications for policy and practice. *Topics in Early Childhood Special Education, 12*(3), 283–306.

Harrison, P.J. (1995). Evaluating programs. In M.J. Hanson & E.W. Lynch (Eds.), *Early intervention: Implementing child and family services for infants and toddlers who are at risk or disabled* (pp. 288–322). Austin, TX: PRO-ED.

Hutt, M.L., Menninger, W.C., & O'Keefe, D.E. (1947). The neuropsychiatric team in the United States Army. *Mental Health, 31,* 103–119.

Individuals with Disabilities Education Act (IDEA) of 1990, PL 101-476, 20 U.S.C. §§ 1400 *et seq.*

Individuals with Disabilities Education Act (IDEA) Amendments of 1991, PL 102-119, 20 U.S.C. §§ 1400 *et seq.*

Individuals with Disabilities Education Act (IDEA) Amendments of 1997, PL 105-17, 20 U.S.C. §§ 1400 *et seq.*

Johnson, B.H., McGonigal, M.J., & Kaufmann, R.K. (Eds.). (1989). *Guidelines and recommended practices for the individualized family service plan.* Washington, DC: Association for the Care of Children's Health.

Johnson, L.J., & LaMontagne, M.J. (1994). Program evaluation: The key to quality programming. In L.J. Johnson, R.J. Gallagher, M.J. LaMontagne, J.B. Jordan, J.J. Gallagher, P.L. Hutinger, & M.B. Karnes (Eds.), *Meeting early intervention challenges: Issues from birth to three* (2nd ed., pp. 185–216). Baltimore: Paul H. Brookes Publishing Co.

Johnson-Martin, N.M., Attermeier, S.M., & Hacker, B.J. (1990). *The Carolina Curriculum for Preschoolers with Special Needs.* Baltimore: Paul H. Brookes Publishing Co.

Joint Committee on Standards for Educational Evaluation. (1981). *Standards for evaluation of educational programs, projects, and materials*. New York: McGraw-Hill.

Katz, K. (1989). Strategies for infant assessment: Implications of P.L. 99-457. *Topics in Early Childhood Special Education, 9*(3), 99–109.

Kaufman, A.S., & Kaufman, N.L. (1983). *Kaufman Assessment Battery for Children*. Circle Pines, MN: American Guidance Service.

Kaufman, A.S., & Kaufman, N.L. (1985). *Kaufman Test of Educational Achievement*. Circle Pines, MN: American Guidance Service.

Krauss, M.W., & Jacobs, F. (1990). Family assessment: Purposes and techniques. In S.J. Meisels & J.P. Shonkoff (Eds.), *Handbook of early childhood intervention* (pp. 303–325). Cambridge, England: Cambridge University Press.

Lamb, M.E., & Bornstein, M.H. (1987). *Development in infancy* (2nd ed.). New York: Random House.

Lifter, K. (1996). Assessing play skills. In M. McLean, D.B. Bailey, Jr., & M. Wolery (Eds.), *Assessing infants and preschoolers with special needs* (pp. 435–461). Columbus, OH: Charles E. Merrill.

Linder, T. (1993). *Transdisciplinary play-based assessment: A functional approach to working with young children* (Rev. ed.). Baltimore: Paul H. Brookes Publishing Co.

Lynch, E.W., & Hanson, M.J. (Eds.). (1998). *Developing cross-cultural competence: A guide for working with children and their families* (2nd ed.). Baltimore: Paul H. Brookes Publishing Co.

Mahoney, G., & Weller, E. (1980). An ecological approach to language intervention. In D. Bricker (Ed.), *New directions for exceptional children: Language intervention with children* (pp. 17–32). San Francisco: Jossey-Bass.

McLean, M. (1996). Assessment and its importance in early intervention/early childhood special education. In M. McLean, D.B. Bailey, Jr., & M. Wolery (Eds.), *Assessing infants and preschoolers with special needs* (pp. 1–22). Columbus, OH: Charles E. Merrill.

McLean, M., & Crais, E.R. (1996). Procedural considerations in assessing infants and preschoolers with disabilities. In M. McLean, D.B. Bailey, Jr., & M. Wolery (Eds.), *Assessing infants and preschoolers with special needs* (pp. 46–68). Columbus, OH: Charles E. Merrill.

Meyer, C., Schuman, S., & Angello, N. (1990). *Aggregating portfolio data*. Lake Oswego, OR: Northwest Evaluation Association.

Mori, A., & Olive, J. (1980). *Handbook of preschool special education*. Rockville, MD: Aspen Publishers.

National Association for the Education of Young Children (NAEYC). (1988). Position statement on standardized testing of young children 3 through 8 years of age. *Young Children, 46*(3), 21–38.

Neisworth, J.T. (1993). Assessment. In Division for Early Childhood (DEC) Task Force on Recommended Practices, *DEC recommended practices: Indicators of quality in programs for infants and young children with special needs and their families* (pp. 11–18). Reston, VA: Council for Exceptional Children.

Newborg, J., Stock, J.R., Wnek, L., Guidubaldi, J., & Svinicki, J. (1988). *Battelle Developmental Inventory (BDI)*. Chicago: Riverside.

Odom, S.L., McLean, M.E., Johnson, L.J., & LaMontagne, M.J. (1995). Recommended practices in early childhood special education: Validation and current use. *Journal of Early Intervention, 19*(1), 1–17.

Parten, M. (1932). Social participation among preschool children. *Journal of Abnormal and Social Psychology, 27*, 243–269.

Patterson, G., & Moore, D. (1979). Interactive patterns as units of behavior. In S.L. Suomi, M.E. Lamb, & G.R. Stephenson (Eds.), *Social interaction analysis: Methodological issues* (pp. 77–96). Madison: University of Wisconsin Press.

Peterson, N.L. (1988). *Early intervention for handicapped and at-risk children*. Denver: Love Publishing Co.

Rehabilitation Act of 1973, PL 93-112, 29 U.S.C. §§ 701 *et seq*.

Rosenblith, J.F., & Sims-Knight, J.E. (1985). *In the beginning: Development in the first two years.* Pacific Grove, CA: Brooks/Cole.

Sameroff, A.J., Seifer, R., & Zax, M. (1982). Early development of children at risk for emotional disorder. *Monograph of the Society for Research in Child Development, 47*(Serial No. 199).

Strain, P. (1987). Comprehensive evaluation of intervention for young autistic children. *Topics in Early Childhood Special Education, 7*(2), 97–110.

Teti, D.M., & Gibbs, E.D. (1990). Infant assessment: Historical antecedents and contemporary issues. In E.D. Gibbs & D.M. Teti (Eds.), *Interdisciplinary assessment of infants: A guide for early intervention professionals* (pp. 3–13). Baltimore: Paul H. Brookes Publishing Co.

Thorndike, R.L., Hagen, E.P., & Sattles, J.M. (1985). *Stanford-Binet Intelligence Scale* (4th ed.). Chicago: Riverside.

Thurman, S.K., & Widerstrom, A.H. (1985). *Young children with special needs: A developmental and ecological approach.* Needham Heights, MA: Allyn & Bacon.

Tjossem, T. (1976). Early interventions: Issues and approaches. In T. Tjossem (Ed.), *Intervention strategies for high-risk and handicapped children* (pp. 3–33). Baltimore: University Park Press.

Turnbull, A.P., & Turnbull, H.R., III. (1990). *Families, professional, and exceptionality: A special partnership.* Columbus, OH: Charles E. Merrill.

United Cerebral Palsy Associations (UCPA). (1976). *Staff development handbook: A resource for the transdisciplinary process.* New York: Author.

Uzgiris, I.C., & Hunt, J.McV. (1975). *Assessment in infancy: Ordinal scales of psychological development.* Urbana: University of Illinois Press.

Vincent, L.J., Salisbury, C.L., Strain, P., McCormic, C., & Tessier, A. (1990). A behavioral-ecological approach to early intervention: Focus on cultural diversity. In S.J. Meisels & J.P. Shonkoff (Eds.), *Handbook of early childhood intervention* (pp. 173–195). Cambridge, England: Cambridge University Press.

Wolery, M. (1989). Using direct observation in assessment. In D.B. Bailey, Jr., & M. Wolery (Eds.), *Assessing infants and preschoolers with handicaps* (pp. 64–96). Columbus, OH: Charles E. Merrill.

Wolery, M., & Bailey, D.B., Jr. (1984). Alternatives to impact evaluations: Suggestions for program evaluation in early intervention. *Journal of the Division for Early Childhood, 9*(1), 27–37.

Woodruff, G. (1980, June). Transdisciplinary approach for preschool children and parents. *Exceptional Parent,* 13–16.

# Activities

1. Review four assessment instruments used in ECE programs. Check the assessment instrument manual for the sample population description, procedures and adaptations for children with special needs, and test item development. Examine the materials for child- and family-friendliness and potential cultural bias.

2. Write a rationale for why you would or would not use these assessment instruments with young children in your area.

3. Observe an ECE program that includes children and families who are from diverse cultural and/or linguistic backgrounds. Identify two ECE program goals. Develop an ECE program evaluation plan based on those two goals.

4. Examine the test items of two or more standardized assessment instruments. What are the similarities between them? How are they different? Which assessment instrument items would be most useful in planning an ECE program?

5. Observe a child and family engaged in play. Which factors that you observe would contribute to your selection of a particular assessment instrument?

# Transitions

*M.J. LaMontagne, Gwen Wheeler Russell, and Mary Janson*

## CHAPTER ORGANIZER

In this chapter, we explore the following ideas . . .

1. Successful transitions are not accidents; rather, they are well-planned, thoughtful actions designed to accomplish specific outcomes.

2. Transitions occur both across and within environments.

3. Transition activities should encourage and sustain collaboration among team members.

4. Planning and communication are essential to ease the transition of children and their families from one environment to another.

5. The transition plan is a road map designed to guide stakeholders through the transition process.

6. Theory, research, and legislation acknowledge the critical role that the transition process plays in the continuum of services for children and families.

Young children experience many transitions during their preschool years. They attend child care programs, receive in-home child care, participate in community play groups, and are taken to preschool centers and multiple other locations as determined by their family. For young children with special needs, these environments may also include hospital and early intervention environments (Rosenkoetter, Hains, & Fowler, 1994). Families of young children with and without disabilities share common concerns as they send their children from the safety of their homes into unfamiliar programs, environments, and systems (Miller, 1996). Even with the most extensive information-gathering efforts, families ultimately must leave their children in the hands of individuals with whom they are barely acquainted. This act of separation can be a most traumatic experience for the family (Miller, 1996). The challenge for all early childhood education (ECE) professionals is the collaborative design and implementation of strategies to support children and their families as they traverse the many community environments to gain access to services.

Transition in the broader sense is viewed as an outcomes-based system (Will, 1985) that focuses on the successful movement of children and families across environments, programs, or service delivery modes (Chandler, 1992). Hutinger (1981) defined *successful transition* as a planned process with a clearly articulated sequence of actions that lead to children and their family making a smooth, calm entrance into another program or environment. Included in a successful transition is the adjustment of the sending and receiving environments so that the receiving program fits the children and their families and the sending program is able to separate from the exiting family members. The entire transition process involves the interaction of many individuals and environments, and, by the very nature of the involvement of a number of people, collaboration must be part of the plan in order for it to succeed. The transition literature and the Individuals with Disabilities Education Act Amendments of 1991 (PL 102-119) have emphasized the need for well-planned transitions that attend to the specific day-to-day details of moving people from one place to another (Bennett, Raab, & Nelson, 1991; Bruder & Chandler, 1996; Katims & Pierce, 1995; Rosenkoetter et al., 1994). The transition process is multidimensional; it involves more than merely physical location (Maxwell & Eller, 1994). Young children and their families in transition have new peer groups, new roles, new systems, new professionals, and new expectations thrust upon them. For many young children with and without disabilities and their families, gaining a sense of comfort and security in what is a new and most often unknown environment creates in them a sense of apprehension and fearfulness rather than anticipation and excitement. ECE educators are charged with the task of addressing all aspects of transition in a successful manner.

A more specific view of transition focuses on the movement of young children as they switch activities within their program environments. These day-to-day transitions occur continuously throughout young children's engagement in the various materials, centers, and learning opportunities that their ECE program provides. The ease and flow of this movement directly affects the individual child's engagement and interest in learning opportunities and can influence the attention and engagement of other children, especially when transitions are disruptive (Miller, 1996). ECE educators face a daily challenge to structure routines, environments, activities, and schedules that support children's quiet and natural exchanges of one learning opportunity for another.

Wolery (1989) described the purpose of the transition process as meeting four basic outcomes. First, transition activities should be designed to ensure the continuity of services to children and their families. A seamless system of interagency services and resources should flow smoothly as children and their families move across environments. A successful transition plan guards children and their families against disruption in programs, services, and resources due to physical change in location. Second, a comprehensive transition program works to minimize the family disruptions and turmoil that can result from the upheaval caused by moving from a familiar environment to an unknown environment. This is not to say that a transition plan successfully protects children and their families from all stress, frustration, or worries. However, a well-planned transition program strives to identify potential problems and provides a systematic procedure for addressing as many challenges as possible in order to make the move minimally disruptive to children and their families. Third, a collaborative transition blueprint supports the success of children in the receiving environment. By working together, ECE educators and family members can identify the strengths and concerns of children and the characteristics of the next environment to create a comfortable fit between the children and the program design. Communication among team members offsets the historical perspective of fitting children into the program and should support a fit among children's characteristics; families' needs, priorities, and concerns; and the characteristics of the new education program. The fourth outcome of transition is tied directly to the legal mandates of the Individuals with Disabilities Education Act Amendments of 1991, which require that the individualized family service plan (IFSP)/individualized education program (IEP) team develop a transition plan for all young children with disabilities.

Transitions across environments or within environments must be well planned for successful movement by young children and/or their families. If transitions are planned in advance and individualized to meet the unique characteristics of children and their families, then transition can be a time of positive interactions and empowering experiences that create a hopeful context for future successful transitions (Bruder & Chandler, 1996; Diamond, Spiegel-McGill, & Hanrahan, 1988; Edgar, McNulty, & Goetz, 1984). When transitions are not well planned or well prepared, families and children may have experiences that are overly stressful, anxiety intensive, and negative in nature (Bruder & Chandler, 1996). The goal of ECE is to support young children and their families as they strive to meet their own unique needs. The partnership between families and professionals supports the delicate balance between enabling and disenabling caregivers as they struggle to successfully maneuver the many education environments that provide services to children and their families.

There is no transition formula in which to insert each child and family for a successful transition (Miller, 1996). When planning transitions, ECE professionals must draw from many sources and models to develop an appropriate individualized process for a specific child and family. It is important that ECE professionals remember that any given model is merely a framework to be adapted, refined, altered, supplemented, or expanded to meet the unique characteristics that each child and family bring to early childhood programs. It is the repertoire of resources across disciplines and communities that enables ECE professionals and families to experience successful transitions.

---

*Consider the following description of transition experiences:*

When Daniel turned 6 years old, his parents were excited at the prospect of his heading for the big, bad world of public school. No longer would they be explaining that their son was attending a classroom for kids with disabilities and environmental risks that was run by the local human services agency—one less stigma for Daniel. On the day of the transition meeting, Daniel's parents were excited and had their dreams and visions all laid out in their minds. With their hearts on their sleeves, Daniel's parents went to Daniel's transition meeting. As always, "the TEAM," as they liked to be called, explained that Daniel was not doing the things that typically developing children were doing at Daniel's age and why Daniel was not there yet. The team never made comments about Daniel's strengths, except that he was "cute." When it came time for Daniel's teacher to speak, she described Daniel with words and phrases like *nonverbal; socially, emotionally, and cognitively at a 3-year-old level;* and so forth. What Daniel's parents were hearing was a description of the same son who they knew was constantly asking for help or for something to eat at home. Needless to say, Daniel's parents both felt like horses that had been ridden hard and put away wet. Another of the teacher's statements was almost the breaking point for Daniel's parents: "We recommend that Daniel stay in this preschool another year. We just don't feel that he is ready for real school." Daniel's mom thought for a minute and looked at her husband, who felt just as she did. Daniel's mom, once composed, told the ECE program's "TEAM" that Daniel's own "team" of two had decided earlier that Daniel would be attending public school the following year and that they appreciated the TEAM's input. The TEAM had not prepared a transition plan for Daniel because they were sure that his parents would see that they were right. Therefore, Daniel's "home team" moved forward with their own transition plan, meeting with public school administrators and working from there. The transition process was very difficult for Daniel because there were no policies or procedures in place to handle someone in his circumstances. Everything was done hastily, ultimately robbing him of the learning environment that could have supported him in his kindergarten classroom.

---

**Reflection:**  After reading the preceding section, how do you think the ECE program described could have better served Daniel?

# TRANSITION MODELS

Several different models for helping children and their families make transitions across education environments have emerged in the literature. Each of these models was created to serve children and families by providing a general set of guidelines that can be modified to fit the unique characteristics of individual children, their families, and the ECE programs that they attend.

## General Education

The General Education Collaboration Model (Simpson & Myles, 1993) is a framework for supporting children with disabilities within the general education classroom through the partnership of educators. Although developed for the process of mainstreaming, this model has applicability for transitions as well. The foundation of this model integrates shared input, shared responsibility, and shared decision making, which are the foundations of the partnership between families and early childhood professionals as they develop, implement, and evaluate transition plans (AASA/NAESP/NAASP School-Based Management Task Force, 1988; Bauwens, Hourcade, & Friend, 1989; Crisci & Tutela, 1990). The General Education Collaboration Model lists five specific components:

1. Flexible departmentalization (Jones, Gottlieb, Guskin, & Yoshida, 1978; Lawrence & Lorsch, 1967; Margolis & McGettigan, 1988)
2. Program ownership (Roubinek, 1978)
3. Identification and development of supportive attitudes (Heller & Schilit, 1987; Hersh & Walker, 1983)
4. Student assessment as a measure of program effectiveness (Jones et al., 1978; Rogers & Saklofske, 1985)
5. Classroom modifications that support mainstreaming (Myles & Simpson, 1989, 1990; Simpson & Myles, 1989)

*Departmentalization* refers to the unique role that each individual plays in the process of providing services to children. The flexibility of departmentalization suggests that the uniqueness of individual roles permits all participants to coordinate actions, communicate information, and determine accountability and responsibility for implementation across family members and educators. In relation to the transition process, each ECE educator, early childhood special education (ECSE) teacher, and parent has a specific role with associated responsibilities. ECE educators have a familiarity with child care and preschool curricula and environments and can help identify community placement options with developmentally and individually appropriate practices. ECSE educators have an extensive knowledge base of disability conditions and their impact on development, so they can contribute methods and techniques for adapting environments to meet the specific characteristics of a child with disabilities. Parents have a comprehensive understanding of their children, other members of their families, and their cultural back-

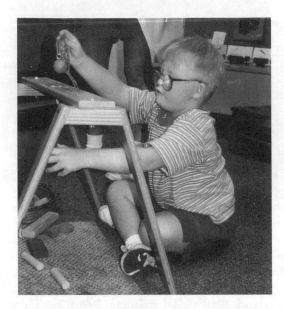

Early childhood professionals need to be aware of and sensitive to children and families as they make the transition from home to school, within a program, and between programs.

ground and can provide the context in which ECE services are appropriate. Together, these team members can work collaboratively to coordinate, communicate, and implement successful transition plans.

*Program ownership* relates to the distinctive areas of traditional emphasis of each team member: early childhood education for ECE educators, early childhood special education for ECSE teachers, and family for parents. Within this model, the lines of distinction become more permeable to allow individuals to seek commonalities, discover differences, and work within a partnership to successfully move young children across early childhood service environments.

Perhaps one of the most remarkable components of this model is the identification and development of supportive attitudes. Successful mainstreaming and transition require supportive attitudes that demonstrate a belief system that the process can work. In the partnership of families and ECE educators, believing that children, families, and educators can design and implement successful transition plans is a critical yet often neglected step in the process. For any team to realize its goal, each team member must be committed to the actualization of the agreed-on goal. Without this support, the details of the most comprehensive transition plan may not be carried out by individual team members, thereby causing the transition to fail. Through shared input, shared responsibility, and shared decision making, families and ECE educators should be able to exhibit the necessary positive attitudes that will contribute to the successful transition of young children and families in education.

Another attractive feature of this model is its focus on student assessment as a measure of effectiveness. Transition efforts are deemed successful based on the behaviors of children, families, and ECE professionals. If their behaviors are positive and the children, families, and professionals are demonstrating successful interactions within the new environment, the assumption can be made that the transition plan worked. Most often in transition planning, it is the day-to-day details of helping children and families make the transition that are carried out and emphasized (e.g., locating and visiting the next education environment, sending written information to receiving teachers and staff, providing a list of children's interests and their "all about me" books, processing the necessary paperwork for children with disabilities). Less attention is given to evaluating the success of the plan by collecting data in the new environment. Is the child able to demonstrate skills and abilities that are developmentally and individually appropriate for him or her? Is the child successful in establishing new peer relationships? Can the child gain access to, explore, and interact with the new environment? Does the child feel comfortable, safe, and secure with new teachers, staff, and children? Is the family satisfied with the child's new learning environment? Is the family comfortable with the communication system of the new program? Does the teacher believe that he or she is meeting the needs of the child and the child's family? Is the teacher getting the support services needed to address the unique characteristics of the child and/or the child's family? Only through the collection of this type of information can ECE professionals accurately determine whether the transition plan for a child and the child's family is successful.

The final component of this model addresses the need for classroom modifications to support the inclusion of a child with disabilities. From a transition standpoint, this component can be applied to all young children. An underlying assumption in ECE is that programs should fit children rather than children fitting programs. In the transition process, sending programs investigate receiving programs to determine expectations and structures. The purpose of this investigation is to support young children and their families by identifying and addressing the unknown characteristics of the new environment. Through the partnership among the ECE professionals and family members, unique information about children and their families is sent to the new program so that needed supports and changes can be anticipated and implemented by the arrival time of the children and their families.

## Early Childhood Special Education

The Individuals with Disabilities Education Act Amendments of 1991 set forth policies and procedures related to the transition of young children with disabilities and their families across education programs. These provisions provide a structure to which ECSE programs must adhere. Of primary concern is the transition between programs for infants and toddlers (i.e., birth through age 2) and programs for preschool-age children (i.e., ages 3–5 years). Programs must plan in advance the graduation of a toddler to a preschool program. Although the federal mandate requires that advance planning occur at least 90 days prior to the child's third birthday, it has been suggested that transition planning needs to start a minimum of 6–12 months before the anticipated transition date in order to effectively produce a successful plan of action (Wolery, Strain, & Bailey, 1992). At the transition-planning parent–teacher conference, participants review options (e.g., child stays in the current program until the end of the year or makes the transition to a new program) for the child from his or her third birthday through the end of the current school year and design a transition plan. Given equal importance in the federal legislation is the inclusion of families in transition planning. Family members must be a part of the planning process, and each program must have a policy statement describing how they will include families in the transition process.

Rosenkoetter and colleagues (1994) developed a transition model, Bridging Early Services, that integrates three major influences on transition practices for young children with disabilities and their families: 1) federal and state polices and trends, 2) family leadership and advocacy, and 3) local issues and practices. Within this conceptual framework are blended two crucial dimensions that can support or shatter transition efforts. The first dimension is the relationship that ECE professionals, families, and children develop. Positive relationships that nurture respect, trust, open and honest communication, and appreciation for individuals and their contributions support transition efforts. Negative relationships serve to undermine efforts and create distrust, miscommunication, and alternative or unspoken needs. The second dimension brings into play the written policies, procedures, and time lines, which provide parameters for ECE agencies and families. Each partner in the transition plan must attend to the guidelines formulated by his or her agency. For ECE professionals, these guidelines are federal, state, and local policies, as well as philosophical and theoretical frameworks that guide their practices. For families, the parameters are defined by family characteristics, interactional patterns, cultural background, and family resources. In order for a transition plan to be successful, it must meet the needs of all partners in the process.

The Bridging Early Services transition model provides a focus for transition planning. According to this model, transition planning should promote interagency collaboration, form partnerships with families, and support individual children. Transition planning is a dynamic process that needs the energy generated from collaborative partnerships. Interagency collaboration provides a system for meeting the needs of children and families by effectively using the human and fiscal resources of the community. Positive relationships with families furnish the context for defining the transition goals that will determine successful entrance into the next education environment. Supporting individual children as they experience learning opportunities in new environments is the fundamental purpose of an IEP.

# RECOMMENDED PRACTICES MODEL
# FOR YOUNG CHILDREN WITH SPECIAL NEEDS

As a result of a national survey of ECSE practitioners, families, and higher education faculty conducted by the Division for Early Childhood Recommended Practices Task Force (1991), the ECSE field validated 22 indicators of recommended practices. These 22 indicators detail the four components of successful transition:

1. Collaboration among state and local agencies
2. Collaboration between families and other caregivers
3. Collaboration between sending and receiving agencies
4. Children (Bruder & Chandler, 1996)

Within this transition model there exists an understanding that successful transition is a comprehensive venture that attends to each of these components during the process of planning, implementation, and follow-up activities (Bruder & Chandler, 1996). There also is the awareness that every action supporting transition should simultaneously promote collaboration among team members, including families.

## Collaboration Among State and Local Agencies

The first component of the recommended practices model relates to collaboration among state and local agencies. Planning for children and families as they move from one agency to another requires communication, collaboration, and cooperation among those agencies involved in the delivery of services to families. Interagency agreements should delineate roles and responsibilities of each agency, the transition team configuration, and transition policy and procedures including time lines for initiating and completing transition activities (Bruder & Chandler, 1996). Formal communication procedures that describe the manner (both written and verbal) in which each agency will share information is a necessity for developing a transition plan that will work. In addition, common time for planning and preparing for transition across agencies is essential to support communication and collaboration and to ensure that the goals of transition are met.

## Collaboration Between Families and Other Caregivers

Families and other caregivers represent the second component of the recommended practices model. The practice of working with young children with disabilities resides in a family-centered perspective toward providing education services. From this interventionist stance, it is acknowledged that families are the lifelong context of the child and that families are the consistent factor in the life of the child. Therefore, transition practices should reflect the awareness that families, not service providers, move with their children across environments and that families have a unique insight into their priorities and concerns relating to transition issues. To support families and children during anticipated transition periods, it is important to share information with family members as soon as possible to ease the way. Collaboration between agencies and families provides a system for passing information that identifies when a child and family are ready for transition and the potential receiving sites to be considered. The information shared should be comprehensive and should outline the activities, steps, and processes for family involvement, as well as time lines (Lazzari & Kilgo, 1989). A true family-centered approach accepts families' choices and recognizes that families may choose to make the transition from one environment to another prior to the start of the program or before the child's chronological age time line. Family choice and decisions may result in a change in the type, frequency, or duration of services, thus requiring transitions to alternate programs, service delivery options, or staffing patterns (Bruder & Chandler, 1996). When planning for transitions, families should be provided the opportunity to visit potential ECE classrooms or programs and meet with staff from both the old and new programs. These types of transition activities provide the structure for acquiring information, sharing information, and supporting the collaboration that is essential in designing and implementing smooth transitions. The identification of a service coordinator greatly assists in the scheduling of meetings, observations, and communications across agencies and family members. In order to develop transition plans that support families and children, it is vital that ECE educators receive the needed training to support their successful interactions in this process. ECE educators need to enhance their collaboration skills; their communication abilities; their understanding of family priorities, resources, and concerns; and their ability to provide family-centered services (Bruder & Chandler, 1996).

## Collaboration Between Sending and Receiving Staff

The third component of the recommended practices model describes the recommended practices for sending and receiving program staff. These ECE educators should have an understanding of the interagency agreements that apply to their programs as well as an understanding of all policies and procedures that may influence the transition process. The required tasks and time lines will be listed in the interagency agreements, but it becomes the task of the ECE educators to tailor the guidelines to fit the unique needs of an individual child and that child's family. To meet this challenge, the sending and receiving program staff must be familiar with local resources and the range of service options available to a specific child and that child's family. As with families, ECE educators should make time for observing each other's programs and discussing their observations and insights as they relate to the child and the child's family. This exchange of information between programs can lead to a common collaborative consensus regarding program strengths and challenges that need to be addressed in the child's transition plan. It also provides a format for gaining insight into skills that can be addressed in the child's current IFSP/IEP to support successful integration into the next environment. Through this collaboration, ECE educators in the next environment can acquire the knowledge that is critical for preparing other staff, personnel, children, and parents in their programs for the arrival of this young child and family.

## Children

Indicators of recommended practice that focus on the child compose the fourth component of this transition model. Once the next environment has been selected, it is critical that the new environment be assessed in order to identify those skills that will support a smooth transfer of the child and the family. These transition skills will vary by program characteristics, staffing patterns, and agency resources. To ensure the attainment of the previously stated outcomes for transition delineated by Wolery (1989), it is imperative that ECE educators work together to define the expectations, challenges, and boundaries of the receiving program. There also is a need to know the current developmental status of the young child and how the child's present strengths, abilities, and challenges fit with the characteristics of the new environment. These child evaluation data provide the transition team with the information for designing a plan to support a congruent match between the child and the child's next educational environment by identifying the potential problems and planning strategies to resolve anticipated transitional bumps. Part of this transition plan is the incorporation of goals, objectives, and outcomes into the young child's IFSP/IEP to support the acquisition of skills and abilities needed for the child's success in the new educational environment. As ECE educators and families gain the understanding that assessment, intervention, and follow-up evaluation are parts of the transition plan, the need for systematic collaborative planning as early as possible becomes very apparent. How well the team works together and communicates serves as an indicator of the level of transition success.

***Reflection:*** We all experience transitions as we grow up. In fact, you made a significant transition when you became a college student. As you read the next section, think about how your transition could have been better supported.

## DEVELOPMENTALLY APPROPRIATE PRACTICES FOR YOUNG CHILDREN

The National Association for the Education of Young Children (NAEYC) has established four key elements to support the successful transition of young children and families across community environments (Administration for Children, Youth, and Families, 1987; Bredekamp & Copple, 1997; Glicksman & Hills, 1981). The first key element in the transition process is attention to implementing DAP in the curriculum for young children in every education program. By teachers' incorporating DAP in the curriculum, children and families encounter age-appropriate materials, strategies, content, and learning opportunities. This program continuity supports easier and more fluid transitions that are more successful rather than more stressful for the young child and the family.

The second critical element for successful transition relates to collaboration between ECE educators and administrators from the old and new programs. Ongoing communication and sharing of information is vital for children and families to experience a positive transition event. Cooperation at the administrative level facilitates the congruent fit between child and program characteristics. Exchange of information among old and new ECE educators better prepares all participants of transition for the unfamiliar aspects of the new environment, as well as identifying those DAP guidelines (e.g., community of learners, reciprocal relationships with parents, constructing appropriate curricula, teaching to enhance learning and development) that will be familiar to the child and family.

Preparing the young child for the transition is the third element that NAEYC recommends. Providing the child with opportunities to experience differences and commonalities between his or her soon-to-be-old and his or her new programs will assist the child in understanding the next environment. This understanding gives the child a sense of familiarity with the new environment, which in turn addresses issues of safety and apprehension. The fourth key element is the effective involvement of parents in the transition process. Once again, communication is the framework for determining types, levels, and preferences for a family's involvement in transition planning and implementation. The partnership among ECE educators, administrators, and family members has a direct influence on a young child's successful transition from one program to another. Interactive communication that provides a comfortable climate for voicing parents', teachers', or administrators' concerns or goals related to the transition plan will support the identification of possible stumbling blocks and strategies for circumventing these roadblocks. The collaboration of all invested individuals ensures that all resources are used and that all parameters are recognized.

## FAMILIES AND CHILDREN

Moving from one environment to another is a process that, by its very dynamics, creates change for all participants. For families, this change can cut across many dimensions in both expected and unexpected ways. Rosenkoetter and colleagues (1994) identified several potential bumps that can be smoothed if teams plan and work together in the transition process. When families and children leave a program, they leave friendships, supports, and familiar systems. This personal aspect of transition can produce additional stress beyond the mechanics of the process. The family and the child are without the individuals who have laughed, cried, and persevered with them through the joys and sorrows. In addition, the rules may change in relation to service delivery, types of services available, and the coordination of those services. The professionals involved in providing education services have new faces and different personalities to which families must become

Providing a supportive environment for children in transition is both essential and helpful to families. Professionals' awareness of the difficulties and challenges of transition is important.

accustomed in order to support their children's educational opportunities. For families of children with disabilities, discrepancies in eligibility criteria across programs may impede enrollment in intervention or related services. For some children, the transition to a new program may result in a new label for their disability. A change from developmental delay to intellectual disabilities or mental retardation, for example, can have a significant impact during a time already known as stressful.

Bruder and Chandler (1996) suggested that bumps in the transition process can be flattened to some extent by following a few guidelines. Beginning the transition process early, with complete information sharing among family members and program staff, is the most effective means of easing the transition process for families. Discussing with families what changes in services, eligibility requirements, and diagnosis may occur gives them time to explore and research this new information without additional time pressures. Given adequate time, families can make informed choices about which service delivery changes are negotiable or nonnegotiable and which names are acceptable to the family and child. Providing opportunities for families to meet with old and new staff begins the process of separation and acquaintance for all individuals. Transition is a natural process and an expected process for families and children. However, transition is not a fast or quick event, and adaptation to change has no schedule for completion; rather, it is an individual process that responds well to collaboration and planning.

## Strategies for Successful Transitions

Effective transitions ensure that continued support and services are provided to the child and the family as they move between or within service delivery systems. Successful transition processes are ongoing and future focused. Therefore, transition should be addressed in every IFSP or IEP, not just when a service change is anticipated.

The components for successful transitions have been identified by the federally supported regional educational laboratories:

- Developmentally and culturally appropriate curricula
- Regular communication and careful collaboration between school staff, including visits back and forth, transfers, and discussions of records
- Family-centered services such as Adult Basic Education, nutrition, health checkups, social services, and transportation
- Thorough documentation of program efforts and outcomes that are communicated to all stakeholders
- Shared decision making by home, school, and community partners
- Joint staff development, planning, and supervision of school staff (in the present program and at the receiving agency)
- Sensitivity to children and families from diverse cultural backgrounds and/or with linguistic differences

Promising transition programs should include these components. Collaboration among home, school, and community creates transitions that ensure the continuity of comprehensive services for young children and their families. The transition process must be clear and include successful activities that address continuity across learning environments.

Planning and communication are essential to ease the transition for children and families from one program to another. The transition-planning process is a key factor involved in successful transitions. The stakeholders in the process (i.e., parents, family members and caregivers, service coordinators, service providers, sending and receiving agencies, and local education agencies) must come together in the planning process. The focus of the initial steps in the process should be to discuss service delivery options, evaluate the need for ongoing service coordination, review records, determine whether additional assessments are needed, discuss specific transition activities, and begin writing the transition plan.

The transition plan is the road map to guide the stakeholders through the transition process. The plan must be detailed enough to include a sequence of activities, the individual responsible for each step, and a time line for completion of each step. The plan should be straightforward and uncomplicated, meeting the needs expressed by the family. The plan must include the following activities:

1. Discussion with the parents about transition
2. Procedures to prepare the child for anticipated changes
3. Signed consents from parents for release of information
4. Discussion of formal and informal supports needed by parents
5. Receiving agency notification
6. Invitations to the receiving service providers to visit the child at the present program
7. Parent–child visit to the receiving program

The El Paso County Collaboration Program in El Paso, Texas, offers a model that can easily be adapted for preschool and child care programs at the local level. The El Paso program model states that after the establishment of the program's mission, goals, and objectives, the transition plan may also address documentation and dissemination of results, the planning of communication and collaboration activities, staff development activities, field trip activities, parent involvement activities, continuity of educational development activities, and continuity of comprehensive services.

Activities that assist in successful transitions include 1) planning meetings that include parents, staff, and personnel from the current learning environment and the receiving agency to exchange ideas about the plan; 2) training of parents, staff, and teachers about the transition process and providing information about each other's program philosophies, goals, curricula, materials, schedules, and assessment instruments; 3) preparing children for the transition process by taking them on a field trip to the receiving learning environment and through appropriate activities that engage the child in learning about the new environment; and 4) implementing transition policies and procedures that are collaborative to avoid expensive duplication of services, reducing time lapses between assessment and services, and providing positive mutual support systems for children and families entering new learning environments.

## TRANSITION ISSUES

Theory, research, and legislation acknowledge the importance of transition and the critical role that this process plays in the continuum of services for children with disabilities and their families. For young children without disabilities and their families, transition is equally important for their successful movement across community and education environments. For any child, education services are not static. Changes occur within programs (e.g., switching to different activities, staffing changes, exiting children and incoming children) and across programs (e.g., from preschool to child care, from home-based to center-based programs, from ECE programs to ECSE programs). In order to be responsive to the fluidness that the transition process requires, early childhood educators, administrators, and families must face a few facts. Most important, they must understand transitions from the perspective of the families they serve. For them, transition is more than a concept; it is a real set of events that affect every aspect of their lives. Consider the perspective of one of the authors regarding transitions, given in the next section.

## A FAMILY'S PERSPECTIVE ON TRANSITION

Before our youngest daughter, Katie, was born with a disability and before service providers in our lives kept telling us to get ready for transition, I personally had gone through hundreds of transitions. However, I called that process something else—life, a transition from one environment or situation to another. Each of us is affected on a daily basis by a multitude of transition processes: Growing up, from infancy to the teen years; going off to college or to work; living on one's own for the first time and getting married; having children of one's own; and raising those children to adulthood so that in turn those children then take care of us in our later years. Moving from one environment or situation to another. From our initial transition at birth to the final transition, I guess, of death, the transitions that we experience are multifaceted and build upon each other. The word *transition* never popped into my head as I went through the process of marrying my husband. Rather, it was something that I thought would happen one day, and I prepared for it. We accept many of the transitions in our lives, usually planning for a transition to take place. Before many of the natural transitions in our lives have taken place, we have more than likely planned or prepared for that transition. We planned and prepared ourselves for which college we would attend or which career path we would take. Baby name books were read and names were decided on, baby clothes were chosen, and diaper pails were purchased in the preparations we made for the birth of a baby. Think of the number of transitions you personally go through when having a baby. Now think of how those transitions affected not only your life but also the lives of the people around you.

Transitions are a way of life in most families. Any time children change, a transition occurs. The fine china that my husband and I received as a wedding gift has not been on any table in our house for more than 14 years—exactly the time when our oldest daughter, Megan, started sitting at the table. As all three of our children became interested in sports, the whole concept of dinner at any table went away. For my husband and me, the whole way we made decisions changed as our children changed. We now take our vacations at a time of the year that does not conflict with softball or soccer. Some of the changes have been immediately embraced and joyously woven into the fabric of our family. Others have been difficult, and it is only with painstaking perseverance that those changes have been woven into the fabric of our lives. There is always the fear of the unknown, the new and different, that can go hand in hand with all transitions, planned or unplanned. Most of us have family and friends who have shared the same types of transitions and changes, which we validate with each other as we go through shared experiences. New mothers can share their experiences with their mothers, sisters, or friends who have had children. Teachers talk to other teachers about how they got through the past week of school. We keep people around us who have had those shared experiences, those shared transitions. How many decisions were based on the experiences of those around us who went through a transition similar to the one that we were facing? What happens when an event occurs in your life, and, when you look around for someone with whom to share that experience, no one is there?

As in all families, with families of children with disabilities or developmental delays, transition is also a way of life. Becoming a family that has in its context a family member with a disability was not a transition for which I had prepared myself or for which I had planned. I never thought about it. None of my friends or family were having kids with disabilities, so why would I? The day the pediatrician told me that he thought that Katie had some form of mental retardation, I went home to do the same thing I did every other time I came home from the pediatrician's office. I was going to call my mother and tell her about weight, length, and so forth. Instead, I just stared at the telephone. I did not know what to say, and I did not think I could get the words *mental retardation* out of my mouth. How could I explain something that I did not understand? Not only did I not understand, with every breath I was taking, I did not want this to happen to my family.

There was no one around me at that time who had to make a life change like this one. The support network that my husband and I had developed was changing. Something in the context of our family was different from others' families, and things started changing. Only in hindsight can I say that, in comparison with our support network, probably my husband and I did the most changing. We were going through what every family goes through when their children change. Over time, our priorities changed, which changed the decisions we were making as a family. The natural progression of transition that you would expect in a typical child's life had become an obstacle course of rules, regulations, referring to changes as *transitions*, and writing a plan for those transitions. The feeling of control that I had felt with my two older children, Megan and Ben, was missing when planning for Katie's transitions. I had no experiences on which to base the decisions we were being asked to make. The feeling of being in control was slowly becoming a feeling of being out of control. With Megan, Ben, and Katie (before Katie's diagnosis), I was very structured with my day. I felt in control with that structure that I had developed, especially with three children under the age of 4. All of a sudden, I was not making the decision about what my day would look like. I had appointments with occupational therapists, physical therapists, geneticists, neurologists, speech-language pathologists, early interventionists, craniofacial teams, eye doctors, allergists, and orthopedic specialists. The activities and routines that I had established for my family were changed, not by my hand, but by the hand of people who really did not know that I preferred the children to nap every afternoon when we completed our storytime.

I became resentful and angry and lonely for a lot of reasons. The wonderful support system that I had in place all of my life with family and friends was pretty much gone. After the years of being too angry, too resentful, and too tired, I became a pain in the neck, I could not even stand myself, and, unfortunately, my husband suffered the consequences of that, too. I was resentful of all of the doctors' and therapists' appointments to which I had to drag Megan and Ben. No one could tell me any differently, but I felt for sure that they would be scarred for the rest of their lives for having to eat so many fast-food meals while riding around in search of a cure for their sister.

I was angry that this whole disability thing was just dropped on me, and, if I could have had some choice in the matter, things would be different today. I was lonely in a roomful of people, because I could not look into the eyes of other mothers. I wished that someone would look at me and say, "Yes, I understand. It's okay to feel all the things your feeling because if you don't, you'll never be able to go on."

A significant transition in my life came when I was asked to sit on my county's early intervention collaborative group. For the first time in a long time, I felt that I was regaining some control. Professionals really wanted to know how I believed a service delivery system for families should look in our county. With that experience came information and knowledge. When I went in to develop Katie's IFSP, informed decisions were made. In collaboration with service providers, we came up with a plan for my family that took into consideration what we needed to put in place for Katie but not at the expense of the rest of her family. At the same time, I was meeting other families who had children with disabilities, and I once again had friends with something in common, shared experiences.

Based on the information that I was gaining, and having a support network again, I started to feel that I was once again in control. My anger and resentment started to diminish as I started to feel comfortable with the new order of things. Looking back, I can identify some of the key elements to that change coming about over a period of time. The significant element that affected my ability to become more proficient with change, which enhanced my family's ability to change, was being given information. Once I felt that I was being given choices and that informed decisions were being made, I started to feel in control again. Another significant element was the opportunity to share with other families, getting to the place where I was feeling validated that we could get through this because other families had. I could once again benefit from the fact that someone had gone through an experience before I had, and I could benefit from their insight.

I came to realize that change is inevitable. Knowing that something is going to change and being able to plan and prepare for change helps reduce one's stress level. Preparation gives voice to the things for which I need to advocate, which is to make meaningful things happen for Katie. Through many transitions and a tremendous amount of practice, we transitioned Katie from fourth grade to fifth grade. We looked forward to this change. Katie's family has become the major component of a transition process. We've learned over the years that transition affects us all. We all are at the meetings, even Megan and Ben. As the family members who will have the longest relationship with Katie, Megan and Ben need to gain information and feel as if they have some control over their roles in Katie's life. More important, they have the opportunity to practice the skills that they will need in the future.

Having a classroom design that fosters
comfort with daily routines provides a
foundation for transitions.

**Reflection:**  As you read the preceding perspective on transition, the overarching
nature of transitions to families became clear. Although this example was from a family
with a child with a disability, all families have a continuing set of transitions that dramatically affect the family. If you think back over the past 10 years of your life, think
of the many significant transitions in your life and use your experiences to understand
why the family's perspective of transition must be central in transition planning.

## COLLABORATION AS TRANSITION

Throughout this chapter, the need for planning and collaboration in the process of
transition has been articulated. However, planning and collaboration do not occur
by accident. There must be support for transition from administrators, practitioners, and families. All participants must set aside time to discuss issues unique to
the child, the child's family, the community, and the agency. Adequate time must
be available to fully examine these issues, explore possible strategies, and develop
transition objectives. Time lines must be adequate to accommodate visits, exchanges of information, and refinements of the transition plan as new information
is gathered. There is no argument that ECE administrators and practitioners and
children's families are busy with the day-to-day demands of their roles. But transition planning cannot be a quick add-on at a parent conference. For transition

plans to be successful, a time commitment by administrators, practitioners, and families must be guaranteed.

During the planning process, the participants must work together to figure out what constitutes a workable transition plan for this child, family, and involved agencies. Collaboration is an interactive process wherein individuals share ideas, concerns, and solutions without fear of judgment, scorn, or ridicule by others. The transition plan should reflect the consensus of the group so that each member is invested in its successful implementation. Reaching a collaborative agreement (i.e., the transition plan) requires that administrators, practitioners, and families listen to each other, successfully communicate their viewpoints and feelings, and negotiate transition strategies and objectives with which they are comfortable. For transition plans to be successful, there can be no hidden agendas that later surface and become a barrier to the effective movement of the child and the family across educational environments.

Another factor is the issue of training individuals to participate in the transition process. ECE administrators, practitioners, and families need training in the technical process of transition (e.g., interagency agreements; writing transitions plans, policies, or procedures of social services agencies, medical professionals, human resources agencies; conducting transition plan meetings) and the interpersonal context of transition (e.g., collaboration, teaming, communication, conflict resolution). Preservice and in-service training for all individuals serves to bring the participants to a common ground in transition with shared language, practices, expectations, and decision making.

## EVALUATION OF TRANSITION

Implementing the transition plan is not the final step in the transition process. To determine the success of a transition plan, it is necessary to evaluate the process and the intended and unintended outcomes for the child, the child's family, and agency practitioners. This information can be used to enhance the likelihood of success with the next transition plan for this child and family, as well as for other children and their families. A triphase approach examines the needs of the participants at the beginning of the transition process and uses the acquired information to shape the transition plan so that it addresses each participant's objectives (Johnson & LaMontagne, 1994). The next phase of this evaluation approach is designed to gather information as the transition process unfolds from planning to implementation. This information is used to alter and change the transition plan so that it is responsive to the many unforeseen variables (e.g., illnesses, family's change of address, slots filled or opening at a certain preschool) that often occur. The final outcome phase evaluates the impact of the transition plan on the child, family, practitioners, administrators, agencies, and any other participant in the transition process. The triphase approach is unique in that it explores the articulated outcomes of the transition process (i.e., transition goals and objectives) and can simultaneously attend to other unexpected outcomes of the transition process (i.e., impact on other children, staff, and families in the program; shifts in knowledge about community services). The evaluation of the transition plan is an important consideration for ECE administrators, practitioners, and families. Evaluation results provide accountability and a foundation for change. If results indicate that more time is needed for planning, then participants have facts to show agencies the need for additional time. If results show that the transition went smoothly and that all individuals were satisfied with their level of involvement and the achievement of transition objectives, then the participants have information that will assist in the development of other successful plans.

## CONCLUSIONS

The process of transition from one environment to another is dynamic and requires the attention of all participants assuming an active collaborative role. ECE educators should remember that the exit of a child and family from their program is just as important as their entrance into and participation in it. The success by which a young child can move among activities within the ECE program is as important as their morning arrival and afternoon departure across environments. The experiences in an ECE program set the stage for future experiences, whether they are successful or unsuccessful. Quality ECE programs are known for their nurturing and supportive approach to learning experiences. Transition to new environments is a learning experience that with nurturing and support can open a new world of opportunities for a young child and his or her family. ECE educators working together with families can successfully open that transition door.

## REMEMBER THIS

1. Successful transitions require the investment and support of families and ECE professionals.

2. Parent–professional partnerships are the cornerstone of ECE transition practices.

3. Across all transition models is the theme of collaboration and communication as the framework for success.

4. The transition plan is the road map to guide the stakeholders through the transition process.

5. Effective transitions ensure that continued support and services are provided to the child and the child's family as they move between or within service delivery systems.

## REFERENCES

AASA/NAESP/NAASP School-Based Management Task Force. (1988). *School-based management: A strategy for better learning.* Arlington, VA: American Association of School Administrators.

Administration for Children, Youth, and Families (ACYF). (1987). *Easing the transition from preschool to kindergarten.* Washington, DC: U.S. Department of Health and Human Services.

Bauwens, J., Hourcade, J., & Friend, M. (1989). Cooperative teaching: A model for general and special education integration. *Remedial and Special Education, 10*(2), 17–22.

Bennett, T., Raab, M., & Nelson, D. (1991). The transition process for toddlers with special needs and their families. *Zero to Three, 11*(3), 17–21.

Bredekamp, S., & Copple, C. (1997). *Developmentally appropriate practice in early childhood programs* (Rev. ed.). Washington, DC: National Association for the Education of Young Children.

Bruder, M.B., & Chandler, L. (1996). Transition. In S.L. Odom & M.E. McLean (Eds.), *Early intervention/early childhood special education: Recommended practices* (pp. 287–307). Austin, TX: PRO-ED.

Chandler, L.K. (1992). Promoting children's social/survival skills as a strategy for transition to mainstreamed kindergarten programs. In S.L. Odom, S.R. McConnell, & M.A. McEvoy (Eds.), *Social competence of young children with disabilities: Issues and strategies for intervention* (pp. 245–276). Baltimore: Paul H. Brookes Publishing Co.

Crisci, P.E., & Tutela, A.D. (1990). Preparation of educational administrators for urban settings. *Urban Education, 11*(4), 414–430.

Division for Early Childhood (DEC) Recommended Practices Task Force. (1991). *Recommended practices in early intervention/early childhood special education.* Reston, VA: Council for Exceptional Children.

Diamond, K., Spiegel-McGill, P., & Hanrahan, P. (1988). Planning for school transition. An ecological-developmental approach. *Journal of the Division for Early Childhood, 12,* 245–252.

Edgar, E., McNulty, B., & Goetz, J. (1984). Educational placement of graduates of preschool programs for handicapped children. *Topics in Early Childhood Special Education, 4*(3), 19–29.

Glicksman, K., & Hills, T. (1981). *Easing the child's transition between home, child care center and school: A guide for early childhood educators.* Trenton: New Jersey Department of Education.

Heller, H., & Schilit, J. (1987). The regular education initiative: A concerned response. *Focus on Exceptional Children, 20,* 1–6.

Hersh, R., & Walker, H.M. (1983). Great expectations: Making school effective for all students. *Policy Review Studies, 2,* 147–188.

Hutinger, P.L. (1981). Transition practices for handicapped young children: What the experts say. *Journal of the Division for Early Childhood, 2,* 8–14.

Individuals with Disabilities Education Act Amendments of 1991, PL 102-119, 20 U.S.C. §§ 1400 *et seq.*

Johnson, L.J., & LaMontagne, M.J. (1994). Program evaluation: The key to quality programming. In L.J. Johnson, R.J. Gallagher, M.J. LaMontagne, J.B. Jordan, J.J. Gallagher, P.L. Hutinger, & M.B. Karnes (Eds.), *Meeting early intervention challenges: Issues from birth to three* (2nd ed., pp. 185–216). Baltimore: Paul H. Brookes Publishing Co.

Jones, R.L., Gottlieb, J., Guskin, S., & Yoshida, R.K. (1978). Evaluating mainstreaming programs: Models, caveats, considerations, and guidelines. *Exceptional Children, 44,* 588–601.

Katims, D.S., & Pierce, P.L. (1995). Literacy-rich environments and the transition of young children with special needs. *Topics in Early Childhood Special Education, 15*(2), 219–234.

Lawrence, P.R., & Lorsch, J.W. (1967). *Organization and environment.* Boston: Harvard Business School Press.

Lazzari, A.M., & Kilgo, J.L. (1989). Practical methods for supporting parents in early transitions. *Teaching Exceptional Children, 22*(1), 40–43.

Margolis, H., & McGettigan, J. (1988). Managing resistance to instructional modifications in mainstreamed environments. *Remedial and Special Education, 9,* 15–21.

Maxwell, K.L., & Eller, S.K. (1994). Children's transition to kindergarten. *Young Children, 49*(6), 56–63.

Miller, R. (1996). *The developmentally appropriate inclusive classroom in early education.* Albany, NY: Delmar Publishers.

Myles, B.S., & Simpson, R.L. (1989). Regular educators' modification preferences for main-streaming mildly handicapped children. *Journal of Special Education, 22*(4), 479–492.

Myles, B.S., & Simpson, R.L. (1990). Mainstreaming modification preferences of parents of elementary-aged children with learning disabilities. *Journal of Learning Disabilities, 23*(4), 234–239.

Rogers, H., & Saklofske, D.H. (1985). Self-concepts, locus of control and performance expectations of learning disabled. *Journal of Learning Disabilities, 18*, 273–278.

Rosenkoetter, S.E., Hains, A.H., & Fowler, S.A. (1994). *Bridging early services for children with special needs and their families: A practical guide for transition planning.* Baltimore: Paul H. Brookes Publishing Co.

Roubinek, D. (1978). Will mainstreaming fit? *Educational Leadership, 35*, 410–411.

Simpson, R.L., & Myles, B.S. (1989). Parents' mainstreaming modification preferences for children with educable mental handicaps, behavior disorders and learning disabilities. *Psychology in the Schools, 26*, 292–301.

Simpson, R.L., & Myles, B.S. (1993). General education collaboration: A model for successful mainstreaming. In E.L. Meyen, G.A. Vergason, & R.J. Whelan (Eds.), *Challenges facing special education* (pp. 63–77). Denver: Love Publishing Co.

Will, M. (1985). Transitioning: Linking disabled youth to a productive future. *OSERS News in Print, 51*, 11–16.

Wolery, M. (1989). Transition in early childhood special education: Issues and procedures. *Focus on Exceptional Children, 22*, 1–16.

Wolery, M., Strain, P.S., & Bailey, D.B., Jr. (1992). Reaching potentials of children with special needs. In S. Bredekamp & T. Rosegrant (Eds.), *Reaching potentials: Appropriate curriculum and assessment for young children* (pp. 92–111). Washington, DC: National Association for the Education of Young Children.

# Activities

1. Visit three local ECE programs, and interview teachers regarding their transition policies and procedures. Identify commonalities and differences across programs, and then compare your findings with the models described in this chapter to determine which model is used by each ECE program that you visited.

2. Interview family members regarding their experiences with the transition process, including transition planning, activities, and documents.

3. Develop three transition activities for a family with a child making the transition from early intervention services to preschool programming. The family must be culturally and linguistically diverse and reside in a rural area. Their 2-year-old daughter has a medical diagnosis of cerebral palsy.

# Epilogue

*Lawrence J. Johnson,*
*M.J. LaMontagne, Peggy M. Elgas, and Anne M. Bauer*

As indicated in the preface, a diverse set of individuals who care a great deal about children and their families came together to share their expertise in this book. The vast majority of the contributors to this book work or have worked at the Arlitt Child and Family Research and Education Center at the University of Cincinnati, Ohio. Although they do not always agree, they have learned to work together and have embraced a unified view of early childhood education (ECE) practices that incorporates practices from ECE and early childhood special education (ECSE). In much the same way that diversity enhances the classroom, incorporating diverse perspectives into a unified approach to ECE has greatly enriched ECE teachers' abilities to meet the needs of the children and families whom they serve. One of the cornerstones of a blended approach to ECE is collaboration. As ECE moves forward as a field and continues to find better ways to support children and their families, it is imperative that collaboration become more than a process. Among those working with young children and their families, collaboration must become a way of being. As such, ECE professionals' dispositions must be geared toward finding ways to share their expertise to better serve children and families. Service providers who work in ECE environments come from diverse disciplines, and, though there are clear differences in their training and theory bases, all are committed to doing their best for the children and families whom they serve. This shared commitment provides the foundation for blending ECE practices into a unified perspective.

Although it is hoped that this book will contribute to a blending of practices, the book's editors recognize that there are serious challenges that the ECE field must meet before a collaborative, unified perspective can become commonplace. The following are some of these challenges:

1.  The ECE field needs to more fully develop a sense of modesty and recognize that working with young children and their families is extremely complex. The questions raised about a blended ECE approach are enormous, and the answers are complex and ever evolving. No one discipline has all of the answers, but the unified collaborative of ECE professionals and families can learn from each other and begin to develop rich approaches to surmount challenges as they emerge.

2.  One of the first steps in meeting ECE challenges is to learn more about the disciplines associated with ECE. ECE and ECSE professionals need to learn about their fields' philosophical underpinnings and professional practices. Through increased understanding, these educators will be better able to translate practices into a common core of practices and find complementary practices that will enhance their ability to meet the needs of the children and families they serve. The more familiar ECE and ECSE educators are with each other, the easier it is for them to remember their shared commitment to young children and their families.

3.  As asserted previously, before a unified perspective of ECE can be embraced, collaboration must become a value. As a value, collaborative thinking and behavior become integral parts of ECE professionals' approaches to their jobs, and individuals within ECE are disposed to seek ways to work together with families to the benefit of the children. Rather than focusing on issues that divide them, ECE and ECSE professionals need to find issues that unify their practices.

4.  Unfortunately, collaboration is difficult and requires effort and ongoing attention to be successful. It is always easier to do something in isolation than it is to do something collaboratively. Although arguments are made that collaborative efforts are almost always superior, some gravitate toward the path of least resistance and avoid collaborative endeavors. Decision makers must recognize this difficulty and allocate the appropriate time and resources to ensure that collaborative efforts can be supported.

5.  There are several practical problems that, on the surface, seem simple but are actually complex and difficult. These problems relate to state licensure and certification for ECE professionals and higher education governance structures that approve programs.

    a.  Whereas many states have begun to adopt a unified perspective and have developed licensure and certification requirements that allow or require ECE programs to blend ECE and ECSE programs, the majority of the states have licensure and certification requirements that make it difficult if not impossible to develop unified programs. Effort needs to be directed at making ECE licensure and certification requirements more flexible without losing rigor. Until that time, ECE and ECSE educators must be creative and find ways to blend programs within the states' licensure and certification requirements.

b.   Another problem relates to affiliations in higher education and governance structures that approve programs. Typically, ECE and ECSE programs are in different administrative units within colleges of education (i.e., teacher education, special education). When proposals are put forward to blend and unify programs, administrators and other faculty within the unit ask which program will get the resources of the programs being blended. If the administrators or other faculty in the unit become concerned about a loss of resources, they may be reluctant to support the unification of programs. As a result, the governance structure of the college can prevent a program from being approved and can keep the programs separate. Moreover, committees that approve programs are often designed to preserve the status quo. Innovative programs that cut across units can make higher education committee members uncomfortable, causing difficulties in the program and course approval processes. Individuals in ECE and ECSE training programs must get past affiliation concerns and fear of reductions in resources so that new programs that are consistent with current recommended practices can emerge.

The preceding list provided is not all-inclusive but presents some of the challenges that have occurred at the University of Cincinnati in blending its ECE and ECSE programs. Perhaps the most serious challenge for ECE and ECSE educators relates to how they conduct themselves as professionals. The challenge they face is to incorporate this blended orientation into their ECE practices. As the reader of this book enters or reenters the ECE field, he or she is likely to be in a program that has not embraced a unified approach and may have minimal levels of collaboration. In such a case, the challenge is to open lines of communication and begin at the grass-roots level to collaborate with colleagues and the families served by the ECE program. An ECE teacher who is able to make a difference in an ECE program enhances that program and makes an important contribution to improving the ECE field.

# Index

*Page numbers followed by "f" indicate figures; those followed by "t" indicate tables.*